Screen
and
Society

The Impact of Television
upon Aspects of
Contemporary Civilization

Screen
and
Society

The Impact of Television upon Aspects of Contemporary Civilization

Edited by
Frank J. Coppa

Nelson-Hall nh Chicago

Library of Congress Cataloging in Publication Data

Main entry under title:

Screen and society.

   Bibliography: p.
   Includes index.
   1.   Television broadcasting—Social aspects—
Addresses, essays, lectures. 2. Television
criticism—Addresses, essays, lectures. I. Coppa,
Frank J.
PN1992.6.S3   301'.16'1   79–13500
ISBN 0–88229–413–X

Manufactured in the United States of America

10   9   8   7   6   5   4   3   2   1

Contents

To my wife Rosina
and daughters Francesca
and Melina

The Explosion of the Eye:
An Introduction to the Promise
and Problems of Television

Frank J. Coppa
Department of History
St. John's University

Soon after Alexander Graham Bell exhibited his discovery in 1876 the song "The Wondrous Telephone" captured the public imagination. "You stay at Home and listen to the lecture in the Hall and hear strains of music from a ball!"[1] the song promised, stimulating the vision of the coming broadcast age. The prophecy was fulfilled at the turn of the century when Guglielmo Marconi's visit to the United States precipitated the wireless mania that ushered in the age of radio. The two decades from 1920 to 1940 were dominated by radio broadcasting. When sight was added to sound on an experimental basis in the interwar period and commercially after World War II, television, which had only been a word coined in 1907, became a reality for millions throughout the world. For the first time in human history it was possible for all people to be within the reach of each other's voice and vision.

First in the United States and the United Kingdom, later in the rest of North America, Japan, continental Europe, Australia, South America, Asia, and Africa, millions were mesmerized by the "talking picture box" as forests of antennas emerged. By the 1970s virtually every American had easy and frequent access to the "electronic wonderland."[2] Television ownership increased dramatically everywhere and the amount of viewing time soared. For four or five hours a day, seven days a week, television had become part of the environment for countless citizens of all ages, colors, classes, and nationalities. For some it defined the environment, becoming their chief source of amusement, information, and education.

Years ago Marconi predicted that telecommunications would become part of an "almost unnoticed working equipment of civilization."[3] This was later reinforced by Marshall McLuhan who explained that the electronic age had created a radically new environment. Television is environmental, he continued, because like other environments, it is imperceptible.[4] Television is almost invisible for all of its visibility.[5] In her book, *The Plug-in Drug*, Marie Winn has argued that children's development is influenced not only by the content of television shows but even more so by the very nature of the television experience. Whether they watch "Sesame Street" or "Magilla Gorilla" cartoons the effect is the same: they are left in isolation, before they have learned the niceties of social relations; they are subject to a medium that systematically destroys the differences between reality and fantasy, before they have learned to separate the two.[6]

More recently Frank Mankiewicz and Joel Swerdlow, in their book *Remote Control: Television and the Manipulation of American Life,* have argued that television regulates our actions, including how, when and what we eat, when we sleep, how we raise our children, what we buy, and how we act on matters of sex and race. More importantly, perhaps, they maintain that television has transformed our perception of what problems can be solved and how to solve them, adding that television is the most powerful external factor in American life.[7]

Very early it was charged that television did more than simply record the events of our age; it created wants and stimulated needs. "In a culture like ours, long accustomed to splitting and dividing all things as a means of control, it is sometimes a bit of a shock to be reminded that, in operational and practical fact, the medium is the message," wrote McLuhan. "This is merely to say that the personal and social consequences of any medium—that is, of any extension of ourselves—result from the new scale that is introduced into our affairs by each extension of ourselves, or by any new technology."[8]

Television is thought to be at once the mirror and motor of contemporary institutions and the prevailing value system. Its importance is attested to by its potential to magnify man's ability to communicate, its pervasiveness, its social and industrial potential, the increasing time the masses devote to it, and the huge sums of money required in its operation. By the late 1960s American advertisers spent some three million dollars on this medium.[9] The total value of receivers in the United States represents an investment of upwards of 10 billion dollars.[10] Furthermore, by the 1970s television reached more people than all the other mass media combined.[11]

The technology of literacy, based on the phonetic alphabet and the Gutenberg press, profoundly influenced western values. But however important its role, its influence was limited. Books and other printed material only reached half of the world's people; the other half remained illiterate or functionally so. Television, combining the two most widely and easily grasped forms of expression, spoken language and pictures, is unique because it is the first medium or extension of man to be shared and understood by virtually all.[12] It has been described as a deeper and more involving form of communication, possessing the potential to unite men psychologically and spiritually. Videoculture, it has been argued, can recreate on a national or even a global scale the mystical unity possessed by primitive tribes.[13] Given its spectacular growth and broad appeal, it is not surprising that speculation should have arisen about its impact.

For the last twenty-five years we have been immersed in a medium never before experienced, and we have yet to understand how it has altered our lives.[14] Like the invention of movable type printing, which made possible the Reformation and the scientific revolution which transformed the societies of the west, television represents a fundamental change in the manner in which people communicate. However, while we can interpret the significance of printing from the vantage point of some five centuries, television has existed for only one generation. The tools to assess its influence have yet to be perfected.[15] Ignored by serious scholars and the television industry itself, the study of television has fallen by default into the hands of journalists and Sunday supplement editors who have not hesitated to make exaggerated and overgeneralized claims and assertions.[16]

In the United States, where television has achieved the same distribution as indoor plumbing, television has supposedly established many unique genres, formulas and traditions.[17] The tube has been held responsible for videodance, a new art form resulting from the translation or transference of dance from the theatre to this electric medium.[18] It has purportedly given ballet a distinctly American flavor and provoked a "ballet boom", making it the fastest growing of the country's performing arts.[19] Attempts have been made to visualize serious music by combining the worlds of music and video art.[20] Indeed television has been seen as the major dramatic outlet for popular culture in America, both reflecting and molding that culture. Some have claimed that television programs are the most significant form of popular art in our time.[21] Television, it has been said, has imposed itself so completely that it would be difficult, if not impossible, to comprehend the present without it.

In certain areas the influence of television has been immediate and apparent. As television viewing increased in the United States the number of newspapers and magazines that were forced to cease publication swelled; among the victims were *Look* and *Life* (both recently resurrected). The fact that by 1963 most Americans named television as their chief and most trusted source of information was considered largely responsible for the retreat from the printed word.[22] "We're living in an age of audio-visually educated readers and competing with much brighter visual products," said the editor of *The Boston Globe*, aware that more Americans were devoting their time to television.[23] Attendance at movie houses decreased dramatically and in the half decade from 1948 to 1953 paid admissions declined by some thirty-seven percent.[24]

The relationship between popular television figures and series and the increasing popularity of celebrity dolls and toys seems quite clear. Dolls representing television characters or personalities, such as the "Six Million Dollar Man," the "Bionic Woman," "Wonder Woman," Sonny and Cher, Donny and Marie, and a host of others, have found a ready market as children, avid television watchers, pressure their parents to purchase them. "You can't just sell a patrol car," said a spokesman for one of the large chain toy stores. "It's got to be an Adam-12 patrol car."[25]

In 1956 the first edition of Leo Bogart's *The Age of Television* was published. It was an heroic attempt to compile all the available studies of the medium into a composite picture. From its tables and charts as well as its commentary a number of facts clearly emerged. Bogart showed that television had already achieved ascendancy over the other mass media and that it had reduced the amount of time the American people spent in reading. He also reported that television viewers tended to be less active in social organizations and were less likely to go out evenings. His findings also showed that television viewers were more inclined to purchase brand name items.[26]

The television industry in the United States, as well as presidential commissions and other independent bodies, have sought to assess the effect of television violence upon viewers. In 1956 the subcommittee to investigate juvenile delinquency, under the leadership of Senator Estes Kefauver, concluded that television was potentially dangerous to its young audience. Despite the industry's commitment to patrol itself, surveys by the Senate subcommittee in 1961 and 1964 revealed that violence on prime time programs had substantially increased. This led to further study. In 1969 the National Commission on the Causes and Prevention of Violence, appointed by President Lyndon Johnson, concluded that television violence might encourage actual violence, especially in the case of children from poor and broken homes.[27]

More recently a study undertaken by the Foundation for Child Development in which some 2,200 children, representing a cross section of seven to eleven year olds, were interviewed, showed the influence of television. The researchers found that television viewing and fear often went hand in hand; children who watched television four or more hours a week were twice as likely to feel "scared often" as those who did not. Furthermore, the study revealed that the more they watched, the more afraid they became.[28]

There are other manifestations of television's influence. Programs about popular television "lawyers" such as Perry Mason and Petrocelli have allegedly distorted the public's image of law and justice by their representation of dramatic episodes and happy endings, and their search for wide audience appeal.[29] The disillusionment that minority communities have with their police has been attributed, at least in part, to the fact that few officers can measure up to the television image of the men in blue. Similarly, sympathetic television doctors have exposed the flaws of our own indifferent and hurried doctors.

The full impact of television was felt later in Europe than in the United States but the results appeared equally severe. It is estimated that between 1957 and 1963 one-third of all British movie houses went out of business. In the decade after 1961 attendance at the cinema decreased by 337 million in Germany and 190 million in Italy and France.[30] A similar trend was visible in the other countries of Europe. By the 1970s television had become so important that in experiments conducted in Germany and England families who were paid not to watch television proved unable or unwilling to do so. After a few months they dropped out of the experiment and insisted that their sets be turned on.[31]

In Italy the *Domenica del Corriere*, the Sunday edition of the

Milanese newspaper *Il Corriere della Sera,* adopted a more compact format, with a new section *La Domenica in famiglia* (Sunday at home with the family), in which weekend entertainment is listed, with television playing a prominent part. In Great Britain pub owners complained that television was a threat to their trade because it led viewers to buy bottled beer and drink at home. Biscuit makers, on the other hand, profited by this development. Supposedly television was responsible for the 22 percent fall in attendance at adult education classes in London, as well as the closing of village halls and literary societies.[32]

In the United States political arena pollster Louis Harris has found, on the basis of survey data from 1963 to 1970, that there is "a definite and distinct pattern of increasing support of a President after he has taken to television to appeal for his position." He found this to be so consistent, aside from a few exceptions, that he has concluded "that the Presidential use of television almost automatically gives him an important advantage."[33] Television was instrumental in the decline and fall of Senator Joseph McCarthy and quite possibly cost Richard Nixon the presidency in 1960. In 1972 George McGovern's image and perhaps even that of the Democratic Party was damaged as a result of television's coverage of the convention events.[34]

Television newsmen have recently shown a greater awareness of their influence in the political process transcending the role of impartial commentators and making frankly political judgments. "It's not exactly the precise figures that will be important," confessed Roger Mudd during the course of the presidential primaries, "it's whether or not the media and the politicians agree that this man won, and this man lost."[35]

The political impact of television is also felt elsewhere in the world. Television in the Soviet Union and Communist China has been seen as an instrument of the state for pacifying its population and pressing its ideological viewpoint. In Franco's Spain, Salazar's Portugal, Nasser's Egypt and even De Gaulle's Fifth Republic, critics charge, television was used as a crutch for a personal regime. In the Republic of South Africa, which only belatedly and reluctantly entered the television age, there are those who fear that this powerful visual medium will become a propaganda weapon for the political party in power. Television has also been held responsible for inciting unrest in the underdeveloped third world by precipitating a revolution of rising expectations that cannot be fulfilled. It has been thought to aggravate class conflicts throughout the world by graphically depicting how the leisure class lives. Finally there was the haunting fear that George Orwell's vision of 1984, where omnipresent television screens fostered control and conformity, was prophetic.

The critics of this medium are legion. Almost everywhere, the allegation has been made that television would impair imagination and dull the creative senses. Some have argued that television has been the opiate of the people, bringing them to a terminal state of stupefication. It has been particularly derided by the intellectual community, which generally has found it detrimental to serious thought and human values.[36] It has been held responsible for declines in reading and writing abilities; diminished socialization, irritability and hyperactivity among children and adults, fragmentation of the nuclear family, the spread of the drug culture, increasing crime, the decline of our cities, growing immorality, and the rise of a new brand of ruthless juvenile delinquent. In the 1960s television, in its quest for the exotic, was charged with inciting minority groups to express their extremism in order to be newsworthy,[37] a theme stressed by Paddy Chayefsky in his screenplay for the movie *Network*.

Although television has poured millions upon millions of dollars into professional sports and greatly increased the incomes of the first-rate teams, in the process transforming the image of professional athletes from that of childish mercenaries to superstars, it has been considered a mixed blessing at best. Those involved in amateur sports argue that television has encouraged armchair fans rather than active participants while those in the minor leagues have witnessed an alarming decrease in interest in sports at that level. In 1949, they point out, there were some fifty-nine minor league baseball teams throughout the country and their games were well attended. Today, there are less than twenty and their fans have steadily declined. In Great Britain where soccer is the national pastime the professional teams that are televised are popular, while the lower level third and fourth division teams are virtually going bankrupt.[38]

Educators and parents, meanwhile, have long maintained that television has interfered with the educational process, curtailing reading of newspapers and books as well as interfering with homework. Some suggest that it has played havoc with the child's sense of time. "One of the things that puzzles people about the television generation is that the children who have been sitting in front of the TV for four or five hours a day have their time sequence routinized," observes Clare Booth Luce. "They expect all of life's problems to be resolved in a half hour or so."[39]

These perceptions and accusations have some factual support. Studies made in England indicate that where television becomes available for several hours per day it subsequently dominates the leisure of children.[40] Bogart in his chapter "Television and the Juvenile Audience" cited studies which revealed that television had disrupted the eating and sleeping schedules of children and led to conflicts with parents over programs to be viewed.[41] In addition there are signs of crumbling achievement in American schools, registered by the College Board's Scholastic Aptitude Test, whose scores have been tumbling for the last thirteen years; the decline in reading levels; and the inability of a large number of young Americans to write coherently. In 1976 the downward trend continued as the average verbal score of high school seniors dropped three points from the last year on the Scholastic Aptitude Test.[42] Although television has been named the culprit, this has not yet been proved.

Noting that the average American spends some 1,200 hours a year watching television and only some five in reading books, one language expert relates some sad consequences.[43] In *American Language Today* Cornelia Nachbar finds family conversation a vanishing art. Others have held television responsible for the steady decline in the level of education, accusing it of producing a sclerosis of the mind and a chronic somnambulism among the masses.

The black tennis star Arthur Ashe, in an open letter to black parents, decried the fact that blacks spent too much time on the playing field and too little time in libraries and like so many others, blamed television. "Which televised events have the greatest number of viewers?" he asked, and answered "Sports—the Olympics, Super Bowl, Masters, World Series, pro basketball playoffs, Forest Hills."[44] The consequence is that the black child gets a massive dose of O. J. Simpson, Kareem Abdul-Jabbar, Muhammad Ali, Reggie Jackson and Dr. J, and dreams of becoming a pro athlete himself. In his letter Ashe called upon parents to counter the influence of television and instill a desire for learning in their children.

Many parents have failed to control the television environment in their homes. According to Eda Le Shan, author, family counselor and educator, with children spending more hours viewing television than in school, parents must carefully evaluate and monitor their viewing. Excessive viewing, she notes, takes time from playing and growth and produces undesirable traits in children. Among the unfortunate consequences may be hyperactivity, which may result when children are virtually bombarded by the sights and sounds from the set. Too many hours spent before the television, she notes, also tends to create passivity in children, who are used to being silent observers rather than active participants. Both these characteristics contribute to a decline in classroom performance.[45]

In the words of Marshall McLuhan the television child is "culturally disadvantaged," for his orientation to this medium renders difficult an accommodation to the older educational establishment.[46] "Next to the H-bomb," said an American professor, "television is the most dangerous thing in the world today."[47]

Critics have observed that adults as well as children seek instant gratification and find a convenient and relatively inexpensive escape mechanism in television, relating to the talking picture box rather than the people around them, with disastrous consequences for personal relationships and family life. Some have suggested that the spiraling divorce rate is in part attributed to the addiction to television. This is the position taken by Clare Booth Luce, who has argued that this medium has done a great deal to break up family life: "TV, radio and movies have helped break up families because mother and daddy are no longer the story tellers, and children aren't conversing with one another. They are watching TV instead."[48]

Clergymen, meanwhile, have decried the fact that television has brought "the demoralizing influence of the music hall right in the home" under the guise of adult entertainment. They challenge the appropriateness of programs focusing on prostitution and perversion. One minister labeled television one of the world's greatest potential dangers.[49] Father George Maloney, S. J., has named excessive, indiscriminate television watching the greatest deterrent to a life of prayer. The recent "Vatican Declaration on Certain Questions Concerning Sexual Ethics" condemns the unbridled exaltation of sex which "through the means of social communication and through public entertainment . . . has reached the point of invading the field of education and infecting the general morality."[50] A number of Protestant and Jewish organizations have concurred that television's emphasis on violence and its preoccupation with sex has contributed to the proliferation of crime and the moral disruption of contemporary society.

Religious groups that have disagreed on basic social and political questions have found a new unity in their demand that viewers should have more say about what is shown on television. The United Methodist Church, the American Lutheran Church, and the Church of the Brethren have a Television Awareness Training Program. The Roman Catholic Conference Office on Film and Broadcasting distributes information on what the churches are doing to increase access to the airwaves.[51]

In the United States television with its massive advertising campaigns and its Madison Avenue approach has been depicted as one of the handmaidens of inflation, encouraging its viewers to buy now and pay later. It has also been accused of engendering racial envy. "I wonder if advertisers and television officials themselves know what they are doing to the public," writes S. I. Hayakawa, the linguist, educator, and more recently United States Senator. "Let them ask themselves as they preview a commercial how it looks and what it means to the 10 percent, or in some parts of the country, the 50 percent of their viewing audience who are Negro."[52]

On the other hand television has not been without its ardent champions, who note that the medium provides fuller and more impressive coverage of current events.[53] Others stress its role in entertaining the elderly, lonely, housebound, and convalescing. They see it as a wonderful invention having immense positive social significance that draws men, women, and children back into the home and thus strengthens family life.[54] At a time when contemporary man is the victim of alienating forces only certain forms of collective communications, above all television, seem to be capable of restoring the lost sense of unity.

Early enthusiasts for television announced that it was a means of bringing about mass enlightenment, offering culture and technique to those craving instruction. Others observed that it could bring expert teachers to hundreds of classrooms and thousands of students simultaneously, and hospitals would find it invaluable in instructing younger doctors in the complexities of intricate surgery. More recently some religious orders in the Roman Catholic Church have experimented with the use of television to recruit priests.

Various groups and individuals have sought to harness the power of television. A new biweekly magazine called *Action,* aimed at American junior high school students reading at the second grade level, contains much material inspired by television—the preview issue featured "Charlie's Angels" on the cover and included an article on the three young actresses in the series. "Television is a predominant interest item to the young and all of our issues will probably have something on it," said the editorial director, no doubt aware that many parents and educators hold the medium responsible for much of the reading problem in the first place. "The trick is not to see television as the bad guy, but to accept it as a reality and know how to use it."[55]

Television's champions have claimed that used at home, it could bring literacy to the adult world, opening new vistas for millions worldwide. It has been observed that more people have been exposed to the plays of Shakespeare by this medium in its few decades of broadcasting than have been in all the audiences of the bard since those plays were first staged. Likewise, the telecast of Giacomo Puccini's *La Boheme* live from the Metropolitan Opera House in New York City in 1977 exposed it to a greater audience than all who had attended its performance since its premiere at the Teatro Reggio in Turin in 1896. Franco Zeffirelli's television movie "Jesus of Nazareth" was seen by some 90 million people in the United States and some 200 million worldwide.

Possessing the potential for educating masses of people, above all in the third world, television has been seen as the means of providing a sense of statehood while offering a basic education to the people of Africa and Asia. It has been heralded as a great boon to the poorer countries of the world, enabling them to overcome the bottlenecks of financial exigency, teacher training, social conditions, and lack of equipment, which have hitherto contributed to massive illiteracy. Television, it has been argued, will provide an effective educational shortcut and thus eradicate illiteracy in the underdeveloped reaches of Asia and Africa.

Some have seen the possibility of creating television schools directly linked with one another, pooling skills and specialists and overcoming the barriers of distance and nationalities.[56] In conjunction with space satellites, television has the potential of reducing the span of time and bringing even remote regions of the world into focus in seconds, making the planet smaller and humanity one.[57]

According to . . . projections, tomorrow's household will contain a
facsimile copier to capture the day's news; a remote learning and
shopping terminal; a videotape recorder for delayed playback of
entertainment and cultural programming; special terminals to
give access to computational services, bank accounts and office
files; a wall size TV screen for viewing abstract art or baseball
games; monitoring systems that will prevent burglaries and heart
attacks; a television camera for two-way video conferences; a
wide variety of other communications services and devices.[58]

Few other inventions have excited such vigorous debate concerning
their potential, their impact and their consequences. Indeed a recent
study by the American Booksellers' Association has indicated that
those who read books watch almost as much television as those who
do not. [59]

Despite comments and speculation about the impact of television,
it remains the medium most taken for granted by scholars and the
public at large. Everyone talks about it, but few have seriously
studied it.[60] Television materialized and spread so quickly from a
lightning-fast technological revolution that there has not always
been adequate time to study the extent of its audience, let alone the
impact of the medium upon that audience. One observer noted that
"trying to gauge the impact of television upon American society
has been something like attempting to understand the dynamics of
a tidal wave—when one is in the middle of it."[61]

The task of students of television has not been rendered easier
by the industry itself, which has often shown little interest in its
own history, as it erased old tapes to make room for new entries.
Not until the end of 1976 was the world's first public library of
broadcasting, the Museum of Broadcasting, opened in New York
City. This institution was the brainchild of William S. Paley, chairman of the board of CBS.[62]

The most common form of television research in the United
States and abroad concentrates upon the number of people watching a particular program. Their impact is great, often provoking
multimillion dollar decisions, for only a single point increase in the
powerful A. C. Nielsen rating system is reported worth about one
million in advertising revenue. Then there are reaction studies,
conducted mainly for private broadcasters, which provide an assessment of public reaction to a specfic program. And of course
considerable time, effort, and money is poured into testing the
efficiency of television advertising. The television industry has in-

vested precious little to determine the long-range impact of its product upon the public at large, or how successful it has been in communicating information and ideas. A great deal is not yet known about the effect of television on opinion, the alteration of public attitudes, and even purchasing decisions. Few studies have objectively and accurately assessed the relationship between modern society and television.

There have, however, been some serious studies of the medium. Researchers decided to take advantage of the fact that the town of McBride, in British Columbia, situated in a blind spot for television reception, did not have transmission until the Canadian Broadcasting Corporation put in a special transmitter. Sensing the importance of this community's belated entrance into the television age, specialists from the University of British Columbia decided to study how television would affect the life patterns of the three thousand residents. They examined the town in 1973, before the advent of television, and then again in 1975, two years after the installation of the transmitter. They noted increased aggressiveness among juveniles, a detrimental impact upon community activity and spirit, and an adverse effect upon educational achievement.[63]

Another important study was initiated in the United States in 1969 when Senator John Pastore inquired of the Secretary of Health, Education and Welfare whether there was a causal connection between televised violence and antisocial behavior by individuals, particularly children. This prompted the Surgeon General's Committee to sponsor a program of research over three years at a cost of 1.8 million dollars—the most far-reaching probe to date of the social consequences of television. The results of this study, published in five volumes, were far from conclusive and did not definitely answer Senator Pastore's inquiry.

> The evidence does indicate that televised violence may lead to increased aggressive behavior in certain subgroups of children, who might constitute a small portion or a substantial portion of young television viewers.[64]

Equally tentative are the conclusions of professors Jerome and Dorothy Singer of Yale University's Family Television Research and Consultation Center, whose study of television violence finds that anti-social and aggressive behavior among three- and four-year-olds is influenced by the amount and kinds of television that children watch *plus* a number of other factors. British professor William A. Belson, who has studied older children, is likewise cautious in his conclusions. His study *Television Violence and the Adolescent Boy* concludes that watching violent television shows does not necessarily make adolescent males more willing to attack others.[65]

The fact that the findings of the Surgeon General's Committee were preliminary and tentative stems in part from the fact that the effects of television take place indirectly and over a long span of time and in part from the limitations of the technique used. "A quite different approach to understanding television as a social force—one that has just begun to be explored—is provided by the perspective of the historian," writes Richard Adler, assistant director of the Aspen Institute Program on Communications and Society. "The historian would seem especially well qualified to place the institution of television in a larger context and to examine its effects on other institutions. Yet very little such work has been done."[66]

Six of the essays included in this volume, all essentially works of synthesis, are by historians. Their contribution is supplemented by the perspective of the three remaining authors, whose fields are education, political science, and telecommunications.

Together these essays address themselves to a number of important questions. Precisely how widespread is television broadcasting worldwide? How has it affected attendance at movie houses, theatres, and sporting events? How has television changed education in the United States and abroad? To what extent, if any, has television altered the political process? What has been the effect of television on popular culture and taste? How has television influenced the urban crisis in the United States? How does public television differ from commercial television in America and abroad? What differences, if any, can be detected when government rather than private enterprise serves as the patron of the most popular of the arts? How does television operate as a business? Finally, what has been the influence of television viewing on the interests and initiative of viewers, as well as on family life and sociability?

These essays do not, indeed could not, provide definitive answers to these questions. In some cases they raise as many new questions as they provide answers. They do expose some of the overarching generalizations about the medium; dwell upon some of the newer developments; examine its impact in particular areas and fields; and cull and synthesize the findings of a number of specialized studies, revealing their broader implications. Collectively they illustrate that television is a full-fledged institution whose impact upon a generation, worldwide, deserves to be assessed.

Notes

1. Erik Barnouw, *Tube of Plenty: The Evolution of American Television* (New York: Oxford University Press, 1975), p. 3.
2. John G. Cawelti, "Some Reflections on the Videoculture of the Future," *Journal of Popular Culture,* 7, no. 4 (1974): 990.
3. Douglass Cater, "Introduction: Television and Thinking People," *Television as a Social Force: New Approaches to TV Criticism,* ed. Richard Adler (New York: Praeger Publishers, 1975), p. 1.
4. Marshall McLuhan, *Understanding Media: The Extension of Man* (New York: McGraw-Hill, 1964), p. viii.
5. John L. Wright, "Tune-In: The Focus of Television Criticism," *Journal of Popular Culture,* 7, no. 4 (1974): 887.
6. Stephanie Harrington, review of *The Plug-in Drug* by Marie Winn, *The New York Times,* 20 March 1977.
7. Daniel J. Boorstin, "The Great Electronic Dictator," *New York Times Book Review,* 19 February 1976.
8. McLuhan, *Understanding Media,* p. 7.
9. Richard J. Barnet and Ronald E. Müller, *Global Reach: The Power of the Multinational Corporation* (New York: Simon and Schuster, 1974), p. 232.
10. Richard Adler, "Understanding Television: An Overview of the Literature of the Medium as a Social and Cultural Force," in *Television as a Social Force,* p. 26.
11. Cater, "Introduction," p. 1.
12. Wilson P. Dizard, *Television: A World View* (Syracuse: Syracuse University Press, 1966), p. 2.
13. Cawelti, "Some Reflections," p. 991.
14. Michael Novak, "Television Shapes the Soul," *Television as a Social Force,* p. 9.
15. Adler, "Understanding Television," p. 23.
16. Benjamin De Mott, "The Viewer's Experience: Notes on TV Criticism and Public Health," *Television as a Social Force,* p. 49.
17. David Feldman, "Tune-Out: The Dynamics of Television," *Journal of Popular Culture,* 7, no. 4 (1974): 1010.
18. Wallace White, "Videodance—It May Be a Whole New Art Form," *The New York Times,* 18 January 1976.
19. Michael Iachetta, "Ballet, with TV's Help, Almost a Pop Dance," *New York Daily News,* 25 January 1976.
20. John J. O'Connor, "Can Serious Music be 'Visualized'?" *The New York Times,* 18 January 1976.

21. Dennis E. Baron, "Against Interpretation: The Linguistic Structure of Television Drama," *Journal of Popular Culture*, 7, no. 4 (1974): 946.
22. Dizard, *Television: A World View*, p. 11.
23. David Gelman with Nancy Stadtman, "The Great Paper Chase," *Newsweek*, 31 May 1976.
24. Robert C. Davis, "The Impact of Mass Communication," *Technology in Western Civilization*, ed. Melvin Kranzberg and Carroll W. Pursell, Jr. (New York: Oxford University Press, 1967), 2: 327.
25. Rona Cherry, "Toying with a Name," *The New York Times*, December 19, 1976.
26. Adler, "Understanding Television," pp. 30–31.
27. David M. Rein, "The Impact of Television Violence," *Journal of Popular Culture*, 7, no. 4 (1974): 934.
28. "Our Fearful Children," *New York Daily News*, 13 March 1977; "Children and their Fears," *The New York Times*, 6 March 1977.
29. Martin Garbus, "The Case Against Perry Mason," *The New York Times*, 28 December 1975.
30. Walter Laquer, *Europe Since Hitler* (Baltimore: Penguin Books Inc., 1972), p. 338; Peter Nichols, *Italia, Italia* (Boston: Little, Brown and Co., 1973), p. 165.
31. Adler, "Understanding Television," p. 33.
32. William A. Belson, *The Impact of Television: Methods and Findings in Program Research* (London: Crosby Lockwood and Sons, Ltd, 1967) p. 225–26.
33. Les Brown, "Albert Says TV Favors Presidents," *The New York Times*, 18 January 1976.
34. Laquer, *Europe Since Hitler*, p. 340; David L. Paletz and Martha Elson, "Television Coverage of Presidential Conventions: Now You See it, Now You Don't," *Political Science Quarterly*, 91 (Spring 1976): 109–31.
35. Paul H. Weaver, "Captives of Melodrama," *The New York Times Magazine*, 29 August 1976.
36. David Littlejohn, "Communicating Ideas by Television," *Television As a Social Force*, p. 63.
37. Laquer, *Europe Since Hitler*, p. 340.
38. Joan M. Chandler, "TV and Sports: Wedded with a Golden Hoop," *Psychology Today*, April, 1977, pp. 75–76.
39. Mary Louise Clancy, "Clare Booth Luce—Feminist with Definite Ideas about Family Life and Best Solutions," *Twin Circle*, 27 June 1976.
40. Wilbur Schramm, "What TV is Doing to Our Children," *Sight, Sound, and Society, eds.* David Manning White and Richard Averson (Boston: Beacon Press, 1968), p. 58.
41. Adler, "Understanding Television," p. 31.
42. Jack Magarrell, "Aptitude-Test Scores: Is the Decline Slowing?" *The Chronicle of Higher Education*, 13 September 1976.
43. Sandi Cushman, "Family Conversation is a Vanished Art," *New York Daily News*, 18 January 1976.

44. Arthur Ashe, "An Open Letter to Black Parents: Send Your Children to the Libraries," *The New York Times*, 6 February 1977.
45. Sandi Cushman, "Parents Should Monitor Children's TV Habits," *New York Daily News*, 1 February 1976.
46. McLuhan, *Understanding Media*, p. ix.
47. Timothy Green, *The Universal Eye: The World of Television* (New York: Stein and Day, 1972), p. 10.
48. Clancy, "Clare Booth Luce."
49. Belson, *The Impact of Television*, p. 226.
50. "Vatican Declaration on Certain Questions Concerning Sexual Ethics," *The Tablet*, January 22, 1976.
51. "Church Groups Seek to Curb TV Violence," *The New York Times*, 6 March 1977.
52. S. I. Hayakawa, "Television and the American Negro," *Sight, Sound, and Society*, p. 73.
53. Laquer, *Europe Since Hitler*, p. 340.
54. Belson, *Impact of Television*, pp. 225–26.
55. Gene I. Maeroff, "New Magazine Seeks to Aid Slow Teen Age Readers," *The New York Times*, 6 March 1977.
56. Henri Dieuzeide, "Possible Uses of Satellites in Education," *Communication in the Space Age: The Use of Satellites by the Mass Media* (Paris: Unesco, 1968), p. 66.
57. Lord Francis-Williams, "Responsible Presentation of the News in the Space Age," *Communication in the Space Age*, p. 42.
58. Kas Kalba, "The Electronic Community: A New Environment for Television Viewers and Critics," *Television as a Social Force*, p. 141.
59. David Manning White and Richard Averson, *Sight, Sound and Society: Motion Pictures and Television in America* (Boston: Beacon Press, 1967), p. 3.
60. Wright, "Tune-In," p. 887.
61. Adler, "Understanding Television," p. 24.
62. Lewis Grossberger. "History Repeats Itself," *Sunday News Magazine*, 26 March 1978.
63. John Scura, "First Television Sets Shake Up Isolated Town," *Twin Circle*, 2 April 1978.
64. Adler, p. 39.
65. Bob Donath, "New Study Finds Some TV–Violence Link," *Daily News*, February 28, 1978.
66. Adler, p. 39.

1. The Global Impact of Television: An Overview

Frank J. Coppa
Department of History
St. John's University

From the dawn of civilization to the onset of the Industrial Revolution mankind had been hopelessly divided, kept apart by geography, race, language, culture, diverse historical development, and above all, by lack of continuous contact. Folk traditions varied from village to village so that parochialism reigned supreme. A culture shared by all was a dream not easily realized even in the nineteenth century when the allure of nationalism became increasingly powerful. The prospect of creating a universal culture or even more modestly of promoting international understanding was deemed utopian, rendered impossible by deep-seated prevailing differences. Unquestionably, common patterns of living have long existed in all societies past and present, but a broad popular culture could not develop until communication had evolved to provide a mechanism for the rapid, broad, and relatively inexpensive dissemination of information. This was to be the task of the Industrial Revolution at the end of the eighteenth century.

The history of man is tied to the development of communication. To communicate in a more complete and effective manner than animals is the first prerequisite of civilization. From the cave paintings of the old stone age to the marvels of the electronic media, as man fashioned new tools, he changed his own image.[1] For more than a million years speech and gesture were the only means of communication among humans. Much later, some six thousand years ago, writing was developed. Only five hundred years ago did printing appear in Europe.[2] Not until the nineteenth century, however, was there an inexpensive mechanism for the circulation of the printed word that could permeate literate societies of the western world. This was achieved by the daily newspaper, which achieved large-scale circulation after the technological innovations of the 1830s.

The electronic revolution of the twentieth century produced the wireless or radio, which transcended the need for literacy and expanded the scope of mass culture. Following the Second World War, radio, which addressed itself to the ears of the world, was to be outpaced by television, which appealed to both ears and eyes. In less than three decades television evolved from a novelty into an instrument of popular diversion, big business, cultural exchange, and more. Its sight and sound have made it the first medium shared and understood by all of humanity, including its lower depth, from Tokyo to the Thames.

This essay will examine television's global dimension: its development in a series of countries from the United States to the Union of Soviet Socialist Republics. It will also provide an overview of the international communications system which links national and regional networks, and examine the international dialogue and interdependence that television has fostered. Finally, it will seek to determine to what extent television has changed the world into a village.

A number of factors have combined to make television the universal eye. They include: the spectacular spread of television transmission and the world-wide distribution of receivers; the export of American programs and the development of "electronic imperialism"; the advances made in media technology, especially the launching of a series of communication satellites; and the development of a number of regional broadcast unions. Each of these warrants consideration in the assessment of television's world-wide impact.

The expansion of television transmission and viewing since the end of the Second World War has been phenomenal. Before Hitler's Third Reich precipitated the war, television existed largely on an experimental basis in the United States, the United Kingdom, France, Germany, and Russia. Transmission was curtailed or terminated everywhere during the course of the conflict, but resumed soon after. The number of receivers in the world rose from less than 200,000 in 1940 to more than 300 million by the early 1970s.[3] By that time there were more than twenty thousand television transmitters operating on a regular basis with some five thousand in America, almost six thousand in Asia, and well over nine thousand in Europe.

The United States very quickly assumed the lead as the number of receivers increased from 186,000 in 1940 to 18,000,000 in 1954. By 1970 their number had soared to 84 million. Whereas in 1950 only slightly more than 10 percent of dwelling units had sets, by 1960 this figure was almost 90 percent.[4] The Soviet Union, the other super-power, also saw the opportunity offered by television. In 1947, the year after the United States resumed commercial transmission, the Russians announced their own broadcast plans. They decided to produce large screen receivers so that educational and entertainment programs could be viewed on a communal basis in factories, army clubs, collective farms, trade union halls, and community centers. The program was successful, for by the 1970s there were some fifty million receivers in the Soviet Union, more than in any other country except the United States.[5] Japan, meanwhile, rose from the ashes of defeat by means of an economic miracle which transformed her into the television giant of the far east. By the 1970s the Japanese viewers were among the most addicted in the world. A government study, "Britain 1978: An Official Handbook," revealed what most had already known—that watching television is Britain's favorite pastime.[6]

The other countries of the world followed suit. By the early 1960s there were 46 sets for every one thousand people in the world. By the early 1970s television stations in some one hundred countries served an audience of more than one billion people. A station was even placed on the Rock of Gibraltar, serving less than 10,000 receivers and surviving on the miniscule budget of $100,000—less than half the cost of one episode of "Bonanza."[7] Nor was television a western monopoly; it had grown from a few hundred transmitters in the North American region to thousands of stations on five continents.[8]

The countries that had enjoyed great power status before the political collapse of Europe viewed the resumption of television broadcasting as one means of asserting their cultural vitality despite the loss of political primacy. Their governments were determined to avoid the excesses of commercial United States television, which subjected the average viewer to some 40,000 commercials annually. They had substantial success. French commercials, for example, are limited to eight minutes per day while in Germany they are crammed into a single twenty-minute segment each evening. In Italy a similar string of commercials is called "Carosello" (Carrousel), and is well-produced and extremely popular.[9]

The European system of television administration rather than that of the United States has provided the pattern for the rest of the world. In France, Norway, Sweden, Denmark, and the Netherlands, television emerged as a strict state monopoly. Most other European countries opted for a state supervised network in which some commercial activity is permitted. In Italy and Switzerland mixed companies were established, while in Western Germany television networks were financed by the various states. Thus the German system, due to the insistence of the Americans and French after the war, is one of the most decentralized in the world. It has been argued that the relative superiority of European to American television has much to do with its greater independence of private sponsors. Only in Luxemburg and Ireland has television remained largely in private hands.[10]

In the mid-1960s there were 13 million sets in England, ten million in Western Germany, another ten million divided equally between France and Italy, and some four million between Sweden and Holland. By 1973 Western Germany had over 18 million, the United Kingdom over 17 million, and in France and Italy the number had doubled so that the French had over 12 million sets and the Italians over 11 million. No European country was capable of avoiding the allure of television; in Italy there were soon more television sets than baths.[11] In all, the countries of Western Europe accounted for more than 80 million sets.

Meanwhile the onset of the cold war prompted the countries of Eastern Europe, which did not wish to be outclassed by the west, to clamor for television broadcasting. They were soon to account for another 20 million sets or one for every six people in the region. "Europe," said Marshall McLuhan "is now getting a unity under the electronic auspices of compression and interrelation."[12]

The vast stretches of the third world, recently freed from European imperialism, saw television as a means of asserting their independence and modernity, especially appreciating the educational and political role that television could play in the creation of a national culture and the consolidation of a national state. To be sure, the developing regions did not have the same number of receivers as the more advanced areas, accounting for some 29 million in comparison to the more than 300 million in the developed areas as late as 1973, but the number was increasing. Transmission even reached some preindustrial areas; Emperor Haile Selassie I of Ethiopia had a miniature station installed in a complex of rooms in the city hall of Addis Ababa.

In Latin America, Colombia, lacking compulsory education and sufficient funds and teachers for an adequate national school system, sought to use "teleclubs" to teach its illiterate masses reading as well as the basics of public health, housing, and agriculture.[13] There and elsewhere, political, economic, educational, and prestige factors combined to contribute to the proliferation of receivers and the increase in transmission.

In the United States during the 1930s the Federal Radio Commission authorized more than two dozen experimental stations, but television's development was hindered by the fiscal impact of the depression and the mentality of the broadcasting industry which continued to concentrate upon radio. Television transmission ended its experimental basis in 1941 with the Commission's decision to permit commercial television to forge ahead with a full-scale national service. In New York the National Broadcasting Company (NBC) and the Columbia Broadcasting System (CBS) commenced operations on a fifteen hour schedule.[14] More ambitious plans were proposed but torpedoed by the Second World War.

It was not until 1947 that telecasting was resumed to the delight of a war weary people. Originally considered a medium for the upper classes, television was enthusiastically received by those in the lower income levels, who early provided a mass audience for the antics of "Mr. Television," Milton Berle. From 1948 to 1952 only a select number of cities including New York and Los Angeles enjoyed a full complex of channels. Most other major cities had only one channel; some had none at all. However, all of this soon changed.

Within the next two decades television receivers multiplied (like cancerous cells, according to the most caustic critics) and the country was virtually blanketed with transmission. The industry estimated that almost 90 percent of the population was exposed to television each week. At the end of 1949 less than 10 percent of American homes contained television sets; within the next decade the percentage soared to 90 percent. By the 1970s more than 60 million households had televisions; over half had more than one. This was accompanied by massive viewing, which tended to steadily increase. The average owner viewed some four hours and thirty-five minutes per day in 1950; by 1970 this had increased to six hours per day. The big three, NBC, CBS, and ABC, accounted for more than 95 percent of the entertainment to which some 90 percent of the population was exposed each week.[15]

NBC, CBS, and ABC soon learned that programs could profitably be exported as television rapidly emerged throughout the world. The Columbia Broadcasting System soon distributed its programs to over a hundred countries while its news service film was to be transmitted to households in more than 90 percent of the nonCommunist world. "Bonanza," in its heyday, was watched by more than 400 million people each week in some eighty-two countries in the Americas, Western Europe, Eastern Europe, Asia and Africa. Lucille Ball's Comedy Series, in its various versions, also found a world-wide market and has been broadcast in French, German, Spanish, Italian, and Cantonese as well as English. "Hawaii-Five-O" has been broadcast in six languages and sold in almost fifty countries.[16] Other American series popular abroad include "High Chaparral," "Gomer Pyle," "Hogan's Heroes," "Perry Mason," "The Mary Tyler Moore Show," "Get Smart," "I Spy," "Ironside," "The Virginian," "Columbo," "The Wonderful World of Disney," "Dr. Kildare," and "Kojak."

In 1965 the sale of such series to some ninety countries brought almost 80 million dollars to American coffers. Since then the rate of export and the amount earned by American companies has steadily increased. By 1971 both NBC and CBS sold such programs abroad for more than half a billion dollars.

The chief attraction of American programs, apart from their technical excellence and their excitement, is their price. While it may have cost $220,000 to produce a single episode of "Bonanza," it can be obtained in parts of Africa for about $50. This practice, which some have termed "electronic dumping," has enabled a number of United States-based firms to dominate the television of countries scattered throughout the world.[17] The impact of such programs has been particularly great in Canada and Latin America, already in so many ways in the shadow of their colossal neighbor.

Thirty-one million Canadians are attracted by the twenty-five American stations whose signals they receive clearly across their sprawling 4000 mile border with the United States. Canadians have shown little loyalty to their home networks, the large public-service Canadian Broadcasting Corporation (CBC) and their independent commercial network CTV, spending up to two-thirds of their time viewing American channels. In the mid 1970s viewers in Toronto gave 60 percent of their time to Canadian stations and 40 percent to the big three in Buffalo, encouraging Toronto advertisers to pour over 9 million dollars a year into commercials on the Buffalo channels, making them among the most profitable stations in the United States.[18]

Cable television, which has spread more quickly in Canada than elsewhere in the world so that by 1970 approximately one quarter of all households had it, brings in American as well as Canadian programs. To make matters worse even the two national channels rely heavily upon imported American programs, spending about 35 million dollars a year for exclusive rights in their areas for the top programs broadcast in the United States, putting them forward as their main attractions.[19]

Australia, with a viewing public of some seven million and over 1500 sets for every 10,000 of the population, also has been an important market for United States telefilm distribution. In the early 1960s Australian local production accounted for only 10 percent of prime-time programming and the remaining 90 percent was largely American.[20]

The situation is similar in South America where 40 percent of the television programs in Peru, half the programs in Bolivia, and an overwhelming 85 percent of the programs in Costa Rica are put together by foreign corporations. Television has a potentially vast market south of the border, but it is not as common as in the United States or Canada. In the early 1960s there were only some 24 receivers per 1000 population, in comparison to 243 for North America.[21]

Initially Latin America was inundated by United States programs, but a number of factors have stemmed the flood. For one thing, there was a language difference that was not present in the Canadian exchange. Furthermore the culture of the people and their level of socioeconomic development often differed markedly from that of their northern neighbors. Programs that had a great appeal in the United States were not as successful to the south. The masses of Latin America seemed more attuned to the native *telenovelas* with their simple plots and unsophisticated language, which were viewed hour after hour. There was also considerable competition from programs produced in Europe, especially Spain, that the Latinos found more *simpatico*.

Nonetheless, critics have charged that the export of American programs and even more the advertisement of American products

have created an unfortunate psychological dependence. Evangelina
Garcia, an expert in social communication at the Central University of Venezuela as well as a consultant to a number of United
States firms, notes that today in Venezuela "the housewife measures her happiness by whether she has a refrigerator."[22] Studies
of the impact of television in Peru indicate that the poor there find
the world of television an easy escape from the unfortunate realities of everyday life, especially the rigid class structure. Many
of the people of Latin America find it difficult to identify with the
blond, blue-eyed heroes and heroines of so many shows produced in
the United States. This has led some to view these programs and
products with suspicion.

Recently a similar suspicion was echoed by the government of
Yugoslavia, which unlike most other communist countries, readily
imported American feature films and television series. The government controlled newspaper *Politika* of Belgrade has criticized the
impact of these films, and even condemned one episode of "The
Wonderful World of Disney" for presenting "an uncritical, ideal-
ized picture of the goodness and the high moral standards of
wealthy Americans."[23] The Belgrade daily feared the effect that
such programs would have on impressionable young minds, while
party members privately questioned the wisdom of showing such
police series as "Columbo" and "Kojak." International diplomacy
and Yugoslavia's precarious position between east and west required that a Soviet adventure series be shown simultaneously
with "Kojak."

A number of American educational programs have been well received abroad—most notably "Sesame Street." Developed under the
auspices of the public service National Education Television
(NET), the series sought to provide the basic skills of reading and
writing to children. In translation, since 1970, "Sesame Street" has
become an international success.[24]

If the United States is practicing a new kind of cultural colonial-
ism in exporting its television programs, an electronic imperialism,
it is not unique. The British BBC has exported biographical studies
of Isadora Duncan, Richard Strauss, Delius, and George Sand, as
well as twenty-six episodes of "The Galsworthy Saga," sold to fifty
different countries, including Russia. The British have also exported historical studies such as the award winning "Six Wives of
Henry VIII," "Elizabeth Regina," Kenneth Clark's personal view
of "Civilisation," "The World at War," and Alistair Cooke's "Amer-

ica: A Personal History of the United States." The English series "Steptoe and Son" and "Till Death Do Us Part," when translated into "Sanford and Son" and "All in the Family" became resounding successes in the United States.

BBC's "Upstairs, Downstairs" was also well received both in the United States and elsewhere. Some have argued that the most common element in European television is the addiction to British adventure series, which are seen in almost every European country on both sides of the Iron Curtain with the exception of Russia. The more successful ones such as "The Avengers," "Danger Man," "The Saint," or "Z-Cars" virtually blanket the continent. British television must share the responsibility for fostering international fantasy, if not dialogue. Paradoxically, while sending their films and series abroad at a hectic pace, the British have restricted both their public and commercial networks, limiting imported programs to fourteen percent of viewing time.[25]

The Egyptians, whose network was established by the Radio Corporation of America and presents many American television programs with Arab subtitles, are clearly attempting to establish their superiority in television throughout the Middle East. Their major competition stems from the United States, whose programs, shown in English with Arabic subtitles, are extremely popular in Jordan and the oil rich states of the Gulf, as well as Egypt itself.[26] The French have sold or given programs and newsreels to the French-speaking countries of Europe, Canada, and their former colonies in Asia and Africa. The Soviet Union sends its programs to its communist allies in Eastern Europe by satellite and coaxial cable.

Spanish television, which is a curious combination of American and European broadcasting, has vigorously exploited the Latin American market, filling the void left by the resentment of North American programs. Utilizing the Atlantic satellites, yearly conversations with South American video executives, and since 1971 the Ibero-American Television Organization (IATO) to promote and facilitate exchange, Spanish television is creating a strong cultural bridge between Europe and South America. At present Spain with almost six million sets ranks fifth in Western Europe behind Western Germany, Britain, France, and Italy. In all of Western Europe there are some 75 million sets, one for every five people. Only in Portugal, Yugoslavia, and Greece has television not become commonplace.[27]

In European broadcasting the British have long enjoyed a number of advantages, certainly since 1936, when broadcasting from Alexandra Palace in London became the first in the world. Greer Garson, then a relatively unknown actress, and the already famous playwright George Bernard Shaw, were among the first to be televised.[28] Initially programs were shown for some thirteen hours per week and there were less than 10,000 sets in the entire country. Even this limited service was terminated with the outbreak of the Second World War and it was only at the end of the conflict after a hiatus of seven years that regular transmission was revived.

In June 1946 the public service British Broadcasting Corporation (BBC) was launched with less than 2000 subscribers. Supported by annual lease fees, the BBC was the sole broadcaster of programs in the United Kingdom and served as an example for the rest of Europe. In 1955 the Independent Television Authority, later rechristened the Independent Broadcasting Authority (IBA), was permitted to begin commercial broadcasting, known as ITV, challenging the BBC's monopoly. To deal with the aggressive competition of the more diversified and popular ITV, the BBC was allowed to open a second channel in 1964, providing an attractive alternative to what was being shown on the first BBC channel. By that time both the BBC and ITV channels had achieved total coverage and were received throughout the country.[29]

On the continent they were considered models to be emulated. The relative openness of British television and the absence of censorship were particularly admired. "The beauty of the position in Britain as opposed to France and Germany is that everyone in this country knows that every major controversy will find its way on to the screen" remarked Anthony Smith, a BBC producer. "British television is organized in such a way that it can't be prevented from making the semiconscious guilts and anguishes of the British conscious and official."[30]

The British primacy in European television broadcasting was also maintained by the technological excellence of the system, especially admired by the West Germans. The latter, possessing the richest public service network in the world as well as superb technological skills, have also been instrumental in the development of European television in the postwar period. Owners of more receivers than any other Western European country, the Germans were the first to limit commercials to a number of minutes per day and to dramatically increase the revenue drawn from license fees. The color system they developed, the PAL, has been adopted by most other Western European countries.

Ironically all television broadcasting in West Germany, a militant champion of the free enterprise system, is publicly owned. In the early 1960s Chancellor Konrad Adenauer sought to undermine both the regional control and strict public service nature of German television by proposing the establishment of a national commercial television channel, but he was frustrated by the German constitutional court.[31]

The French, who demonstrated a thirty line system of transmission as early as 1929 and introduced studio experiments from 1932 onwards, resumed their telecasting soon after the liberation of Paris in 1944. French television, thereafter, developed slowly for a number of reasons including the protracted debate over the merits of a private versus a state controlled system. The resolution of this issue did not bring immediate expansion to France's television facilities, for in the late 1940s the government decided to give priority to the rehabilitation of the national radio network. Small wonder that in the early 1950s France had one of the lowest ratios of sets per family in Europe.[32]

It was only in 1954 that the French Chamber of Deputies approved a five year plan for the national television network. A decade later the National Assembly transferred radio and television from the control of the Ministry of Information to the autonomous Office de Radiodiffusion Télévision. Nonetheless the government still maintained a firm control over broadcasting and this was increased during the years of Charles de Gaulle, who used it as an extension of his own colorful, towering personality, enabling him to bypass Parliament and appeal directly to the people in accordance with his use of the referendum. One of his ministers justified the General's use of the medium by asserting, "La télévision, c'est le gouvernement dans la salle a manger."[33]

The French developed their own color system, SECAM, which is not easily compatible with the PAL system. Undoubtedly this played a part in the Soviet Union's decision to adopt the French system. It has also been adopted by the Communist countries of Eastern Europe with the exception of Yugoslavia. Since sets made for the SECAM system cannot receive programs from the PAL and vice versa, the French have contributed to the creation of an electronic barrier in Europe. PAL color is received from Italy to Scandinavia and Britain, while France and the Communist countries in the east embrace SECAM.

The vitality of French television is attested to by its large revenue—the second largest in Europe—and by its exportation of programs to former colonies in Asia and Africa as well as Belgium, Switzerland, Luxemburg, Monaco and French Canada. The two Italian stations of the RAI, the last of the big four networks, have cooperated with the French on a number of projects, especially the production of historical films made especially for television.[34]

Even though there were experiments with the transmission of images in Mussolini's Italy in the later 1920s, it was only at the beginning of 1954 that television service officially commenced with one channel which was received nationwide. This was complemented by a second channel in 1961 which soon reached some ninety percent of the population. These two channels are controlled by the public service Radio Televisione Italiana (RAI), which unlike many other broadcasting organizations in Europe is not an autonomous state corporation but rather is owned by the state's Institute for the Reconstruction of Industry (IRI), a holding company. Television programming is supervised by the Parliamentary Supervisory Commission which must assure the political independence and objectivity of the information on radio and television, and by a committee of the Ministry of Posts and Tele-Communications.[35] In 1977, despite the fear that complete color transmission would contribute to the spiraling national inflation, RAI-TV announced Italy's entry into the color age.[36]

Although there were only six million sets in Italy in the mid-1960s and transmission time was limited to some nine hours on the first RAI channel and two hours on the second, the evening audience was high.[37] It sometimes reached as many as thirty million because sets were placed in coffee houses, bars, public squares, and other places where crowds congregated. The premium placed on social interaction in Italy plus the obsession with talk has meant that television has not had the devastating effect on conversation and sociability that it has had in much of Western Europe and the United States. Television is extremely popular, but few Italians are isolated by it. Many prefer to watch it in company, in a bar, pensione, or dining hall rather than a private parlor.[38]

Over the years the largest audience has been attracted by "Tele-giornale," a lively news program which is very important in the peninsula, for television news is the main source of information for some ten million Italians. Whereas some 30 percent of the population over eighteen years of age in postwar Italy purchased and read books regularly, and some 31 percent frequently attended the cinema, some 63 percent of this population watched television with some degree of regularity. For this reason, among others, the RAI has used television as an educational device for Italian schools.[39]

Unlike the BBC and France's RTF, which dabbled with programs of educational enrichment in the 1950s, the RAI looked upon television as more than an instrument of enrichment and proposed that it be used to supplement the chronic lack of secondary school facilities, particularly in the *Mezzogiorno* or South. From this hope there emerged *Telescuola* or television school, operated by RAI in cooperation with the Ministry of Education, the first attempt to employ direct instruction via television to a mass audience.

Commencing with one hour and two vocational courses which enrolled some 50,000 students in 1958, by the early 1960s *telescuola* was broadcasting over thirty hours per week with a range of courses which then included history, mathematics, geography, French, art, and civics. Interestingly enough, about one third of its students were high school dropouts, more than half of them female. In 1961 the overwhelming majority of those who completed the course and presented themselves for the examination at a state school, passed. Equally successful was the *telescuola* program "It's Never Too Late," a reading and writing course for hard-core illiterates. The Italians, and others, have presented abundant evidence that there can be effective teaching via television.[40]

In Italy, long the land of provincialism and *campanalismo,* where the first loyalty had traditionally been to the village and its vicinity, television has had a unifying effect. Thus one finds among the younger generation a tendency to affect the Roman accent typical of newscasters and actors on television. Viewers in the Lucania, in the *Mezzogiorno,* said that television made them realize that they were cut off from the other Italy where people lived better and life was less burdensome. Undoubtedly this has played a part in the flight from the land and the migration from the South to the North. The young girls of the South imitated the ladies of this other Italy and their parents did not object, considering that this was the way of the future.[41]

Although the pace of European television has been set by the British, Germans, French, and Italians, who alone have the resources to create and distribute large scale productions and hire satellite time for the transmission of important news stories, the smaller states have not been idle. In the smaller multinational states of Europe broadcasting is done in several languages: Flemish and French in Belgium; German, French and Italian in Switzerland. The Dutch have evolved an extraordinary system, providing all organizations with more than 15,000 members who have purchased television licenses with air time on the country's two television networks. The Norwegian "Idebanken," the bank of ideas, is a unique program which seeks the advice of its viewers upon a series of problems, just as "The file on XY" in Germany relies upon its viewers to aid the police in solving open criminal cases.[42]

The television transmission of the smaller states as well as the pacesetters has been aided by the European Broadcasting Union. The English championed the establishment of the Union which finally emerged following a conference convened at Torquay in 1950. Its program exchange system, known as Eurovision, links twenty-eight active members and thirty-two associates and extends to North Africa and Eastern Europe. The European Broadcasting Union, the world's largest and most important, has its technical center in the Palais de Justice in Brussels and its headquarters in Geneva. Transmission from Brussels can be relayed instantly to more than 75 million television sets in Western Europe. A non-political, multinational organization, the EBU serves the needs of professional broadcasters. It acts as a clearing house for its members' programming, especially sports and news, which accounts for the greater part of its efforts.

When an outstanding news story breaks, an international soccer or tennis match is played, there is a moon shot or an Olympics, the Europeans rely upon Eurovision rather than their independent broadcast organizations to provide them with coverage. As early as 1953 at the coronation of Queen Elizabeth II, cameras at the site combined with transmitters on the continent to relay this pageant to millions of curious viewers. The following summer the world football championship match mesmerized more than 60 million Europeans. The broadcasting of sports events such as Wimbledon tennis, sports car racing, Olympic games and the tremendously popular soccer have remained important. Recently, however, there has been an increasing emphasis on news coverage.[43]

Avoiding needless duplication, the European Broadcasting Union is more efficient and less expensive in its coverage of outstanding events. The Union's news exchange, which occurs twice daily, enables the smaller, less wealthy systems to enjoy the same calibre of coverage attained by the big four. Television permits an almost complete synthesis between fact and news: information on the death of President Kennedy was diffused throughout the world in about half an hour. Most Eurovision transmission centers on news or sports, where the pictures can readily tell the story and language is not an obstacle. The exchange and coproduction of programs carried on within the European Broadcasting Union has shown that the language barrier is less difficult to overcome than certain patterns of thought and logic.[44]

A number of outstanding events have been televised throughout most of the continent and have captured the imagination of Europeans. The death of the Kennedys, the funeral of Churchill, the World Cup finals have all had a profound impact. The great museums of the world such as the Louvre and the Vatican, as well as the Kremlin and the White House have been seen by millions throughout the world through the television camera's eye. One of the most popular Eurovision linkups has been the annual song contest which has attracted audiences of upwards of 200 million in some seventeen European countries. The victorious song is usually released in several languages, providing it a truly common market.

The European Broadcasting Union acts as the representative of European customers for telecommunication facilities requiring the use of the satellites and negotiates on behalf of its members the conditions of utilization. The members of the EBU are linked to Intervision, the broadcasting union of the Communist bloc, which ties stations in seven Eastern European countries. Coordinated in Prague, it is, like its counterpart in the west, a center for the exchange of news and sports, which are popular and well-received, and political propaganda, which is not popular but remains one of the staples of the system. Eurovision countries can purchase any of the items on the Intervision list, which is sent from Prague to Geneva. Since the early 1970s the European Broadcasting Union's news exchange has also been linked with television stations in Latin America through the Spanish network in Madrid. This has made the special news items of Brazil, Colombia, Peru, and Venezuela available to the members of the European Broadcasting Union and in turn provides for the transmission of their top stories by satellite to these Latin American states.[45]

As early as July 1962 experimental telecasts were exchanged

between Western Europe and the United States. Such exchange has
since continued on a regular basis via the Telstar satellite which
established the first bridge across the Atlantic. In the following
year the Europeans transmitted 100 programs to the United States
and received some 40 in return.[46] The European Broadcasting
Union has increased contact with the far-flung Asian Broadcasting
Union established in 1964 under the auspices of Japan and including such countries as India, New Zealand, South Korea, the Philip-
pines, and Australia. Relations between the European Broadcasting
Union and the more politicized Arab States Broadcasting Union,
established in 1969, have been good. Unquestionably Europe, east
and west, has derived the greatest advantage from the establishment of regional television networks.

The barriers separating Eurovision from Intervision remain far
more political than technical. This is largely the case because the
Soviet Union, one of the pioneers in television transmission and
possessing more sets than any other country except the United
States, remains aloof from the European Broadcasting Union. The
Russian determination to remain outside of the EBU as well as its
decision to adopt SECAM rather than PAL color seems to be part
of a general Russian attempt to control what Soviet subjects see
and hear. If American television can be said to be mainly concerned
with selling goods, and Western European television is by and large
inspired by the public service concept, television in the Soviet
Union has as its main goal political education not to say Communist indoctrination.

Unlike the Communist states of Eastern Europe which have
shown American, British, French and Italian productions and
series, the Soviet Union has only on occasion taken news or sports
items from the West. This, however, has not prevented the Soviet
government from selling broadcast rights for the 1980 summer
Olympic games in Moscow to the National Broadcasting Company
of the United States for a reported eighty million dollars. In 1969
the Russians purchased "The Forsyte Saga" and collaborated with
the French to film "The Battle of Moscow." The detente diplomacy
practiced by Secretary of State Kissinger has made the Soviet
Union somewhat less wary of the West, although the programs
they have purchased have been the politically neutral—"Casals at
88" and the documentary on the plight of the Indians, "Now that
the Buffalo's Gone." The only nonCommunist programs that the
Russians regularly see are the international soccer matches and ice

hockey.[47] In turn, they have permitted world telecasts of the Bolshoi Ballet and the Moscow Circus.

Some have argued that the practices of the Soviet Union are not so far removed from what occurs elsewhere. Television in the United States has traditionally been concerned with increasing material consumption while that of the Soviet Union has been obsessed with increasing socialist production. Likewise it has been claimed that censorship on the Soviet Union's stations and its manipulation of news and programming was similar to the practices of Gaullist France, Franco's Spain, or governmental control over media in many countries of the third world. Others, however, have insisted that the Soviet practices are different in kind and that they have sought to reinforce their "iron curtain" by electronic surveillance.

What cannot be contested is the fact that the Soviets have until recently discouraged exchange with the west. The space age is also the missile age and though there have been many proposals to utilize space communications for international harmony, competition has in fact prevailed. The Russians early expressed an interest in space communications, predicting in 1957, the year that Sputnik was launched, that they would develop the capability to broadcast television worldwide via satellite. They were less enchanted by the American vision of using space communications to serve government and business needs than by the opportunity to exploit their success as a means of enhancing the reputation of the Soviet Union.[48]

The Soviets abstained when in 1964 the United States, following a congressional mandate, began international negotiations for the establishment of a global system of space communications. "The Congress hereby declares that it is the policy of the United States to establish, in conjunction with other countries, as expeditiously as practicable a commercial communications satellite system as part of an improved global communications network," read the Communications Satellite Act of 1962, "which will be responsible to public needs and national objectives, which will serve the communications needs of the United States and other countries, and which will contribute to world peace and understanding."[49]

In the summer of 1964 nineteen countries including the Vatican signed an agreement establishing the International Space Communications Consortium (Intelstat) which soon had well over fifty members. The fact that the United States acquired more than

three-fifths of the consortium's shares at the outset and exercised
a virtual veto power over its operations made the Russians reluctant to join. The Soviet Union and the other Communist bloc countries condemned Intelstat as a device for placing space communications in the hands of private American capital. In 1965 when Intelstat launched its first satellites over the Atlantic, Pacific, and
Indian oceans, the Russians launched their first Molninya (light-
ning) satellite. Subsequently more than thirty of these craft were
launched, making the Soviet Union the first country to use communications satellites as an integral part of their domestic network.

In 1968 the Russians in conjunction with Bulgaria, Cuba,
Czechoslovakia, Hungary, Mongolia, Poland, and Rumania approved a draft treaty for Intersputnik, their own international
communications system to challenge United States leadership in
space communications. At the end of 1975 the Soviets launched
their first Stationstar toward a stationary orbit above the Indian
Ocean, filing with the Frequency Regulation in Geneva their inten-
tion of launching seven more such craft in 1978–1980, placing
them along the equator above the Indian, Atlantic and Pacific
oceans. Very clearly they intend to create a global network that will
rival that of Intelstat, which presently carries all intercontinental
television and a good part of the transoceanic telephone traffic.[50]

Perhaps the Soviets desire to monitor television transmission
and control the satellites because they understand television's
impact. Undoubtedly the spread of student revolt in the 1960s was
facilitated by television, which communicated unrest from country
to country with an urgency possessed by no other medium. Another
unfortunate example of its influence, from the Russian vantage,
was its use by former First Secretary Dubcek in Czechoslovakia.
The Soviets concluded that Czech television, by permitting free
speech, open criticism, and all types of arguments, played a major
role in creating the atmosphere of questioning, independence and
defiance which they found necessary to suppress.[51]

For all of their aloofness, surveillance, and secrecy the Soviets
have not been able to completely elude the scrutiny of the probing
camera eye, oftentimes with startling consequences. The immediacy
of television and the importance of the satellites hovering in space
above the equator was made manifest in the summer of 1968 when
millions of viewers throughout Europe and the Americas were
startled to see Russian tanks roll into Prague. This was the first

invasion to be witnessed as it occurred by millions throughout the world.

The following summer the global impact of television was even more clearly appreciated when Neil Armstrong's first steps upon the moon were witnessed by upwards of 723 million people in some fifty different countries. Never before had so large a portion of mankind shared a common experience, as viewers from the industrial and underdeveloped worlds, those from Communist as well as capitalist countries were spellbound by that historic walk.[52]

The future of global television is inextricably intertwined with the linkage of land cables and microwave systems as well as the development of space communication satellites or comsats. The latter, once the fantasy of science fiction writers who envisioned bringing all the people of the world together, had become a reality by the mid-1960s when American technology, followed by Soviet engineering expertise, succeeded in orbiting satellites capable of transmitting telephone communications across the continents of the world and television communication to the most remote regions. Comstar, a domestic satellite in synchronous orbit above the United States, has for years transmitted long distance calls through seven earth stations.

Space communication still retains the aura of science fiction not only because it developed so quickly but also because of the new horizons it has opened for international exchange and its potential for influencing daily lives everywhere. It has enabled television to circle the globe in less than a second, ending the social isolation which had persisted from the dawn of history and bringing every group no more than a few milliseconds from any other.[53]

Communication satellites are not so much a new form of technology as a tremendous extension of existing telecommunications, a great leap forward in existing technology rather than the formation of a new one. As such they have had far-reaching results. In conjunction with computer technology they can assemble and process information on such topics as weather and distribute it worldwide. They have made regional and intercontinental networks possible, linking most of the world together. Time differences do present problems, so that only the most urgent matters and material of vital concern will be broadcast immediately without some delay or retransmission.[54] Nonetheless the satellites' tremendous capacity to promote international dialogue has reminded some that the word communication derives from the Latin *communicatus*—share.

Electronic experts are predicting that by the 1980s space satellites utilizing the energy of the sun or possibly nuclear reactors will be able to transmit vast amounts of material directly from their orbits to sets at home, so that a viewer in New York might be able to tune in at will to London, Paris, or Rome and vice versa. The obstacles to such transmission are clearly economic and political rather than technical.

Almost any broadcast from a satellite will cross several boundaries, especially in Europe, and this infringes upon the prevailing concept of national sovereignty. So long as the satellites are only used to transfer programs between ground stations as is currently the case, it is quite simple for a particular country's government to refuse access to programs it does not wish its population to view. When the satellites develop the capacity to bypass the ground stations and transmit directly into home receivers, new problems will arise and new regulations will be required. That will effectively end the present barriers to the free flow of information, for no wall can be built high enough to keep out voices from space.[55]

It has been predicted that by 1985 more than forty international and domestic satellites will be competing for stations along the equator, leading to orbital crowding. Since broadcasting satellites cover such enormous areas they are bound to impose upon existing frequency allocations and might eventually require a worldwide frequency allocation plan. The prospect of possible radio interference between domestic and international communications satellites has already prompted a dialogue between representatives of the Soviet Union and the ninety-one member global communications consortium, Intelstat.[56]

The technology of the satellites can increase the dialogue between peoples of diverse cultural heritages, alleviating spiritual isolation while contributing to the enhanced realization of a common humanity. With the aid of these complex but compact mechanisms, television can bridge the barriers of time and space so that we may have a greater opportunity to see how the rest of humanity lives. Television, by means of these satellites, can serve as a window on the world, contributing to the formation of a collective conscience. It could reach into areas where there are few schools, increasing literacy and providing the basics of social education and hygiene.[57]

To date the extraordinary capability of the comsats for cheaper and more efficient service between any two points on the globe has been only partially realized although there has been an important reduction in the cost of satellite communication. A company in California has developed a prototype two-way transmitting and receiving terminal which sells for $50,000 while the Japanese have built a prototype receiver which costs only $1,500 to build.[58] However, the prospect of a worldwide system of communication satellites has created tension among the existing sovereign states rather than advancing the notion of a world community. Not surprisingly, concern for national prestige and rivalry have posed serious obstacles to the creation of a unified communications network. Noncapitalist countries, most notably the Soviet Union, have serious reservations about cooperating with a privately owned communications satellite company heavily influenced by the United States, the stronghold of the private enterprise system.[59]

On the other hand in Europe and North America the satellites have had an impact marked by an increase in the number of live broadcasts from abroad. The "Town Meeting of the World," which brought together government and opposition spokesmen from European and American countries to discuss foreign policy, provided a magnificent preview of what the satellites could do when properly used.[60] Television also played a key role in bringing about the extraordinary visit of President Sadat to Israel, and the resulting worldwide television coverage provided new hope for a negotiated solution to the problems of the Middle East. The signing of the Israeli-Egyptian treaty in March, 1979, in Washington was virtually seen throughout the world by means of television and the satellites.

Will the potential of the satellites and television transmission to bring mankind together be realized in the future? Will international television serve as an ambassador of goodwill, fostering understanding and harmony between the peoples of the world? This is contingent upon a number of factors and especially the attitudes of the national governments and private interests. Undeniably too many politicians in the developing countries as well as the more advanced industrial states have regarded television as their particular preserve. Franco, Salazar, and De Gaulle in the west; the Communist regimes in the east; Castro in Cuba; and a series of dictators or leaders of "guided democracy" elsewhere have used television as a means of control rather than communication. Perhaps the Mexican government has been most honest in its determination to use television, enacting specific legislation that entitles it to 12.5 percent of all television time to justify its policies to the masses.[61]

Television as a medium is neutral. Without proper direction international television might well degenerate into an instrument of propaganda and cheap entertainment governed exclusively by the profit motive and parochial interests. Distorted presentations of violence and appeals to the baser instincts can harden heart and soul and pervert rather than uplift man, rendering him more bestial and less human.

Television can open the world to its audience, or it can present a monstrous caricature of reality. Its ubiquitous images can promote peace and understanding or incite jealousy, rivalry, and hatred. The magic mirror reflects the images we choose to project. These are vitally important not only as a barometer of our priorities but also as a mechanism in shaping international opinion.

During the seventeenth session of the General Assembly of the United Nations the representative of Brazil, citing the dangers of radio and television transmission by satellite and anxious to exclude propaganda, the call for religious or class conflict, or even excessive and therefore offensive nationalism, urged that satellites be placed under United Nations supervision. Others have echoed his call. In a series of resolutions the United Nations has concerned itself with measures to promote international cooperation in the development and use of space communication, pressing for its use for the improvement of humanity and the benefit of all the countries of the world.[62] Unfortunately, national rivalry and international tension, among other factors, have frustrated attempts to use television to promote international exchange and harmony.

The Greeks accomplished great things by their exploitation of the phonetic alphabet. The Americans based their republic on the foundation of the Europeans' printing revolution. The United Nations, if it is to have a meaningful existence, may have to control satellite communications.[63] There is wide agreement that the extension of the mass media by space communication imposes a great responsibility upon those who prepare the programs to be seen instantaneously world-wide. It may be that the communications industry has outpaced man's ethical development; that technology has outrun morality.

Notes

1. Lord Francis-Williams, "Responsible Presentation of the News in the Space Era," in UNESCO's *Communication in the Space Age: The Use of Satellites by the Mass Media* (Paris: UNESCO, 1968), p. 41; Neil P. Hurley, "The Role of Communications Technology in Democracy," *Communications Satellites in Political Orbit*, ed. Lloyd D. Musolf (San Francisco: Chandler Publishing Co., 1968), pp. 179-80.
2. Robert C. Davis, "The Impact of Mass Communication," *Technology in Western Civilization*, ed. Melvin Kranberg and Carroll W. Pursell, Jr. (New York: Oxford University Press, 1967), p. 323.
3. *UNESCO Statistical Yearbook, 1974* (Paris: Unesco Press, 1975), p. 855.
4. Derek Horton, *Television's Story and Challenge* (London: G. Harrap and Co., 1951), p. 65; Davis, *Technology in Western Civilization*, 2: 327.
5. *UNESCO Statistical Yearbook, 1974*, p. 856; Horton, *Television's Story*, p. 76; Timothy Green, *The Universal Eye: The World of Television* (New York: Stein and Day, 1972), p. 156.
6. *The New York Times*, 19 February 1978.
7. *Unesco Statistical Yearbook, 1974*, p. 856; Green, p. 11.
8. Wilson P. Dizard, *Television, a World View* (Syracuse: Syracuse University Press, 1966), pp. 1-4; Morris L. Ernst and Judith A. Posner, *The Comparative International Almanac* (New York: Macmillan Co., 1967), pp. 166-67.
9. Richard J. Barnet and Ronald E. Müller, *Global Reach: The Power of the Multinational Corporation* (New York: Simon and Schuster, 1974), p. 232; Anthony Sampson, *Anatomy of Europe* (New York: Harper and Row, 1968), p. 294; Green, *The Universal Eye*, p. 117; Dizard, *Television, a World View*, p. 40.
10. Walter Laquer, *Europe Since Hitler* (Baltimore: Penguin Books, Inc., 1972), p. 339; Sampson, *Anatomy of Europe*, p. 294; Dizard, *Television, a World View*, pp. 27, 37.
11. *UNESCO Statistical Yearbook, 1974*, pp. 863-64; Sampson, *Anatomy of Europe*, p. 293; Laquer, *Europe Since Hitler*, p. 339.
12. Sampson, *Anatomy of Europe*, p. 293.
13. Green, *The Universal Eye*, p. 62.
14. Dizard, *Television, a World View*, p. 23.
15. William A. Belson, *The Impact of Television: Methods and Findings in Program Research* (London: Crosby Lockwood and Sons, Ltd., 1967), p. 215; Barnet and Müller, *Global Reach*, pp. 231-32; Green, *The Universal Eye*, p. 218.

16. Barnet and Müller, *Global Reach*, p. 144; Green, *The Universal Eye*, p. 11.
17. Dizard, *Television, a World View*, p. 3; Barnet and Müller, pp. 144–45; Green, *The Universal Eye*, p. 249.
18. Jack Miller, "U.S.—Canada TV War Is in the Air," *New York Post*, 21 January 1976.
19. Miller, "U.S.—Canada War," Green, *The Universal Eye*, pp. 43, 49.
20. David Wallechinsky and Irving Wallace, *The People's Almanac* (Garden City, New York: Doubleday and Co., 1975), pp. 823–24; *The Comparative International Almanac*, p. 16; Dizard, *Television, a World View*, p. 162.
21. *The Comparative International Almanac*, pp. 166–67; Barnet and Müller, *Global Reach*, p. 145.
22. Barnet and Müller, *Global Reach*, p. 176.
23. Malcom W. Browne, "Yugoslavia Steps Up Criticism of U.S. Television Programs," *The New York Times*, 21 December 1975.
24. Erik Barnouw, *Tube of Plenty: The Evolution of American Television* (New York: Oxford University Press, 1975), p. 437.
25. Sampson, *Anatomy of Europe*, pp. 303–4; Green, *The Universal Eye*, pp. 70, 81.
26. Thomas W. Lippman, "Midwest TV with Western Color," *The Washington Post*, 28 December 1976.
27. *UNESCO Statistical Yearbook, 1974*, pp. 863–64.
28. Dizard, *Television, A World View*, p. 23.
29. Belson, *Impact of Television*, pp. 212–15; Green, *The Universal Eye*, p. 87.
30. Sampson, *Anatomy of Europe*, p. 300.
31. Ibid., p. 295; Green, *The Universal Eye*, p. 104.
32. Dizard, *Television, a World View*, pp. 25–28.
33. Sampson, *Anatomy of Europe*, p. 296.
34. Ibid., p. 301; Green, *The Universal Eye*, p. 117.
35. Donato Goffredo, *Psicologia del Divismo Televisio* (Rome: Fratelli Palombi Editori, 1968), pp. 81, 86; Servizi informazioni della Presidenza del Consiglio dei Ministri, *Questa e L'Italia* (Rome: Istituto Poligrafico dello Stato, 1971), pp. 180–81.
36. Istituto Italiano di Culture, *Newsletter*, 53.
37. *UNESCO Statistical Yearbook, 1974*, pp. 863–64; Green, *The Universal Eye*, p. 128.
38. Peter Nichols, *Italia, Italia* (Boston: Little, Brown and Co., 1973), p. 44.
39. Green, *The Universal Eye*, p. 128; *Questa è L'Italia*, pp. 180–81.
40. Dizard, *Television, a World View*, pp. 210–13; Wilbur Schramm, "What TV Is Doing to Our Children," *Sight, Sound and Society*, ed. David Manning White and Richard Averson (Boston: Beacon Press, 1968), p. 60.
41. Goffredo, *Psicologia*, p. 75.
42. Green, *The Universal Eye*, pp. 144–47; Sampson, *Anatomy of Europe*, p. 295; *The People's Almanac*, p. 826.
43. Dizard, *Television, a World View*, pp. 82–83, 85–86.

44. Ibid., p. 90; Henri Dieuzeide, "Possible Uses of Satellites in Education," *Communication in the Space Age,* p. 63; Goffredo, *Psicologia,* p. 63; Green, *The Universal Eye,* pp. 74–75.
45. J. Treeby Dickinson, "Telecommunication Satellites and the European Broadcasting Union," *Communication in the Space Age,* p. 101; Sampson, *Anatomy of Europe,* pp. 302, 305.
46. Arthur C. Clarke, "Prediction, Realization and Forecast," *Communication in the Space Age,* p. 33; Dizard, *Television, a World View* pp. 5, 87.
47. *The People's Almanac,* p. 827; Green, *The Universal Eye,* p. 160.
48. Jonathan F. Galloway, *The Politics and Technology of Satellite Communications* (Lexington, Mass.: D.C. Heath and Co., 1972), pp. 122–23.
49. "Communications Satellite Act of 1962," *Communications Satellites in Political Orbit,* p. 117.
50. Herbert I. Schiller, "Communications Satellites: A New Institutional Setting," ibid, pp. 152–53; Galloway, *Politics and Technology,* p. 128.
51. Sampson, *Anatomy of Europe,* pp. 299, 304.
52. Green, *The Universal Eye,* pp. 9, 184.
53. Clarke, "Prediction, Realization, Forecast," *Communications in the Space Age,* p. 32.
54. Wilbur Schramm, "Some Possible Social Effects of Space Communication," *Communications in the Space Age,* pp. 12–13, 17, 19; Dizard, *Television, A World View,* p. 1.
55. Ibid., pp. 13, 24; Clarke, "Prediction, Realization, Forecast," p. 37; Green, *The Universal Eye,* p. 14; Leo Bogart, "Mass Media in the Year 2000," *Sight, Sound and Society,* p. 413.
56. Victor K. McElheny, "Orbital Crowding Expected by 1985," *The New York Times,* 7 December 1975.
57. Dizard, *Television, a World View,* pp. 257–58; Schramm, "Some Possible Social Effects of Space Communication," p. 27.
58. "Linking Communities through Space," *Self-Reliance,* 4 November 1976.
59. Musolf, *Communications Satellites,* p. 1.
60. Schramm, "Some Possible Social Effects of Space Communication," *Communication in the Space Age,* p. 16.
61. Green, *The Universal Eye,* p. 63.
62. A Communication Prepared by the United Nations, "The Peaceful Uses of Outer Space: Role of the United Nations Committee in General and Concerning Space Communication in Particular," *Communication in the Space Age,* pp. 155–59.
63. Hurley, "The Role of Communications Technology," *Communications Satellites in Political Orbit,* p. 180.

Bibliography

Within the last twenty years a substantial number of books have examined the phenomena of television and the communications revolution. A good number of these take the form of Erik Barnouw's *Tube of Plenty: The Evolution of American Television* (New York: Oxford University Press, 1975). This is a good chronological history of American television and broadcasting, long on narrative but short on analysis. As its title indicates, it considers American developments. Among its useful features are a chronology of events affecting the industry and the "Bibliographical Notes." The annotated bibliography is particularly good and is conveniently divided along chapter lines.

Similar volumes have been compiled for the major television powers of the world. Donato Goffredo's *Psicologia del Divismo Televisio* (Rome: Fratelli Palombi Editori, 1968), following a short analysis of the psychological impact and needs filled by television, provides a chronology of the development of television in Italy from 1954 to 1967.

Just recently published is the fourth volume of Asa Briggs's *History of Broadcasting in the United Kingdom.* Volume 1: *The Birth of Broadcasting* (New York: Oxford University Press, 1961); vol. 2: *The Golden Age of Wireless* (1965); vol. 3: *The War of Words* (1970). The fourth volume, *Sound and Vision* (1979), examines the decade after World War II. The last volume of this detailed study examines both the rise of television broadcasting as well as the end of the BBC's monopoly.

Derek Horton's *Television's Story and Challenge* (London: George G. Harrap and Co., 1951) provides a short survey of television's history to the 1950s and is therefore dated. Nonetheless it is useful for an examination of the early years of the medium, particularly in Great Britain. More narrowly focused and more scholarly is William A. Belson's *The Impact of Television: Methods and Findings in Program Research* (London: Crosby Lockwood and Sons, Ltd, 1967). Although this volume attempts to measure the social impact of television in Great Britain, some of its findings have a broader applicability.

The broad sweep of global television is presented in such works as Timothy Green's *The Universal Eye: The World of Television* (New York: Stein and Day, 1972). This is a readable survey which examines the history and current state of television in some forty countries on five continents. Somewhat older yet no less useful or scholarly is Wilson P. Dizard's *Television, A World View* (Syracuse, New York: Syracuse University Press, 1966) which examines the potential and pitfalls of international television and provides a good survey of worldwide television and its networks. Both books have a bibliography but Dizard's is fuller and more varied.

Robert W. Sarnoff, Chairman of the Board of the National Broadcasting Company, spoke before the European Broadcasting Union in New York in October, 1962, and suggested that the Union form a study group to explore the possibility of a global organization of television broadcasters and possibly the formation of a World Broadcasting Union. His talk, "Global Television: A Proposal" is included in *Problems and Controversies in Television and Radio* (Palo Alto, California: Pacific Books, Publishers, 1968), edited by Harry J. Skornia and Jack William Kitson.

UNESCO's publication *Television: A World Survey*, originally issued in 1952 and supplemented in 1955, is statistical, dated, and out of print. Nonetheless it is an invaluable guide to the medium's early development abroad even though the facts in its pages provide more information about the spread of television than about its influence and impact. The same must be said of the *UNESCO Statistical Yearbook, 1974* (Paris: UNESCO Press, 1975). A good survey entitled "Television around the World" is found in *The People's Almanac*, edited by David Wallechinsky and Irving Wallace (Garden City, New York: Doubleday and Co., 1975).

Among the most original and imaginative works on the impact of television are those of Marshall McLuhan, including his *Understanding Media* (London: Routledge and Kegan Paul, Ltd, 1964) which is concerned with the influence that television, by virtue of its mere existence, has upon our daily lives and thought patterns. McLuhan's work, which is brilliant at times, raises far more questions than it answers.

There is also considerable speculation found in a number of the works which examine the impact of satellites upon television and world communication. Outstanding among these is the UNESCO volume *Communication in the Space Age: The Use of Satellites by Mass Media* (Paris: UNESCO, 1968). This contains a series of papers presented by a broad range of experts at a conference arranged by UNESCO on the topic of space communication. Included are studies of the social implications of the space age, education in the satellite age, the cultural opportunities offered by the use of space communication, the prospects of such communication for the developed and third world countries, the need for an international framework controlling communication, and others.

The volume edited by Lloyd D. Musolf, *Communications Satellites in Political Orbit* (San Francisco: Chandler Publishing Co., 1968) concentrates upon the political implications of the space age, paying particular attention to the birth of the Communications Satellite Corporation in 1962. Likewise Jonathan F. Galloway's study *The Politics and Technology of Satellite Communications* (Lexington, Mass.: D. C. Heath and Co., 1972) examines the impact of satellite communication upon public opinion, particularly the impact of satellite communication upon public opinion and the formation of domestic and foreign policy. Meanwhile Herbert M. Frenkel and Richard E. Frenkel in their study *World Peace Via Satellite Communications* (New York: Telecommunications Research Associates, 1965) seek to determine if American telecommunications can actually contribute to understanding and peace among the peoples of the world.

The political impact of television is stressed in such works as Sig Mickleson's *The Electric Mirror: Politics in an Age of Television* (New

York: Dodd Mead and Co., 1972) which examines the powerful role of the medium, from the time the Eisenhower forces used it to break the hold of the Taft forces upon the Republican party in 1952 to the present. Joe McGiniss's *The Selling of the President 1968* (New York: Trident Press, 1969) and Theodore White's *The Making of the President 1960* (New York: Atheneum, 1961), *The Making of the President 1964* (New York: Atheneum, 1965) and *The Making of the President 1968* (New York: Atheneum, 1969) concentrate upon the American experience. John Whale's *The Half Shut Eye: Television and Politics in Britain and America* (London: Macmillan, 1969) employs a comparative approach.

2. Television and the Urban Crisis

Robert Muccigrosso
Department of History
Brooklyn College

In 1927 Philo T. Farnsworth, a young pioneer in technology, transmitted the first television image without wires from a San Francisco apartment. Fittingly, the test pattern chosen was the dollar sign. That same year Edward Arthur Burroughs, Bishop of Ripon, struck a blow for standpattism in a sermon delivered before the British Association for the Advancement of Science. "After all," he suggested, "we could get on very happily if aviation, wireless, television and the like advanced no further than at present...."[1] The prelate, of course, lost his battle. By 1970 there were an estimated 175 million television sets in the world. Even a few years before this Marshall McLuhan had asserted with utmost confidence that "as electrically contracted, the globe is no more than a village."[2]

While there is no doubt as to the enormous growth of television there are serious and disturbing questions about the precise effect this twentieth-century form of mass communication has had on the individual and society alike. Professor McLuhan opened a lively hornet's nest and added a significant phrase to the lexicon of communications in the mid-1960s when he decreed that "the medium is the message." "In a culture like ours," he argued, "it is sometimes a bit of a shock to be reminded that, in operational and practical fact, the medium is the message. That is merely to say that the personal and social consequences of any medium—that is, of any extension of ourselves—result from the new scale that is introduced into our affairs by each extension of ourselves, or by any new technology."[3] What more specifically fanned the embers of controversy, however, was McLuhan's contention that it was tele-

vision qua television, not particular program content, which produced revolutionary effects on audiences. Like the telephone but
unlike photography, the radio, or movies, television represented a
"cool medium" which invited—no, demanded—highly active audience participation. The very mosaic quality of the transmitted
video image compelled viewers to become involved, irrespective of
the specific program which "is like the juicy piece of meat carried
by the burglar to distract the watchdog of the mind."[4]

Guru to the confused generation of the 1960s, Professor Mc
Luhan, while continuing to hold an appeal for certain academicians
and intellectuals, has seen his position as the seer of communications decline during the 1970s. Yet other serious scholars have
also questioned the effectiveness of television as a vehicle for conveying important matters of content. Differing in his approach
from that of McLuhan, the prominent American historian Daniel
Boorstin, for example, voiced his fear that the medium might degenerate into a forum for the "pseudoevent." "Will public affairs,"
he asked, "be reduced to a series of performances researched by
psychological warriors, contrived by scenario writers, and enacted
by public figures who are trained to create artificial scenes before
the camera?"[5] Harley Parker, agreeing with McLuhan's assessment that television presents a "cool" medium, has warned that
"active participation or involvement in the communication process
is, naturally, inimical to the dispassionate survey which is so necessary to the critical and analytical stance developed by two thousand
years of literacy."[6] In other words, one cannot reflect at leisure
and with any degree of depth when one is constantly being bombarded with a plethora of rapidly changing audio-visual configurations. The problem becomes more stark upon considering that the
word content of a typical half-hour news program totals less than
that of a single page of the *New York Times*.[7] Perceived in this
manner, the difficulty of reflection becomes even more exacerbated by the necessarily high selectivity of news demanded by
television coverage. One journalist, not surprisingly, has held out
more hope for radio than television as a conveyor of news and a
reporter of public opinion.[8]

And yet no matter how strongly one might question or deplore
the impact of television reportage on audiences one must accept the
certainty that there is an effect, that television does try—and
successfully—to influence people. In 1949 the Federal Communications Commission granted the medium the right to present editori-

als, a right first seized upon by Miami's WTVJ eight years later. Within a decade a full fifty-six percent of the nation's stations were editorializing on a sporadic or regular basis.[9] Both Harris (1969) and Roper (1971) polls confirmed the widespread effect of television reportage. According to the former, nine out of ten adults reported watching televised news on a regular basis, with two out of three claiming to be better informed than five years previously. The latter poll ascertained that a full forty-nine percent of those questioned found television to be the "most believable" of the news media, while newspapers, magazines, and radio achieved primacy only for twenty, ten, and nine percent respectively.[10] Critics argued that the news on television was slanted, politically manipulated, incomplete in its facts due to the nature of the medium, a handmaiden to illiteracy, and so forth. But despite these criticisms, the visual society had come of age.

Nearly a century ago the distinguished British visitor to this country, Lord James Bryce, observed that "the government of cities is the one conspicuous failure of the United States."[11] Were he alive to make his pilgrimage again today, in all likelihood he would amend his observations—but not offer more sanguine conclusions. He might or might not find municipal government more corrupt and inefficient than in the late nineteenth century; he could not fail to note new and, *mutatis mutandis,* intensified problems of crime, squalor, poverty, environmental pollution, fiscal insolvency, overcrowding, racial animosity, traffic congestion, and general human anomie. He would, in sum, encounter the modern urban crisis.

Television both shapes and, in turn, is shaped by the nation's temper, needs, and problems. Sometimes outdistancing, sometimes lagging behind the tempo of contemporary life, it usually has tried to respond to what seem to be the wishes of its audience. In part this has resulted from the exigencies of commercial broadcasting; in part it reflects an understandable and sincere desire to give the people more or less what they want. In the 1950s, for example, when quiescence seemed to be the desire of the nation at large, television cheerfully provided a surfeit of light-hearted diversions, ranging from the Milton Berle show to "Kukla, Fran, and Ollie." Came the domestic and international turmoil of the sixties, however, and television sharpened the focus on serious news and documentary features. Long hidden from satisfactory recognition and understanding, the sores of the nation's cities began to fester with alarming rapidity. As a commentator upon the public scene, television had little choice but to confront these grave developments.

While it is clearly impossible to render anything remotely approaching a detailed account of how television has tried to deal with the urban crisis, it is possible to examine certain areas in which the medium has covered, analyzed, and put forth suggestions for solving urban issues. The story is one of triumph, failure, and mixed results. Above all, it is one of the problems which have continued to defy adequate solution.

Whether or not violence is indeed a way of life for Americans, it has widely been held to be so. As a purveyor of a great (some would say inordinate) amount of violence, television has been castigated as a contributor to one of the cities' and nation's greatest problems. At the time of the assassination of Robert F. Kennedy, Morris L. Ernst, the eminent lawyer who in the 1920s successfully fought the legal battle against the censorship of James Joyce's *Ulysses,* cried out on a popular talk show (the Merv Griffin program): "We're being murdered by TV, not by the guns."[12] Even before Ernst's outcry there was putative evidence that television may have been abetting crime and violence. The murder rate had shown a downward trend in 353 of the nation's cities in the twenty years between 1937 and 1957 but had begun a steadily upward swing commencing in 1958, the year that television reached what was commonly regarded as a near-saturation figure of fifty million sets in American households.[13] When the robbers of a New York bank admitted in 1961 that they had learned their particular techniques from watching a television program entitled "The Perfect Crime," critics of the medium had further ammunition.[14]

The critics feared the effect of televised aggression on children and youths as much as on adults. In 1961 the Senate Subcommittee to Investigate Juvenile Delinquency, chaired by Senator Thomas J. Dodd, a former member of the FBI, pointed to the exposure of young people to violence and sex, manifested fear for its consequences, but offered no panacea. A worried psychiatrist subsequently warned that "by the time he's sixteen, a boy may have seen some twenty thousand homicides on TV and in the movies. He hears talk of five, ten, and fifteen million deaths in case of nuclear attack. This symbolizes the devaluation of life which has resulted in an increasing number of murders among juveniles, and at an earlier age."[15] Another critic took a more skeptical but still concerned stance: "To say that television is *the* cause of delinquency and mental and physical unfitness would be unfair; to say that television is not *a* cause, and an important one, in view of the evidence now available, is no longer acceptable."[16] Others remained unconvinced of the medium's causative or contributory role in the nation's pandemic of violence. Televised violence, insisted one psychiatrist, simply reflected audience interests and when frankly portrayed did not inculcate hostility in viewers not already so prone. He warned, moreover, that "the sooner we get off the kick of falsely blaming American violence on American television, the sooner we will start grappling with the true causes of our national violence."[17]

Responding to the growing controversy, the government in the late 1960s authorized Surgeon General Jesse L. Steinfeld to investigate for possible links between violence in the medium and aggressive behavior on the part of children. After consuming two years of work and one million tax dollars, a twelve-member Scientific Committee on Television and Social Behavior reported its findings in 1972.[18]

After citing the enormously widespread enjoyment of television by the public (ninety-six percent of American homes had one or more television sets which were turned on for an average of six hours a day), the Committee noted that there had been no significant change in the prevalence of violence between 1967 and 1969. While violence had increased in comedy and cartoon programming, it had become generally less lethal in nature, with fewer characters involved.[19] Although there were approximately eight violent scenes per hour, the Commission found no correlation between the actual percentage of violent programs and the data on violence issued by the Federal Bureau of Investigation's Uniform Crime Report in 1971.[20]

As its major finding the Surgeon General's group agreed that "the accumulated evidence ... does not warrant the conclusion that televised violence has a uniformly adverse effect nor the conclusion that it has an adverse effect on the majority of children."[21] The evidence, as analyzed, indicated that children already in possession of hostile tendencies acted more aggressively than those whose proclivities were less hostile. The Commission raised the related question of environment as a determining factor but reached no definite conclusion: "The family, the church, the legal system, and the military, among other institutions, communicate codes, ethics, and guidelines for aggression and violence. The extent to which television reinforces or weakens these codes or guidelines is not presently known."[22] Unable to ascertain the effects of environment, the members logically asked the pivotal question of what changes in programming might guard against any penchants toward violence on the part of the audience, and what possible side effects might then accrue. Again, the Commission offered no sure answers, suggesting only that additional studies should be compiled in order to fathom why children did not appear to react uniformly.[23]

Though unable or unwilling to draw hard conclusions, the Commission did put forth some useful warnings and recommendations: "Since television may play a role in shaping opinion and attitudes, it is important to pay attention to which persons, groups, and interests are presented in a favorable light and which are presented unfavorably. Televised content can suggest who may be considered benign and who may be considered a threat to society." More explicitly, it noted that "in general, the powerful, influential, and elite have opportunity to initiate and control the content and uses of television in ways that the powerless, the poor, and the nonelite do not."[24] Underscoring this extremely important point, the group advised:

> Since the media compete with one another for the attention and involvement of the audience, they must choose emotionally involving content. The more emotion and conflict connected with an issue, the more newsworthy that issue is, and by the same token the more are false beliefs apt to be evoked in relation to it. Unconscious identification and projection mechanisms from early childhood, as well as many vaguely conscious attitudes and interests which impute "good" and "right" to one's own views and "evil" and "wrong" to outsiders, may be important determinants of viewer responses to television content. It is quite possible that television can arouse responses in adults that can facilitate violent behavior much later in time. This possibility should be explored by appropriate research methods, including longitudinal case studies with psychoanalytic methodology.[25]

More than one critic of television violence, had they not done so already, would now draw the conclusion that the Commission was obliquely hinting at, namely, that children and other members of disadvantaged families, rather than advantaged ones, were the persons in whom television might reinforce violent tendencies.[26]

Appearing before the Senate Subcommittee on Communications,

which was chaired by Senator John O. Pastore and which had initiated the study, Surgeon General Steinfeld appealed both to the networks and to the states to guide perplexed parents on the subject of violence and to aid the federal government in its decisions regarding the renewal of broadcasting licenses. Perhaps having scented the unmistakable odor of censorship in the air, the major networks already had committed more than one million dollars for their own private studies of violence.[27]

Today the problem of televised violence and its exact effects on audiences, particularly pre-adults, remains a moot point. Networks have worked to eliminate some of the worst excesses by introducing a proliferation of nonviolent programs and by relegating many violent episodes to late-hour viewing. Still, the criticism continues largely unabated. Very recently the National Citizens Committee for Broadcasting stingingly rebuked the leading networks and their sponsors for depicting too much bloodshed and brutality. Nicholas Johnson, a former member of the Federal Communications Commission and chairman of the group, referred to this visual violence as a "national tragedy" and suggested that television "has become the college of criminal instruction." Both networks and sponsors remonstrated against the findings of the Committee. The president of Gillette North America insisted that his company vigorously policed the programs that it sponsored. He conceded, however, that the standards which Gillette and the Committee were using might simply be different. An executive for the Clorox Company was less defensive, bluntly asserting that "the viewing audience ultimately determines the kinds of programming the networks carry." Nonetheless, he did invite viewers to articulate their feelings to sponsors.[28] With the alarming rise in violent crimes among juveniles and the sobering fact that today's children become tomorrow's adults the invitation increasingly may be accepted.

Another major problem, one by no means unrelated to that of violence, which forms an integral part of today's urban crisis concerns ethnic minorities, especially blacks, and race relations. Once again television's record has been mottled with both success and failure, and once again its overall effect has been called into question.

Precisely what meaning television had for blacks during the 1950s and the early 1960s is difficult to pinpoint. Certainly programs and commercials warmly invited blacks to share the better life of the Affluent Society. Yet when hard-core economic realities failed to change, frustration may have grown immeasurably. Did television coverage of the battles for civil rights in Little Rock, Selma, Oxford, and on the Freedom Marches serve to inspire blacks with renewed hope or only to augment a sense of racial division? Did it have relatively little consequence? Eric Sevareid, for one, felt that the momentous Civil Rights Act of 1964 could not have reached fruition without the beneficent role of television. Indeed, the highly respected reporter discerned a close and positive link between the efforts of the medium and the civil rights movement for the entire "decade of revolution" following the 1957 events in little Rock, where President Eisenhower sent troops to enforce integration over the protests of a reluctant Governor Orval E. Faubus.[29] Yet another writer, also knowledgeable about the communications media, flatly declared that "the black revolution in America and its acceptance by the white majority was not a product of mass communications, but of forces more fundamental to the formation of private and public attitudes. . . . In racial matters, as elsewhere, the media merely acted as a mirror of society, not the 'molder' of its opinions, as the cliche would have us believe."[30]

Some Americans remained essentially unmoved by the early civil rights movement. Few, if any, retained their equanimity with the onset of urban upheavals commencing in the mid-sixties. Urban riots were not new to Americans, whose history was rife with such outbreaks from colonial times onward. There was, however, one element in particular which set apart the modern tumults from their predecessors: widespread television coverage.

During the summer of 1964 New York's Harlem and Bedford-Stuyvesant, two of the nation's most notorious slum areas, were rocked by riots. Television not only duly covered these riots but also, in the opinion of one observer, directly fostered them: "During spring and early summer, almost daily interviews with 'Negro leaders' predicting a holocaust were visible on television. Many of these men were spokesmen without a following, ambitious activists eager for exposure. But their words created an air of tension and expectancy, convincing the ghetto dwellers that violence was indeed imminent. Nobody was surprised when it came."[31] The riots, for all their pain and ferocity, drew relatively little attention or concern outside of New York and brought forth only sparse criticism of the media. The next summer, however, was to witness another major urban riot, this time on the opposite coast of the country. Very soon Watts would become a household name and television would be embroiled in fierce controversy over its handling of the episode.

On August 12, 1965, Watts, a Los Angeles ghetto nearly fifty square miles in area, erupted. Within a few hours three dozen persons lay dead, more than seven hundred and fifty were injured, twenty-five hundred were arrested, and two hundred business buildings were destroyed. Later estimates placed property losses for these two hours of pandemonium in excess of forty-four million dollars.[32] National as well as local television responded to the riot and the subsequent deployment of police and national guardsmen. Los Angeles television station KTLA managed to take close-ups from a helicopter and then offered the footage to other stations. Some accepted, but some did not, displaying a wariness that reportage might worsen an already grim situation.

Questions concerning the manner in which television covered the rioting immediately arose. Did the cameras accelerate the tempo of violence? Should the stations have reported all the events? Did they employ judicious rhetoric and should they have omitted catching and sometimes literally inflammatory phrases such as "Burn, baby, burn?" FCC Chairman E. William Henry applauded coverage by the medium.[33] Others reacted adversely. John Gregory Dunne, a regular contributor to *The New Republic,* for example, castigated the performance: "Consciously or not, electronic journalism is essentially show business, and show business demands a gimmick. With its insatiable appetite for live drama, television turned the riots into some kind of Roman spectacle, with the police playing the lions, the Negroes, the Christians. The angle, in this case, was that the Christians were winning. Not only did television exacerbate an already inflammatory situation, but also, by turning the riots into a Happening, may even have helped prolong them." Accusing television reporters of shooting "from the lip," he added: "In fact broadcast coverage of the riots only deepened my own conviction that a thousand words are worth one picture. The most disturbing effect of televised news coverage is that, like LSD, it tends to create a heightened and often spurious reality of its own."[34]

Critics both within and without the industry hoped that television had profited from its mistakes in covering the disorders in Watts but also hoped that it would not be put to the test again. The latter hope proved short-lived. In the summer of 1967, two years after Watts, violence broke out in fifteen American cities, most severely in Detroit and Newark.

Detroit's television stations tried to react in a useful manner. Earlier in the year they had given free time to Mayor Jerome Cavanaugh, who appealed to the inhabitants of the city not to purchase guns. When the riots did erupt in July, the stations voluntarily blacked out coverage of what they considered incendiary news and provided local athletes with time to answer phone calls from youths, who otherwise presumably might be roaming the streets and further contributing to the havoc.[35] Yet Police Commissioner Ray Girardin, responding to the deaths of forty-three persons killed during the mayhem, angrily contended that "TV could have performed a civic duty by informing people to stay away from dangerous sections." A Newark police official hurled a similar accusation during the riots which occurred in his city that same summer.[36]

Commissioner Girardin and the Newark official were not the solitary voices crying in the wilderness against television's purported mishandling of the riots. Max Lerner denounced both the medium and his fellow countrymen, fulminating that "Americans seem to have struck a Faustian bargain with the big media, by which they have received total and instant coverage and have in turn handed themselves over the vulnerable chances of crowd psychology and of instant infection."[37] Carl T. Rowan, a black journalist and onetime State Department official, voiced the concern of moderate blacks when he complained: "The truth today is that someone who legitimately speaks for thousands of Negroes, who articulates their hopes and frustrations, can show up in most American cities and get no better than routine press coverage. But let a Negro show up who says: 'If you don't do this or that we're going to burn down this damned town.' I guarantee you he'll make front page headlines and all the TV shows."[38] Others concurred that televised appearances by radicals like Stokely Carmichael and H. Rap Brown should be minimal.[39]

Television was not bereft of defenders, however. Eric Sevareid reminded his listeners that the nation's worst race riots had taken place before the advent of either radio or television. Moreover, he cited word-of-mouth communication as the principal culprit in the present situation.[40] CBS president Richard S. Salant, while agreeing that television could and should use greater restraint in certain cases, posited a classical defense of the medium by arguing that it simply could not avoid confronting problems which fell under the rubric of news.[41] Certainly one of the most compelling defenses of television's responsibilities was offered by the veteran journalist, John Hohenberg, who saw the fatuity of blaming it for ills whose cure it could not singlehandedly effect. "The brutal truth," he argued, "is that even where there is partial or total local self-censorship, and it has been done, the news of the rioting is circulated promptly outside the affected area and the playback is sometimes instantaneous." Concluded Hohenberg: "Without doubt, there are serious risks to the continued coverage of civil rights disturbances by the news media without major limitations; yet, these risks are unavoidable in a democratic society that is committed to the principle of a free press."[42]

However eloquently voiced, the pleas that television had performed satisfactorily under difficult conditions fell on many, mostly deaf, ears. As one writer observed: "Frustrated with the helplessness in stemming civil disorder, people question whether or not television might not be the cause of it all. Get the medium is their message."[43] That, too, was the message conveyed by various members of Congress to President Lyndon B. Johnson, who responded in timeworn American fashion by calling for a committee to investigate the situation. Headed by Illinois Governor Otto Kerner, the President's Commission on Civil Disorders speedily completed its study and drew three basic conclusions: (1) despite various inaccuracies and misrepresentations, the medium had honestly tried to give a balanced version of the riots, (2) it had been guilty of exaggeration, and (3) it had "failed to report adequately on the causes and consequences of civil disorders and the underlying problems of race relations."[44]

After viewing nearly a thousand sequences of the rioting as filmed by local and network stations, the Commission, avowing that it had earlier thought otherwise, opined that the industry actually had reported many more "calm" than "emotional" scenes and had concentrated on showing more moderate than militant black spokesmen. While there were isolated incidents of irresponsibility —the helicopter coverage of the Watts riot, the interference with law enforcement by cameramen in Newark, the instance of a New York newspaper photographer persuading a youth to throw a rock in order to achieve a more sensational story—reporters had behaved well.[45]

For all its positive achievements, the medium had sometimes exaggerated or misread what had actually happened. It had, according to the Commission, portrayed the disorders as instances of black-white confrontation. Since the preponderance of rioting had occurred in black areas, the Commission reasoned, with less than compelling logic, that there had been no *race* riots.[46] Further—and worse—television had failed to inculcate in both its black and white viewers any deep sense of the problems the nation faced, along with possible solutions. This failure was not accidental: television had been guilty of the same racial bias and paternalism so deeply rooted in society at large. And while the Kerner group found this situation "understandable," it also found it inexcusable "in an institution that has the mission to inform and educate the whole of our society."[47] Citing the blacks' distrust of the medium, a distrust intensified by experiencing one reality while witnessing another on television, the Commission further berated the industry for failing to give whites a true understanding of the nature of ghetto life.[48] The Commission viewed potential codes for the communications media with skepticism. Useful they might be; a cure-all they assuredly would not be. Instead, Kerner and his associates proposed establishing an Institute of Urban Communications, which would be constituted on a private basis and comprised of journalists and assorted public figures. The purpose of the Institute would be to improve media-police relations, review media performance on matters relating to riots and race relations, and provide other urban affairs services. Perhaps most important, the Institute would recruit, train, and then secure positions for black journalists.[49]

Certain findings of the Kerner Commission were disputable. Its charge that television's practice of hiring blacks was a demonstrable example of tokenism was not. In St. Louis, for example, a city where blacks formed approximately one-half of the population, there were no blacks in the medium in 1960. Ten years later they represented a meager five percent of all the media workers in the municipality.[50] More to the point, St. Louis was by no means unique in this respect among the nation's cities.

Part of the problem has been a sheer lack of adequately trained blacks; part—perhaps most—has been simply a case of racial prejudice. While the number of blacks in the medium has generally remained small, there have been sure signs that changes are taking place. Actual or threatened challenges to deny relicensing by the FCC has helped. Station WLBT in Johnson, Mississippi, lost its license in 1969 for failing to accept black workers. With the handwriting clearly discernible on the wall, station KTAL in Texarkana, Texas, quickly agreed to having two black reporters shown on camera and promised to listen more carefully to the needs and wishes of the local community. Meanwhile a host of different groups, including the United Church of Christ and the National Citizens Committee for Better Broadcasting, gave legal and financial assistance to minorities in their struggle to gain greater acceptance by the medium.[51] As television executives came to understand that blacks were trusted in their communities as whites were not, more blacks received employment.[52] To safeguard and extend their gains in the industry, blacks organized the National Association of Black Media Workers in 1970. At the same time, more blacks were receiving more extensive education. Black congressmen meanwhile have been fighting the battle in Washington. Calling for more blacks in television, studies of television's effects on blacks, and the end of medium discrimination through legal action and the power of license renewal, they scored a symbolic victory in the early 1970s when President Richard M. Nixon appointed Benjamin L. Hooks as the first black to serve on the FCC.[53] While much work must still be done to achieve true racial integration within the industry, tokenism has gradually given way to progress. Pressure from within and without the medium has not proved pointless.[54]

Although television has had a mixed impact on the urban crisis with respect to violence, minorities, and race relations, there have been specific instances when its effect has been decidedly benign. During the disastrous forest and brush fires that swept through southern California destroying several suburban communities in 1964, helpful reporting and repeated urging for calm by local stations may have been instrumental in preventing widespread panic.[55] Several years later this spirit of "good neighbor" reporting had increased in tempo. Whether it was Geraldo Rivera's sympathetic interview with drug addicts conducted on the rooftops of tenement buildings in East Harlem for New York's WABC-TV in July, 1971, or the splendid program on ecology, "The Eighth Day," presented by station KING-TV in Seattle, local television was proving itself increasingly responsive to local needs.[56] Few local programs, however, were able to equal in dramatic intensity the superb documentary Rivera compiled in early 1972 (again for WABC-TV) on the deplorable conditions at Willowbrook State School for the mentally retarded.

Technically a school, Willowbrook, pleasantly situated on Staten

Island, was in actuality a hospital for the mentally retarded. On January 5, 1972, Rivera agreed to visit the premises at the request of a friend, a physician who had been dismissed for having asked the parents of the patients to seek improved conditions. When young Rivera reached Willowbrook he was shocked to find sixty or seventy naked or nearly naked children living in Building 6 in the midst of rank filth and disease. The institution could comfortably accommodate three thousand patients; it was then housing over five thousand. Sharing the same scarce toilets and contracting one another's diseases, patients were dying at the appalling rate of three or four a week. Only twenty percent of the children, moreover, attended any classes whatsoever—this in what was ostensibly a school.[57]

Dr. Jack Hammond, who had served as director of Willowbrook since 1965, warned Rivera the following day about presenting certain televised footage and refused to permit recognizable faces to be shown. Nevertheless, WABC did offer seven minutes of Rivera's handiwork on its 6:00 P.M. news and received roughly three hundred phone calls from concerned viewers that same evening. The number of calls soared to seven hundred by the following afternoon. On the next day the station showed film clips of a Willowbrook tour conducted by Dr. Hammond. Somehow—perhaps not surprisingly —the children appeared healthy. When Rivera returned to the institution on January 10 he learned that many children had received drugs, that the food was poor, and that there were not enough attendants to care for the patients. By the next day Willowbrook had captured the city's attention. Parents rallied at the site; Assemblyman Andrew Stein offered his services; televised clips of the late Senator Robert F. Kennedy's visit to the school in 1965 served to increase popular demand for reform.[58]

Inaction now had become impossible. Willowbrook agreed to rehire three hundred employees, although the school would still remain six hundred employees short of authorized strength, a condition necessitated by severe cuts in the state's budget. Rivera, meanwhile, had gone to California to study that state's decidedly superior system for caring for the retarded. Returning to New York on January 21, the reporter took more film of Willowbrook for his upcoming special, "The Last Disgrace." Ten days later the Staten Island Chapter of the Society for the Prevention of Cruelty to Children began hearings and at the same time called for the state and national governments to investigate conditions. On February 2 Rivera's special was aired. Two and one-half million people watched, making the program the highest rated local news special in television history. Looking back upon his endeavors, Rivera noted some change for the better; wards were cleaner and most of the children were wearing clothes. He remained unimpressed, concluding that "we've got to close that goddamned place down."[59]

With a bit of reflection one can easily extend the list of useful services television provides for beleaguered denizens of the cities: warnings about impending bad weather, reports on traffic congestion, emergency appeals, programs intended to stimulate the social conscience, to enlighten the citizenry, and to impart miscellaneous information, to name a few. It even has been argued that the power of urban bosses has visibly declined thanks in no small part to the efforts of local stations. At the very least, so the argument runs, television has prevented a worse breed of politician from taking office.[60] Given the obvious benefits brought to urban milieus by local programming, critics have raised the central question of why not more.

Radicals have found little difficulty in explaining the subordination (some would say "subservience") of local to national television. As Herbert I. Schiller viewed the situation: "Communications, which could be a vigorous mechanism of social change, have become, instead, a major obstacle to national reconstruction. They have been seized by the commanding interest in the market economy, to promote narrow national and international objectives while simultaneously making alternative paths seem either undesirable or preventing their existence from becoming known." "Television," he added, "the most educative force in existence[,] has been left almost entirely to private considerations and the vagaries of the marketplace. . . . Failure to reshape domestic communications to a form which makes room for human development and environmental adaptability can only deepen the disorders already wracking American society."[61]

Though Schiller's criticism may be valid to some extent, depending on one's political and socioeconomic proclivities, it does need tempering. National television is not the monolith that Schiller describes, nor is it the fabulously opulent capitalist enterprise that many posit. As late as 1973 the three major networks combined ranked only 113th on *Fortune*'s list of the five hundred largest industrial corporations in the United States. Figures for the same year, moreover, indicated that newspaper revenue was more than twice that received by television, and indeed newspapers owned more than one-quarter of all the nation's stations. It must also be understood that the relationship between network and local television has not been a one-way street. While local affiliates do provide free access to the major networks to reach local viewers, in turn they receive free programs and, again based on 1973 figures, twelve percent of the total advertising revenue accumulated by the networks. This twelve percent accounted for eleven percent of the affiliates' total revenue.[62] Still, few would probably care to argue that local television has not received a certain short shrift over the years.

That national television would dwarf local television was by no means a foreordained conclusion, though given the contours of the nation's history at least a slight inevitability should have been discerned. The Federal Communications Act of 1934 explicitly called for television (and radio) programming to be "in the public interest, convenience, and necessity." For nearly twenty years local service seemed to be the lodestar of government policy in the field of mass communications.[63] Despite official acceptance of the desirability of grass-roots programming, however, local television failed to grow perceptibly. At times it scarcely seemed to grow at all. By the 1950s network television began to move far ahead in its quest for viewer popularity and hence, power. Noted one critic: "The genius of the federal system, from the start of the nation's history, has been an equilibrium between local diversity and basic national values. Where this equilibrium has failed there have been tragic consequences."[64]

"Tragic consequences" may not have been an apt phrase to describe an imbalance between national and local television, but at the very least the situation disquieted a number of individuals and groups. The Carnegie Commission of Educational Television worked to remedy the deficiency with what at first seemed heartening results. Largely as a result of the Commission's report, which was, according to Arthur L. Singer, "a plea for pluralism, a plea for localism, a plea for an escape from the ponderousness and the pedagogy that had afflicted most of Educational Television,"[65] the Public Broadcasting Act of 1967 established the private, nonprofit Corporation for Public Broadcasting. Subsidized by a ten million dollar grant from the Ford Foundation and directed by the innovative Fred W. Friendly, former director of CBS-TV News, the project began under favorable auspices. Two years later disillusion set in after a bitter fight with National Educational Television over the question of programming. Friendly resigned, and while localism remained the credo, the organization suffered from an increased centralization of control, lack of funds, and an overall resistance to experimentation.[66]

By the early 1970s the dominance of national television remained unshaken. In 1971, for example, while local programming accounted for thirteen percent of all television content, national programming devoured a full ninety-five percent of all prime-time viewing (7:00 P.M. - 11:00 P.M.).[67] There was (and still is) a further problem, according to Edward Jay Epstein. Rather than preserve the local setting of the news, the major networks have tended to nationalize it, often meshing related but individual stories from several cities into one general account. With permanent lines in New York, Chicago, and Washington, moreover, the networks will choose, all other things being equal, stories from these cities rather than assume additional expenses (renting lines, for example) necessary for broadcasting accounts from other localities.[68] National dominance notwithstanding, local television has fairly stood its ground in more recent years. In 1972 the Public Television System subsumed two hundred and forty stations with an estimated potential audience of seventy-five percent of the country's population. Twenty-five percent of these stations were owned by the local communities themselves.[69] Holding ground is not tantamount to gaining ground, of course. To achieve the latter, proponents of local television have increasingly turned their attention to what they regard as the medium's wave of the future: cable television.

The benefits—real and assumed—of cable television are impressive. Its two-way features can provide the viewer with a sense of genuine engagement in both local and national news. Participating in cable television discussions by calling in one's opinions or voting simply by pressing a button, the viewer, in the comfort of his or her home, can be part of a modern-day town meeting.[70] As one enthusiast perceives the benefits: "The present lack of neighborhood and community cohesiveness would be diminished. Small local enterprises would have an information outlet that would help sustain them in the face of massive regional merchandisers. Local groups with special pleading and debates would not have to enter the ad hoc publishing business or obtain time on metropolitan channels to air their ideas. Neighborhood and community amateur youth and adult activities would have an outlet that would be less expensive than hiring a small hall."[71]

The costs of cable television certainly are not cheap, with estimated installation expenses for each city ranging from two to twenty million dollars. Yet, as it has been suggested, model cities programs and community development corporations might and perhaps should come to the rescue. Since cable television probably would achieve a monopoly or near monopoly on local programming, the resulting market potential for advertising could be a lucrative incentive to induce the business community's participation.[72] Any surplus channels that remained would, in turn, provide access to more people and at a relatively low cost.[73]

Cable television has also promised urban communities added benefits, including police, fire, and other assorted protections. With scanning and cable emergency signaling devices both the police and firefighters can move more rapidly to scenes of trouble. In 1969, for example, the police of Cedar Rapids, Iowa, apprehended forty burglars thanks to these alarms.[74] Should it happen that fire and burglar alarms were to be installed in all homes so that the alarms worked on the same cables that transmitted video signals, the possibility of reducing loss by crime and fire would increase enormously. Citizen grievances against both police and fire units, moreever, could be discussed on cable television, thus increasing the chances of better understanding between the community and those entrusted with its care.

The list of real and theoretical services accruing to urban centers through the proper deployment of cable television extends itself to a variety of areas. In the field of education, for example, there exists an enormous potential for correspondence and adult education courses; computerized tests and grades which would permit greater time for actual teaching and teacher preparation; courses for such selected groups as the elderly and infirm, housewives, and unskilled laborers; and the exchange of video-taped programs. In the area of health services cable television's uses are largely untapped. The distribution of medical and dental information; consultative medical services for those without the means of transportation to doctors' offices and/or hospitals; the distribution of information pertaining to garbage and rat control, sewage and sanitation are some possibilities. Consumers, especially uneducated ones, would also derive benefit from cable broadcasting. Contracts and leases could be discussed, as could general housing problems and problems relating to a wide spectrum of consumer goods. Home meters could be read; disaster warnings and reports could be efficiently transmitted.[75] In addition to providing specialized cultural programming earmarked for specific groups within the community, the cable holds out the promise of ownership and control of broadcasting facilities by minorities and hence, of increasing the numbers of minorities hired. Admittedly, much of the usefulness of cable television and local television in general remains decidedly more potential than kinetic at this point. Yet it may not be an exaggeration for one of its defenders to boast that "the job the best local stations are doing today in electronic journalism has earned them extraordinary loyalty and trust from their audiences."[76]

Not all would agree that cable television possesses magical curative powers for urban maladies. Even granting that it might provide redress for some of the worst grievances, this new development in communications poses difficulties of its own and might easily create new problems while attempting to solve existing ones. For example, while cable television could and does make possible more diversified viewing for its audience, there is no guarantee that it would not be turned against the interests of the community. Control is vital in this case, and control of programming in the hands of hostile or even indifferent owners could easily prove, to use the language of today, counterproductive.

But what should be the proper role of minority groups vis-à-vis local programming? Should they have equal access to the new cable stations or must they gain outright ownership and control in order to fulfill their needs and aspirations? If there is a failure to achieve the latter, there is some fear that the ghettos ironically will be footing even more of the bill for their own lack of power.[77] From other quarters comes the warning that black-owned or black-controlled stations will in reality merely reinforce current patterns and modes of segregation.[78]

The question of ethnicity and local differences versus national homogeneity and identification relates very much to the whole question of cable television, which, in this instance, may prove to be a mixed blessing, with the emphasis perhaps better placed on "mixed." As one journalist has cautioned: "Highly localized television could further the present cultural separation if neighborhoods and communities themselves were sharply separated, as they tend to be. If mass communications serve only their own withdrawn segments of society, it will increase national alienation and aggression. National and regional mass media will help overcome this sense of separation, but they will not be enough, as they are not enough to overcome today's mutual isolation of special groups."[79] Ithiel de Sola Pool, a seasoned observer of the communications scene, agrees with this warning. Admitting that cable television would offer people a greater voice for self-expression, he questions: "Is this a good thing or a bad thing? Like all trade-offs, it is some of each. It makes meaningful and intensive citizen participation possible—far more possible than it can be at the national level, except sporadically. But on the other hand, a devolution of the focus of politics to the local and interest-groups level may make this already inchoate nation even harder to unify and govern than it is now."[80] The answers to these vexing problems will not come easily—if they come at all.

"In urbanized society," observed Ben Bagdikian, "the medium is no longer face-to-face contact but a technological apparatus. If the mass media are not put to use in achieving a maximum flow of ideas, there is no other effective alternative for public discourse."[81] Cities grow more impersonal; individuals, losing their sense of communal identification, grow more lonely and isolated. Television has the burden of bridging the gap—sometimes seemingly a chasm —which separates people from their environment. But what, in the last analysis, should the proper role of television be as it confronts the urban crisis? Should that role be a relatively active or passive one? And to what degree? Should television, in short, attempt to be an arbiter of the destinies of American cities? Sensing the possible misuse of the medium, Bagdikian cautioned that "electrons have no morals. They serve free men and dictators with equal fervor."[82] Were television to eschew a policy of commitment for one of non-partisan objectivity would it thereby better serve the commonweal? Perhaps so. Still, Edward R. Murrow succinctly captured the opposite point of view when he advised his fellow professionals that "we have no right to leave people with the impression that every truth has a truth of equal weight on the other side."[83]

From the 1950s onward television has occupied a central position in an American society which has become increasingly aural and visual in its tastes. Responding to the multivarious problems of that society, television has moved—sometimes rapidly, sometimes haltingly, sometimes scarcely at all—to fulfill a responsible role. The record shows both triumphs and defeats and a good deal left to do. Depending on one's promptings, one will judge the record accordingly. Regardless of the particular judgment rendered, one conclusion seems inescapable: television inexorably has the power to effect conditions of change or stasis. Precisely because of this it is necessary to remember that television is a mechanical apparatus subject to human will and direction. "The danger always exists," Rollo May recently observed, "that our technology will serve as a buffer between us and nature, a block between us and the deeper dimensions of our own experience. Tools and techniques ought to be an *extension* of our consciousness, but they can just as easily be a *protection* from consciousness."[84] Technology, in short, is no substitute for ideas and moral effort.

Notes

1. John Bartlett, ed., *Familiar Quotations,* 14th ed. (Boston, 1968), p. 966.
2. Edwin Emery, Phillip H. Ault, and Warren K. Agee, *Introduction to Mass Communications,* 4th ed. (New York, 1973), p. 227; Marshall McLuhan, *Understanding Media: The Extensions of Man* (New York, 1964), p. 5.
3. McLuhan, *Understanding Media,* p. 7.
4. Ibid, pp. 9, 18, 22–23, 230.
5. Ben H. Bagdikian, *The Information Machines: Their Impact on Men and the Media* (New York, 1971), p. 285.
6. Harley Parker, "The Beholder's Share and the Problem of Literacy," in *Media and Symbols: The Forms of Expression, Communication, and Education,* ed. David R. Olson, Part I of *The Seventy-Third Yearbook of the National Society for the Study of Education* (Chicago, 1974), p. 86.
7. William A. Wood, *Electronic Journalism* (New York, 1967), p. 31.
8. John Hohenberg, *The News Media: A Journalist Looks At His Profession* (New York, 1968), p. 84. Hohenberg cities (p. 83) New York's WMCA as a model radio station for conveying news.
9. Emery et al., *Introduction to Mass Communications,* pp. 242–43. Those that did not choose to present editorials offered lack of time or manpower and general inappropriateness as their reasons.
10. Ibid., pp. 160, 236.
11. James Bryce, *The American Commonwealth,* 3rd ed. (New York, 1895), 1, p. 637.
12. Erik Barnouw, *The Image Empire* (New York, 1970), p. 318.
13. Jerome Ellison, "Stimulant to Violence," in *Violence in the Streets,* ed. Shalom Endleman (Chicago, 1968), pp. 110–11.
14. Harry J. Skornia, *Television and Society: An Inquest and Agenda for Improvement* (New York, 1965), p. 173.
15. Ellison, "Stimulant to Violence," p. 113.
16. Skornia, *Television and Society,* p. 146.
17. Ner Littner, "A Psychiatrist Looks at Television and Violence," in *Mass Media and Communication,* ed. Charles S. Steinberg, 2nd ed. (New York, 1972), pp. 544, 554.
18. Surgeon General's Scientific Advisory Committee on Television and Social Behavior, *Television and Growing Up: The Impact of Televised Violence. Report to the Surgeon General, United States Public Health Service.* Washington, D.C., 1972.
19. Ibid., pp. 2, 5.

20. Ibid., pp. 5, 77–78. The Commission did conclude, however, that there might be a connection between real airplane hijackings and bomb threats and those fictionalized by the medium.
21. Ibid., p. 11.
22. Ibid., pp. 18, 39.
23. Ibid., pp. 9, 12–13.
24. Ibid., pp. 44–45.
25. Ibid., pp. 196–97.
26. Ellison, "Stimulant to Violence," p. 116.
27. Emery et al., *Introduction to Mass Communications*, p. 105.
28. *New York Times*, 30 July 1976, p. D9; *New York Post*, 29 July 1976, p. 55.
29. Wood, *Electronic Journalism*, pp. 89, 101. The author believes that television did the American people living outside the South an important service by pointing to "the short fuse burning in their own communities." (pp. 107–8)
30. Martin H. Seiden, *Who Controls the Mass Media? Popular Myths and Economic Realities* (New York, 1974), p. 11. Seiden, however, did credit television for giving blacks a greater role in the medium after the civil rights movement of the 1960s.
31. Neil Hickey, "A Look at TV's Coverage of Violence," in *Television: A Selection of Readings from TV Guide Magazine*, ed. Barry G. Cole (New York, 1970), p. 66.
32. William Small, *To Kill a Messenger: Television News and the Real World* (New York, 1970), p. 59.
33. Wood, *Electronic Journalism*, p. 88.
34. John Gregory Dunne, "The Television Riot Squad," *The New Republic*, 153 (11 September 1965): 27–28.
35. Neil Hickey, "Detroit: Television on Trial," in *Television*, ed. Cole, p. 72; Small, *To Kill a Messenger*, pp. 64, 69.
36. Hickey, "A Look at TV's Coverage of Violence," p. 64. A year later Girardin decided that television was maturing in its handling of dangerous situations. (pp. 75–76)
37. Ibid., p. 65.
38. Carl T. Rowan, "The Mass Media in an Age of Explosive Social Charge," in *Mass Media in a Free Society*, ed. Warren K. Agee (Lawrence, Kansas, 1969), p. 46.
39. Theodore F. Koop, "Television: America's Star Reporter," in *Ibid.*, pp. 56–57.
40. Small, *To Kill a Messenger*, p. 64.
41. Hickey, "A Look at TV's Coverage of Violence," p. 68.
42. Hohenberg, *The News Media*, pp. 154–57.
43. Small, *To Kill a Messenger*, p. 74.
44. *Report of the National Advisory Commission on Civil Disorders*, with an Introduction by Tom Wicker (New York, 1968), p. 363.
45. Ibid., pp. 363–64, 368–69, 372, 377.
46. Ibid., p. 365.
47. Ibid., p. 366.
48. Ibid., pp. 374, 383.

49. Ibid., pp. 382, 386–89.
50. James Aronson, *Deadline for the Media: Today's Challenges to Press, TV and Radio* (Indianapolis, 1972), pp. 164–65.
51. Emery et al., *Introduction to Mass Communications*, pp. 120–21.
52. Aronson, *Deadline*, p. 23.
53. Emery et al., *Introduction to Mass Communications*, p. 121.
54. Yet as Douglass Cater and Stephen Strickland have warned, such pressure, when applied to programming, "may help to curtail abuses but it may also discourage the freedom and diversity in which creative television can flourish." Douglass Cater and Stephen Strickland, *TV Violence and the Child: The Evolution and Fate of the Surgeon General's Report* (New York, 1975), p. 6.
55. Wood, *Electronic Journalism*, pp. 86–7.
56. *Survey of Broadcast Journalism, 1970–1971*, ed. Marvin Barrett (New York, 1971), pp. 24–5.
57. Geraldo Rivera, *Willowbrook: A Report on How It is and Why It Doesn't Have to Be That Way* (New York, 1972), pp. 9–27, passim.
58. Ibid., pp. 29–56, passim. On January 13, Rivera, accompanied by Congressman Mario Biaggi, visited the Letchworth Village Rehabilitation Center in Rockland County. Both found conditions worse than at Willowbrook.
59. Ibid., pp. 93, 99, 129, 142, 146–47.
60. Seiden, *Who Controls the Mass Media?*, pp. 69–76, 223.
61. Herbert I. Schiller, *Mass Communications and American Empire* (New York, 1969), pp. 29, 151, 163.
62. Seiden, *Who Controls the Mass Media?*, pp. 22–23, 39, 41, 63.
63. Ibid., p. 101.
64. Bagdikian, *The Information Machines*, p. 241.
65. Aronson, *Deadline*, p. 276.
66. Ibid., pp. 153, 277.
67. Bagdikian, *The Information Machines*, pp. 171–72.
68. Edward Jay Epstein, *Between Fact and Fiction: The Problem of Journalism* (New York, 1975), pp. 206, 208–9.
69. Seiden, *Who Controls the Mass Media?*, p. 203.
70. Neil Hickey, Richard K. Doan, and David Lachenbruch, "Here Come the '70s!" in *Television*, ed. Cole, p. 573; Skornia, *Television and Society*, p. 212.
71. Bagdikian, *The Information Machines*, p. 284.
72. Charles Tate, "Community Control of Cable Television Systems," in *Talking Back: Citizen Feedback and Cable Technology*, ed. Ithiel de Sola Pool (Cambridge, Mass., 1973), pp. 60, 62.
73. Bagdikian, *The Information Machines*, p. 260.
74. Gilbert Cranberg, "Cable Television and Public Safety," in *Talking Back*, ed. de Sola Pool, pp. 123–24. There does remain the problem of false alarms, however. (p. 126)
75. Tate, "Community Control," pp. 59–60.
76. Wood, *Electronic Journalism*, p. 124.
77. Tate, "Community Control," p. 55.
78. "The Negro on TV," *The Nation*, (November 22, 1965), pp. 374–75.

79. Bagdikian, *The Information Machines*, p. 257.
80. Ithiel de Sola Pool, "Citizen Feedback in Political Philosophy," in *Talking Back*, p. 245.
81. Bagdikian, *The Information Machines*, pp. 299–300.
82. Ibid., p. 303.
83. Wood, *Electronic Journalism*, p. 81.
84. Rollo May, *The Courage To Create* (New York, 1975), p. 70.

Bibliography

There is no single full-length study which deals primarily with television and the problems of American cities. The student of the subject simply must sift through a variety of diverse sources in order to find the necessary information. There do exist, however, a number of these useful works, so many, in fact, that only a very partial list may be offered to supplement those cited in the footnotes of the chapter.

In terms of background, the standard and probably most objective study of the medium is Erik Barnouw's three-volume *A History of Broadcasting in the United States* (New York, 1966–1970). Leo Bogart, *The Age of Television* (New York, 1958) adequately covers the rise of the industry in the 1950s, while Gilbert Seldes, *The New Mass Media* (Washington, D.C., 1968) treats the whirligig of developments in the 1960s and does so in a lively, critical spirit. The annual *Reports* of the Federal Communications Commission, while generally dull reading, are, of course, also important.

Many studies exist which deal with problems affecting both the cities and the nation at large. Such is the case with the topic of violence, which is surveyed in a collection of essays edited by Otto N. Larsen, *Violence and the Mass Media* (New York, 1968). Though dated by the swiftness of events, Paul L. Fisher and Ralph L. Lowenstein (eds), *Race and the News Media* (New York, 1967) analyzes the problems and lack of representation of minorities in the industry from various points of view.

The question of television's responsibility to the general public is nearly as inchoate as it is difficult. John H. Pennybacker and Waldo W. Braden have edited a useful book, *Broadcasting and the Public Interest* (New York, 1969), which aids in defining the problems and in suggesting possible answers. Though at times overly hostile to the medium, Nicholas Johnson, *How to Talk Back to Your Television Set* (Boston, 1970) contains relevant information and provides enjoyable reading. Those interested in developments pertaining specifically to cable television should consult the various issues of *TV Communications: the Professional Journal of the Cable Television Industry*.

3. The Political Use and Abuse of Television in America and Abroad

Frank Paul Le Veness
Department of Government and Politics
St. John's University

The advent of the age of electronic communications has dramatically altered political life in the United States, and indeed, throughout the entire world. In many respects, radio and television broadcasts have permitted candidates to contact, on a regular basis, far larger numbers of constituents than could have been dreamed possible prior to the formation of the broadcast industry. In addition, the candidate may be seen and heard by potential supporters with a minimum of disruption of the latter's daily activities, and often in warm and friendly surroundings, such as the home or neighborhood tavern. Thus, the candidate may realistically hope for an increased degree of receptivity by voters, and has an opportunity to persuade those who are unlikely to make significant efforts to receive his message—people with little interest in the contest, or those presently committed to other candidates.

In the United States, where freedom of speech is protected by the First Amendment to the Constitution, candidates seeking political office have the opportunity to utilize the pervasive presence of television. Nevertheless, since most broadcast stations are privately owned, and the majority are operated for profit, and due to the public nature of the air waves, and limited number of available channels, the government has found regulation of radio and subsequently television to be in the public interest.

The New Deal administration of President Franklin D. Roosevelt established the present regulatory agency, the Federal Communications Commission (FCC), in 1934. This quasi-autonomous regulatory agency has the duty of regulating the industry, protecting the rights of both broadcaster and the general public. As a result, the FCC regulates both technical operations, such as broadcast frequencies, station power, hours of operation, and the like; and programming, in that the station is required to conform to regulations established for the public welfare. It is, perhaps, this latter area which causes the most significant conflict. Broadcasters have at times charged that the FCC is engaged in censorship, and therefore is in violation of the First Amendment.

Although radio and television station licenses are awarded for specific periods—usually three years—and various groups may compete for the license when it expires, it appears to be exceptional for a station to be denied renewal on the basis that it is not addressing itself to public needs. Although the Commission establishes regulations, such as prohibiting dishonesty in broadcasting, and seeks to establish bases upon which to judge the public interest, most if not all scholars appear to conclude that the Commission does not in fact engage in the prior restraint that would be classified as censorship.[1] Nevertheless, the FCC is not merely a passive governmental bureaucracy. Many Americans will recall FCC Chairman Newton N. Minow, who gained fame for his description of television as a "vast wasteland," and who took an extremely active role in encouraging improvements within the industry.[2]

One of the most burning issues concerning the Federal Communications Commission is its fairness doctrine which requires equal opportunities for all political candidates seeking the same office and the careful delineation of all aspects of political issues (Federal Communications Act, Sec. 315). This regulation has a substantial number of concrete consequences. If, for example, advertising time is sold to one candidate, all others seeking the same office must be afforded the opportunity to buy similar time. If one candidate is invited to participate on a panel or discussion show, then all must be offered similar arrangements. Since the regulation extends to all minor candidates, it appears to have led to a reluctance on the part of broadcast stations to involve themselves in certain types of political programs. An excellent illustration is the presidential campaign debates in 1960 between John F. Kennedy and Richard M. Nixon. Despite the fact that over one hundred million people watched at least a portion of those debates, they were not repeated until the equal opportunities rule was waived for such debates. Even live broadcasts of news conferences of a president seeking reelection were not looked upon favorably by broadcasters.[3]

In 1959, Congress moved to exempt legitimate news programs

from the "fairness" doctrine. Since then the Commission has decided questions as cases arose, rather than by issuing specific directives. The result has been an apparent trend towards limiting the doctrine, which culminated in a 1975 decision exempting news conferences and political debates from the equal opportunities requirement. However, significant difficulties remain, including the tendency of the Commission to issue vague rulings by the case, rather than to establish precise regulations.[4]

The effects of television on the American political scene are, as indicated above, numerous and highly controversial. Certainly television can be said to have become the main source of news and political information for the majority of Americans. In addition, it has raised national consciousness and has assisted regional groups in bringing their causes to the attention of the entire nation.[5] Strong evidence also exists that television advertisements are particularly effective in informing people who have little interest in political campaigns.[6]

Considering the variety of news programs, political panel and discussion shows, special election campaigns, reports, the reinstituted presidential candidate debates, and the like, it would appear that the American public is likely to be extremely well-informed. However, there appear to be a number of obstacles which at least partially prevent the viewer from obtaining a full share of political information.

Attorneys Newton N. Minow and Lee M. Mitchell argue that incumbent candidates for presidential and congressional posts have substantially greater access to free or at least inexpensive television coverage. They note that during the election campaign, the president may still issue official statements which will receive wide media coverage, but to which the equal opportunities right of reply does not apply. United States senators and congressmen have relatively inexpensive television production facilities for their official use, and tapes may be presented to stations as news items or the like, again exempt from the equal opportunities doctrine. Opponents, on the other hand, either have to await invitations to free broadcasts, or spend substantial campaign funds on advertisements. As campaign expenses become more strictly regulated and limited, the difficulties for the opponents of incumbents will increase. Minow and Mitchell suggest that the problem may be alleviated through the allocation of broadcast time to the opposition. In a previous study they suggested three avenues of assistance to opponents. First, the utilization of quarterly televised debates. Second, granting equal time to the national committee of the opposition party in instances where, with ten months or less remaining prior to an election, the president remains undeclared or utilizes an exempt statement. Third (originally a suggestion of the Twentieth Century Fund), that each candidate for the presidency be granted free television periods, with the total time proportionate to the party's strength.[7]

Election campaign expenses have been an increasingly oppressive burden for candidates in recent United States elections. A substantial portion of the increase has been due to expensive television advertisements. Fortunately, the Federal Election Campaign Act of 1974, despite the fact that it was partially overturned by the United States Supreme Court two years later, restricted the funding of the 1976 presidential candidates, so that they spent considerably less than one-half the funds available to President Nixon in 1972.[8] It has been estimated that the total campaign expenses for 1972 may have exceeded $400 million, nearly triple the cost of the campaigns of 1956.[9] Television costs alone rose nearly two and one-half times between 1960 and 1964.[10] Part of this increase can be attributed to the fact that large sums are being spent on creating candidates' images.[11]

In addition to expense, a number of other difficulties arise concerning the use of television in political campaigns. Contrary to the expectations of many, a number of emerging media studies indicate that both specific types of television exposure and the total impact of this medium on campaigns may be considerably less than was anticipated. For example, there is considerable evidence that television news programs inadequately inform the public.[12] This carries over into the realm of the campaign, and exposure to candidates through news programs appears to accomplish little toward changing voter loyalty.[13] However, that same study indicates that paid political advertising has greater effect, particularly with the less-interested and less-committed voters. It concludes that one effect of campaign news stories presented on television is to encourage viewers to consider politics to be as unimportant as the brief news analyses would appear to indicate. Despite their increasing popularity, television spot commercials have also been described as inappropriate for advertising an important item such as a political candidacy.[14]

Over the years complaints have been voiced concerning biased news reporting by television networks in the United States. In 1971 a CBS special, "The Selling of the Pentagon," drew heavy fire. CBS was accused of unfair reporting concerning the United States military.[15] The Institute for American Strategy conducted a study of CBS news for the years 1972–1973, and concluded that these programs lacked sufficient explanations and were definitely biased.[16]

Members of the executive branch of the federal government have also been critical of their administration's treatment by the media, but government endeavors to control media organs are also not unknown.[17] As a matter of fact, media organs must exercise care to ensure that in the process of utilizing information supplied by government sources, they do not change a government opinion into what appears to be a factual report.[18]

A final note should be made with regard to television financing in the United States. As indicated above, the vast majority of television outlets are privately owned and operate under a profit incentive. They are financially supported by means of advertising revenues, and receive no governmental subsidy. Many join one of the nation's three largest networks, CBS, NBC, or ABC, and combine network broadcasts with their own local programs. A second category of stations is classified as nonprofit public broadcasting outlets, which receive government, foundation, viewer, and similar donations. They feature public events, cultural, and educational programming, and do not accept advertising revenues. Public broadcasting stations are organized into the Public Broadcasting Service. Only a few media outlets, such as New York City's Municipal Broadcasting System, are governmentally owned and operated. All are the property of local governments and compete with all other stations for their audiences. The federal government operates stations which operate outside the national borders for personnel and families of the United States armed forces through a network known as the Armed Forces Radio and Television Service. The United States Information Agency, a federal government service, prepares programming about the United States for viewing abroad through its Voice of America outlet.

The role of advertising in the media has become a matter of concern to many Americans, and is at least one reason for the rise of public broadcasting. In the United States, advertisers can directly sponsor programs, and since television is very costly, can exercise substantial control over programming simply by granting or with-holding financial backing. There is normally a direct relationship between popularity of shows and advertiser revenues. Shows which may not interest or may even offend substantial portions of the viewing public, or at least those who are likely to buy the adver-tiser's product or service, may have difficulty in either acquiring or maintaining sponsors. Consumers may either not watch the program, and thus the advertising, or may even refuse to purchase the product that is advertised. Of less dramatic impact are those shows which, though significant, traditionally draw somewhat lower viewer ratings. These include many educational, documen-tary, and cultural offerings. Public broadcasting has become an important vehicle for presenting these productions. However, that does not suggest that all public broadcasts consist of less popular shows. They also feature foreign productions, and a number of both domestically and foreign produced programs have had wide viewer appeal.

The United States has also become an international leader in the television industry. Networks and stations purchase foreign pro-grams, but far more importantly, American-produced programs are viewed all over the world, often with the indigenous language dubbed in. The United States has also been a pioneer in interna-tional broadcasts, which have been significantly increased with the use of communications satellites. Events from virtually every cor-ner of the earth can now be viewed live by United States and other television viewing audiences. It is extremely difficult to categorize the television broadcast patterns of nations throughout the world. However, one study classifies these patterns into four distinct groups. The first includes all totalitarian governments, the second, governments which exercise strict control over media, but which do permit private enterprise, the third, democratic governments in which there is freedom of speech and press, but in which signifi-cant portions of the electronic media are operated by the govern-ment, and the last, the group into which the United States is placed, that in which private enterprise dominates the entire scene.[19]

Into the first category must be placed most of the Communist bloc nations including the Soviet Union; the People's Republic of China; and Cuba. Freedom of speech is strictly curtailed and cen-sorship extends to all forms of communication, from television and radio to the printed word to the arts. Private ownership of media is totally proscribed.

The second category includes nations that often have dictatorial regimes and undoubtedly operate media outlets, but that also permit operation of media (newspapers, radio, and television) by private groups, both public service and profit-oriented. Such organs are normally expected to be supportive of the government and its policies. Freedom of speech and press are limited, and deviant media outlets may well be closed and their operators fined or incarcerated.

The third category includes Canada and democratic states of Western Europe and throughout the world. The governmental services often endeavor to maintain unbiased news reporting services and political programs, and private broadcasting services remain free of governmental interference.

The second section of this essay examines two extremes: the services of the United Kingdom, which include the government-operated British Broadcasting Corporation, but which are guaranteed freedom of speech, and those of the Union of Soviet Socialist Republics, operated in totalitarian fashion.

Broadcasting in the United Kingdom

Broadcasting in Great Britain is similar to that of the United States. Ninety-five percent of the households in Britain have television receivers (a total of 17.5 million receiver licenses were granted by February 1975).[20] A second major similarity is the emphasis placed upon fairness and impartiality in political broadcasting.

Television broadcasts in Great Britain commenced during the 1930s under the auspices of the British Broadcasting Corporation (BBC), a public corporation chartered in 1927. Transmissions were suspended during World War II but were resumed in 1946 and have continually expanded and improved over the subsequent decades.

The BBC was established to provide a monopoly service for all broadcasting in the United Kingdom. As a public corporation, it is financed through receiver license fees, government subsidies for its external programming, and sale of BBC productions. It is prohibited from accepting either advertising or payments for broadcasting specific programs. Under its initial charter, ultimate control was exercised by the Postmaster-General, and government departments could require the corporation to broadcast specific programs. Nevertheless, the BBC did not merely evolve into "a subsidiary Government department under another name" because:

> it was the agreed policy of successive governments, accepted by
> Parliament, to treat their powers as major reserve powers only
> and to grant the corporation absolute independence in the day-
> to-day conduct of its business, vesting it with full responsibility
> over general administration and programme content for audi-
> ences both at home and abroad, and partly due to the personalities
> of successive Directors-General, who have maintained political
> independence and freedom from commercial pressures for the
> corporation, and have upheld its standards of integrity and effi-
> ciency and its place in the international field of broadcasting.[21]

Today the BBC operates under a new Royal Charter of 1965.
Supervisory authority has been transferred to the Home Secretary,
who is in turn responsible to Parliament. Although the Secretary
retains the power to revoke the BBC license, in practice the corporation is independent with regard to its programming, and the
Secretary really only involves himself with broad questions of
policy, technical subjects, and the like.[22] "In 50 years of broadcasting no formal veto has ever been placed by the Government on the
broadcasting of a particular item."[23] There appears to be a general consensus that the above analysis, drawn from British government sources, is indeed accurate, and that there has been little
governmental interference with the BBC, which has truly retained
an impartial character.

The BBC corporate officers consist of twelve governors, including governors for Scotland, Wales and Ulster. National Broadcasting Councils for Scotland and Wales and the Northern Ireland
Advisory Council assist by supervising the BBC policies and programs offered in their respective lands. They are assisted by a
sixty-member General Advisory Council, nine regional advisory
councils, and additional councils established by the BBC to advise
on particular types of programming. In 1971, the Corporation established a Programme Complaints Commission to which persons
who believe they have received unfair treatment due to BBC programs can bring their complaints if they do not receive satisfaction
through dealing directly with the appropriate BBC officials. The
chief executive officer is the Director-General, who is in turn assisted by managing directors who collectively comprise the Board
of Management.

Due to a significant, though by no means overwhelming, demand
for an end to the BBC monopoly of broadcasting in Britain, and the

creation of private enterprise television broadcasting, and due to support of this issue by members of the Conservative Party, statements by Labour Party leaders which led to a partisan struggle,[24] and the efforts of the advertising industry,[25] an Independent Television Authority (ITA) was established "... to provide ... television broadcasting services additional to those of the British Broadcasting Company and of high quality...." Programs were to be produced not by the ITA, but rather by private producers "who, under contracts with the authority, have in consideration of payments to the authority ... the right and duty to provide programmes or parts of programmes to be broadcast by the authority, which may include advertisements." The ITA commenced broadcasts the following year.

The now renamed Independent Broadcasting Authority (IBA) is wholly supported through advertising and the sale of programs to foreign television services. Unlike United States practices, advertisers may not sponsor programs. Advertisements must be inserted between programs or during what are described as natural breaks during programs. Thus, advertisers have no immediate voice over program content, and the quality of programming is maintained. Naturally, the Authority is restricted in programming from the standpoint that it must offer sufficiently attractive programs to draw sizable audiences, and thus, advertisers.[26]

Advertising is limited to a maximum of seven minutes per hour and is also regulated by a code established by the IBA with the advice of its Advertising Advisory Committee, its Medical Advisory Panel, and the Home Secretary. The actual advertisements are checked by the Advertising Control Division of the IBA, which examines them in light of the advertising code. The division rejects approximately twenty-five percent of the eight thousand advertisements it receives each year. All advertisements of a religious or political nature, and those advancing the use of cigarettes or gambling, are proscribed. Advertisements "must be clearly distinguishable as such and be recognizably separate from the programmes, and the time given to them must not be so great as to detract from the value of the programmes as a medium of information, education and entertainment."[27]

The Independent Broadcasting Authority consists of ten members, including representatives from Scotland, Wales, and Ulster, all of whom are appointed by the Home Secretary. It constructs and operates its own transmitting stations, but as previously noted, chooses private production companies to actually develop programming. However, programs submitted by these companies are carefully scrutinized, and must include, for example, news and current events shows, weekly documentaries, and nine hours per week of school programs (except for vacation periods). The Authority is assisted by a General Advisory Council, committees on educational and religious broadcasts and advertising, and an advisory panel on medical questions. Special committees advise concerning programming for Scotland, Wales, and Ulster, and in 1971 the IBA established its own Complaints Review Board. The Director-General serves as chief executive, and is assisted by the eight divisions of the Authority.

There is little doubt but that one of the most important functions of British television lies in the field of current events and political broadcasting, a role which has been steadily increasing. However, as indicated above, one of the most pressing issues with regard to politically-oriented broadcasts is that of fairness and impartiality, which both the BBC and IBA have continually striven to maintain. Several illustrations follow:

Government requests for broadcast time, during which a minister speaks "in order to provide information or explanation of events of prime national or international importance, or to seek the co-operation of the public in connection with such events"[28] must be followed by an offer of reply to the main opposition party. It is likely that additional discussions by lesser officials of government, the opposition, and the smaller Liberal Party will also be aired. During the annual budget debates, both the BBC and the IBA, on successive evenings, also present the Chancellor of the Exchequer and an opposition leader. Both organizations offer numerous current events and public affairs shows, including interviews of officials and other political leaders, discussions, and findings of expert reporters on various issues.

The BBC operates two television channels, and during 1975–1976, BBC-1 broadcast over 350 hours of news, which represented over seven percent of its total broadcasts (BBC-2 does not broadcast news), and that same year broadcast over 800 hours of public affairs programs, representing in excess of seventeen percent of its total output. BBC-2 broadcast nearly 800 hours of public affairs programs, over twenty-one percent of its total.[29] The IBA has increased its informational programming over the years and is reported to have excellent current events and public affairs programs. IBA programming has also emphasized news, with particular stress placed upon regional happenings. Each IBA station has had a nightly local news program for well over a decade. In addition, in 1967, IBA presented Britain's first half-hour nightly news program, added the "First Report" news program at lunch during 1972, and last year, inaugurated the "News at 5:45 to 6" featuring Alastair Burnet.[30]

The emphasis given news and public affairs broadcasts is considered

> ... the more important as many people turn to the broadcasting authorities for information and explanation about current affairs, and particularly to television for the greater vividness of watching events happening or seeing the person concerned.[31]

A word should also be said concerning the political party broadcasts which are jointly aired on all three television channels (BBC-1, BBC-2, and IBA). The BBC, the IBA, and the major political parties negotiate agreements which permit each party a stated number of broadcasts of specific duration. For example, one recent agreement provided:

Party	No. of Broadcasts	Duration of Broadcasts[32]
Conservative	6	10 minutes each
Labour	6	10 minutes each
Liberal	3	10 minutes each
Scottish National	3	10 minutes each*
Welsh Nationalists	1	10 minutes each*

*In Scotland and Wales respectively.

Each party is free to choose its own speaker and topics, and may utilize its time to reply to the broadcast of another party. It has been suggested that with regard to political broadcasting, British television is most effective during election campaigns.[33] In 1959, over sixty percent of the public viewed at least one of the political party programs, and the average audience for those shows in 1964 was nearly four million greater than it had been in that earlier year.[34]

Although it goes beyond the scope of this essay to consider the impact of British television on the electoral process, there is indication that this impact may be somewhat less than imagined. Professor Richard Rose notes, for example, that programs tend to be evaluated by viewers in terms of the viewers' own political affiliation. Thus, confirmed party supporters of long duration tend to favor the broadcasts of their own party regardless of the material contained therein.[35]

BBC programs have by no means always been met with praise. One complaint about news programs is that they are often rather uninteresting. Professor Rose has noted the objection raised by members of various political persuasions that insufficient attention is paid to the activities of Parliament, though he adds that the MPs are at least partly to blame since they have resisted televised sessions.[36] The opening of Parliament by Queen Elizabeth II has been televised, and the House of Lords did experiment for a short period in 1968 with closed-circuit television broadcasts of its sessions. However, Professor Sydney D. Bailey has pointed out that all the results of broadcasting parliamentary sessions may not be beneficial. Members, aware that they are on camera, may change the entire style of parliamentary debate.[37]

Both the BBC and IBA are members of the European Broadcasting Union (EBU) and the former also regularly participates in the EBU's Eurovision television network as well as in the International Telecommunications Union (ITU). The BBC also works closely with Commonwealth nations and broadcast organizations and provides considerable technical assistance and training. Both the BBC and IBA exchange television programs with foreign nations and have involved themselves in satellite communications.

Broadcasting in the Soviet Union

Political television broadcasting in the Union of Soviet Socialist Republics follows a pattern similar to that of most other Communist powers, and is usually copied by them. Under the Marxist-Leninist system of government of the Soviet Union, the Communist party is the repository of virtually all political power. The Party has been established as the vanguard of the proletariat which, during the early stages of communist development subsequent to the overthrow of the bourgeoisie, supposedly will lead the masses on the correct path in establishing the new egalitarian, and indeed, virtually flawless society. The new society's first stage, the dictatorship of the proletariat, is one during which emphasis is placed upon the elimination of bourgeois elements and reeducation of the masses, and one that, as a result, relies upon strict discipline, and that refuses to countenance opposition political movements and organizations since they are considered counter-revolutionary.

Needless to state, the organs of mass media are envisioned as playing a leading role in the reeducation process, and broadcasts are carefully screened and censored by the propaganda section of the Party's Central Committee. The Party is basically organized on a strictly hierarchical pattern, one in which loyalty to the party and its policies is paramount, and in which taut discipline is continually maintained. The Communist party of the Soviet Union is one of the most pervasively developed political forces in the world, with primary organs extending the length and breadth of the land, and reaching virtually all political, social, economic, and cultural groups and mass organizations.

Despite its stated doctrine of "democratic centralism," in which democracy, at least as defined in Western terms, appears rather illusory, the party system is based upon the concept of mass participation in the governmental and other national processes. Popular input is also permitted, at least to a limited extent and until a final decision is reached, though never to the detriment of Party policy.

The mass media is thus viewed by the Communist party and Soviet government as a principal method of extending influence and control over the population; of propagandizing as well as of entertaining. Views in opposition to Party policy are rarely aired. While Professor Robert G. Wesson has noted that the Soviet media do not endeavor to print false facts and figures,[38] there is no doubt that they take liberties with less tangible statements. They are also known to fail to report or to devote minimal coverage to both internal and external events which cast negative light on the nation or its allies, and to have the same policy with regard to those which favorably portray the West or other nations with which the Soviet Union has relatively poor relations.[39]

All organs of mass media are directly operated by the state, and control emanates from the Ministry of Culture's State Committee for Radio and Television. Similar organizations exist in each of the nation's fifteen republics. Any opposition media or media operated for profit by private enterprises are totally proscribed.

Television broadcasting commenced in the Soviet Union during the early 1930s, and increased rapidly after the Second World War. By 1973 there were nearly fifty million receivers, almost two hundred for every one thousand Soviet residents.[40] A substantial number of cities currently have multiple viewing channels, and even remote regions of that vast nation are connected via satellite broadcasts. Television stations throughout the country broadcast programs produced by the Moscow Television Center as well as their own local programs.[41]

The USSR also participates in several external broadcast organizations. Included are the International Television and Radio Organization (OIRT), which was founded in 1946. During subsequent years, Western European members withdrew so that today OIRT is primarily, though not exclusively, composed of Eastern European and other Communist bloc nations. The goals of OIRT include furthering the development of the radio and television industry in member nations, including broadcasts to regions with technical barriers, and fostering cooperation among members, including informational and program exchanges.[42] An outgrowth of OIRT is the Intervision network, composed of Eastern European nations, in which the Soviet Union has developed an active role. To a lesser extent, the Soviets also have program exchanges with a number of foreign television services, including the Eurovision network.[43]

Interestingly, the Soviet Union has not employed television to the same degree that it has engaged other media outlets in its political drives. Studies indicate that the preponderance of Soviet television time is devoted to entertainment, ranging from educational and cultural programs to films and children's productions. It has been estimated that only twenty-five percent or less of Soviet television viewing hours are devoted to political broadcasting (including news).[44] There is, however, a considerable emphasis on educational endeavors, and David E. Powell has noted that due to the mandate to conform to Party policies, even the cultural and entertainment programs have a political impact upon their audiences.[45]

Professor Powell concludes that television in the Soviet Union has a tremendous potential to contact a vast audience which might otherwise be missed by the media, and to do so in a manner conducive to receptivity.[46] The Soviets do not appear to have taken full advantage of this opportunity. It has been suggested that this may be in part due to the elitist attitudes of the government and Party leadership, which does not perceive the necessity for popular persuasion. Rather, it is maintained that the citizenry owe loyalty to their leaders, and support need not be won through convincing appeals.[47] A different study emphasizes the fact that Soviet propaganda specialists are less familiar with television usage, and therefore, prefer to concentrate on other, more familiar, forms of mass media. One distinct problem encountered by Soviet television is that in its endeavors to maximize its audiences, it attempts to please as many people as possible, to the end that few, if any, are really pleased.[48]

It should be recalled that the Soviet Union is undergoing political as well as social and economic modernization. One result is bound to be increasing demands upon the government, including demands for increased information concerning the possibilities of Soviet life. The government will have to discover how to at least partially meet these demands while avoiding disclosures which would dangerously erode its basis of support.[49]

Television has the opportunity to reach more senses of a larger audience than perhaps any other single form of communication. Nevertheless, its uses, while varied, are still controversial. The best methods for maximizing television's positive uses in the political arena remain the subject of study, and the limits of its influence on politics, while considerable, are still undefined.

True to its democratic principles and heritage, the United States has one of the most open television systems in the world, which seeks, under equal opportunities and fairness regulations, to maximize political exposure for all candidates and political viewpoints. Other democratic nations, such as Great Britain, have developed similar traditions.

However, many of today's nations have established strict control over this medium, or have devised governmental monopolies in the industry. While it is readily agreed that some control of this area of public interest and domain is essential, all too often such control or monopoly can perpetuate unpopular governments or ideologies, thereby violating the rights and dignity of the nation's citizenry.

Notes

1. For a more detailed discussion, see Walter B. Emery, *National and International Systems of Broadcasting: Their History, Operation and Control*, (East Lansing: Michigan State University Press, 1969), Chap. 1. For an in-depth description of the role of the FCC see Sydney W. Head, *Broadcasting in America: A Survey of Television and Radio*, 2nd ed., (Boston: Houghton-Mifflin, 1972), Part IV. For an opposing view see, John Tebbel, *The Media in America*, (New York: Thomas Y. Crowell, 1974), Chap. 20.
2. Erik Barnouw, *Tube of Plenty: The Evolution of American Television*, (New York: Oxford University Press, 1975), pp. 299–301.
3. Michael J. Petrick, " 'Equal Opportunities' and 'Fairness' in Broadcast Coverage of Politics," *The Annals of the American Academy of Political and Social Science*, 427 (September 1976): 74.
4. Ibid., passim.
5. Michael A. Krasner, Stephen G. Chaberski, and D. Kelly Jones, *American Government: Structure and Process*, New York: Macmillan, 1977, p. 294.
6. Thomas E. Patterson and Robert D. McClure, "Television and the Less-Interested Voter: The Costs of an Informed Electorate," *The Annals of the American Academy of Political and Social Science*, 175 (May 1976) pp. 88–97. For additional information concerning media costs see Joseph Napolitan, "Media Costs and Effects in Political Campaigns," *The Annals of the American Academy of Political and Social Science*, 427 (September 1976), pp. 114–24.
7. Newton N. Minow and Lee M. Mitchell, "Incumbent Television: A Case of Indecent Exposure, *The Annals of the American Academy of Political and Social Science*, 425 (May 1976), 74–84.
8. Gerald Pomper, et al., *The Election of 1976: Reports and Interpretations*, (New York: David McKay, 1977), p. 70.
9. Bernard Rubin, *Media, Politics, and Democracy*, (New York: Oxford University Press, 1977), p. 151.
10. Sig Mickelson, "The Candidate in the Living Room," *The Annals of the American Academy of Political and Social Science*, 177 (September 1976), p. 28.
11. For two interesting studies see, Dan Nimmo, "Political Image Makers and the Mass Media," *The Annals of the American Academy of Political and Social Science*, 427 (September 1976), pp. 33–44, and Joe McGinnis, *The Selling of the President 1968*, (New York: Trident Press, 1969).

12. Robert M. Batscha, *Foreign Affairs News and the Broadcast Journalist,* (New York: Praeger, 1975), p. 236.
13. Thomas E. Patterson and Robert D. McClure, *The Unseeing Eye: The Myth of Television Power in National Elections,* (New York: G. P. Putnam's Sons, 1976), p. 22.
14. William J. Crotty, *Political Reform and the American Experiment,* (New York: Thomas Y. Crowell, 1977), p. 109.
15. Ernest W. Lefever, *TV and National Defense: An Analysis of CBS News, 1972–1973,* (Boston, Virginia: The Institute for American Strategy), p. 13 and Louis S. Loeb and Daniel M. Berman, *American Politics: Crisis and Challenge,* (New York: Macmillan, 1975), pp. 120–21.
16. Lefever, *TV and National Defense,* p. 139.
17. Krasner, Chaberski, and Jones, *American Government,* pp. 289–93.
18. Louis S. Loeb and Daniel M. Berman, *American Politics: Crisis and Challenge,* (New York: Collier Macmillan, 1975), pp. 121–22.
19. William Ebenstein, C. Herman Pritchett, Henry A. Turner, and Dean Mann, *American Democracy in World Perspective,* (New York: Harper and Row, 1967), p. 291.
20. United Kingdom, British Information Services, *Broadcasting in Britain,* (New York: June 1975), p. 1.
21. Ibid., pp. 3–4.
22. Ibid., p. 9.
23. United Kingdom, British Information Service, Policy and Reference Division, "Television Broadcasting in Britain," (Policy Background), #12/76, (New York: September 3, 1976), p. 2.
24. Burton Paulu, *British Broadcasting,* (Minneapolis: University of Minnesota Press, 1956), pp. 44–45.
25. Douglas Verney, *British Government and Politics: Life without a Declaration of Independence,* 2nd ed., (New York: Harper and Row, 1971), p. 29.
26. Graeme C. Moodie, *The Government of Great Britain,* 3rd ed., (New York: Thomas Y. Crowell, 1971), p. 85.
27. United Kingdom, British Information Services, *Broadcasting,* p. 34.
28. Ibid., p. 26.
29. United Kingdom, British Broadcasting Company, *BBC Handbook 1977,* (London: 1976), Appendix II, p. 117.
30. United Kingdom, Independent Broadcasting Authority, *Television and Radio 1977,* (London: January 1977), pp. 11–13.
31. United Kingdom, British Information Services, *Broadcasting,* p. 28.
32. Ibid., p. 27.
33. Gwendolen M. Carter, *The Government of the United Kingdom,* 2nd ed., (New York: Harcourt, Brace, and World, 1967), p. 18.
34. Ibid.
35. Richard Rose, *Politics in England,* 2nd ed. (Boston: Little, Brown, 1974), p. 232.
36. Ibid., p. 231.
37. Sydney D. Bailey, *British Parliamentary Democracy,* (Boston: Houghton-Mifflin, 1968), p. 268.

38. Robert G. Wesson, *The Soviet Russian State*, (New York: John Wiley and Sons, 1972), p. 250.
39. For interesting illustrations see Ibid.
40. United Nations, Department of Economic and Social Affairs, Statistical Office, *United Nations Statistical Yearbook, 1975*, (New York: 1976), table 218.
41. Emery, *National and International Systems*, pp. 390, 392.
42. From Art. II, cited in Emery, *National and International Systems*, p. 520.
43. Emery, *National and International Systems*, p. 392.
44. David E. Powell, "Television in the USSR," *Public Opinion Quarterly*, 39, 3 (Fall 1975), pp. 287–88.
45. Powell, "Television in the USSR," p. 288.
46. *Ibid.*, p. 287.
47. Frederick C. Barghoorn, *Politics in the USSR*, 2nd ed., (Boston: Little, Brown, 1972), p. 146.
48. Powell, "Television in the USSR," pp. 289, 297.
49. Barghoorn, Politics in the USSR, p. 146.

Bibliography

There is an ample and ever-increasing amount of material available concerning television, and particularly television and politics, which has appeared in sources ranging from popular publications to those which are more scholarly or professional. Listed below are some of the more recent and readily available publications. Examination of these may challenge readers to pursue additional source materials.

Among works of particular interest with regard to television in the United States are: Erik Barnouw, *Tube of Plenty: The Era of American Television* (New York: Oxford University Press, 1975); Robert M. Batscha, *Foreign Affairs News and the Broadcast Journalist* (New York: Praeger, 1975); Robert J. Blakely, *The People's Instrument* (Washington, D.C.: Public Affairs Press, 1971); Edward W. Chester, *Radio, Television and American Politics* (New York: Sheed and Ward, 1969); Edwin Diamond, *The Tin Kazoo: Politics, Television, and the News* (Cambridge: MIT Press, 1975); Fred W. Friendly, *Due to Circumstances Beyond Our Control . . .* (New York: Random House, 1967); Sydney W. Head, *Broadcasting in America: A Survey of Television and Radio* (Boston: Houghton-Mifflin, 1972); Kurt Lang and Gladys Engel Lang, *Politics and Television* (Chicago: Quadrangle Books, 1968); also by the Langs, *Voting and Non-Voting: Implications of Broadcasting Returns before Polls are Closed* (Waltham, Massachusetts: Blaisdell, 1968); Robert MacNeil, *The People Machine: The Influence of Television on American Politics* (New York: Harper and Row, 1968); Harold A. Mendelsohn and Irving Crespi, *Polls, Television and the New Politics,* (Scranton: Chandler, 1970); Thomas E. Patterson and Robert D. McClure, *The Unseeing Eye: The Myth of Television Power in National Elections* (New York: G. P. Putnam's Sons, 1976); Bernard Rubin, *Political Television* (Belmont, California: Wadsworth, 1967); by the same author, *Media, Politics, and Democracy* (New York: Oxford University Press, 1977); Solomon S. Simonson, *Crisis in Television: A Study of the Private Judgment and the Public Interest* (New York: Living Books, 1966); Harry J. Skornia, *Television and Society: An Inquest and Agenda for Improvement* (New York: McGraw-Hill, 1965); William Small, *To Kill a Messenger: Television News and the Real World* (New York: Hastings House, 1974); Robert E. Summers and Harrison B. Summers, *Broadcasting and the Public* (Belmont, California: Wadsworth, 1966); and John Tebbel, *The Media in America* (New York: Thomas Y. Crowell, 1974).

Articles concerning television and other public media have appeared in several recent issues of *The Annals of the American Academy of Political and Social Science.* In the May 1976 issue (Vol. 425) entitled "Political Finances: Reform and Reality," two articles of particular interest are

Newton N. Minow and Lee M. Mitchell, "Incumbent Television: A Case
of Indecent Exposure," and Thomas E. Patterson and Robert D. McClure,
"Television and the Less-Interested Voter: The Costs of an Informed
Electorate." The September 1976 issue (Vol. 427) is entitled "The Role
of Mass Media in American Politics." Each of the articles in this issue is
of interest, and among the most pertinent are Edwin Emery, "Changing
Role of the Mass Media in American Politics," L. John Martin, "Recent
Theory on Mass Media Potential in Political Campaigns," Sig Mickelson,
"The Candidate in the Living Room," Joseph Napolitan, "Media Costs and
Effects in Political Campaigns," and Michael J. Petrick, " 'Equal Oppor-
tunities' and 'Fairness' in Broadcast Coverage of Politics."

Biased television coverage of politics has been the subject of a number
of authors, and included are Joseph C. Keeley, *The Left-Leaning Antenna: Political Bias in Television* (New Rochelle, New York: Arlington
House, 1971) and Ernest W. Lefever, *TV and National Defense: Analysis
of CBS News, 1972-1973* (Boston, Virginia: The Institute for American
Strategy Press, 1974). The issue of political images is also under current
discussion. See, for example, Joe McGinniss, *The Selling of the President
1968* (New York: Trident Press, 1969); Dan Nimmo, "Political Image
Makers and the Mass Media," *The Annals of the American Academy of
Political and Social Science*, Vol. 427 (September 1976); and Gene
Wyckoff, *The Image Candidates*, (New York: Macmillan, 1968).

Information concerning British and Soviet television and its influences
on politics can be found in a number of sources, including government
and politics books concerning each nation, some of which were cited in
the body of this essay. Of particular bibliographic interest with regard
to the United Kingdom is: United Kingdom, British Broadcasting Corporation, *British Broadcasting, 1922-1972: A Select Bibliography* (London:
1972). A. William Bluem and Roger Manvell have edited an excellent collection of essays comparing American and British television development
in *Television: The Creative Experience* (New York: Hastings House,
1967). Additional sources include: Jay G. Blumler and Denis McQuail,
Television in Politics (Chicago: University of Chicago Press, 1969);
Krishan Kumar, "Holding the Middle Ground: The BBC, the Public, and
the Professional Broadcaster," *Sociology* 9 (1975); Burton Paulu, *British
Broadcasting: Radio and Television in the United Kingdom* (Minneapolis:
University of Minnesota Press, 1958); and by the same author, *British
Broadcasting in Transition* (Minneapolis: University of Minnesota Press,
1961); and United Kingdom, British Information Service, *Broadcasting
in Britain* (New York: 1975). Both the BBC and IBA issue yearbooks
which are quite informative: United Kingdom, British Broadcasting Corporation, *BBC Handbook 1977* (London: 1976); and United Kingdom,
Independent Broadcasting Authority, *Television and Radio 1977*, Eric
Croston, ed. (London: January 1977).

A source which includes both Britain and the Soviet Union among a
substantial number of other nations is Walter B. Emery, *National and
International Systems of Broadcasting: Their History, Operation and
Control* (East Lansing: Michigan State University Press, 1969). Soviet
TV is analyzed in David E. Powell, "Television in the U.S.S.R.," *Public
Opinion Quarterly*, 39, 3 (Fall 1975).

4. Sugar Daddy or Ogre? The Impact of Commercial Television on Professional Sports

Richard Harmond
Department of History
St. John's University

Television has brought far-reaching changes to the world of professional sports. By pumping large sums of money into them, TV has promoted the expansion of the professional games. In turn, television money and expansion have led to inflated salaries for athletes and rising incomes for the owners of sports franchises. Moreover, by telecasting hundreds of hours of sports each year, the networks have made celebrities of athletes, and created new fans for football, baseball, basketball, and hockey, as well as for golf, tennis and bowling. Through the instrumentality of what Eric Barnouw calls the "tube of plenty," the professional sports world, it would seem, has entered the lushest era in its history—its golden age.

Or has it? The enlarged leagues, fat salaries, and network exposure are only a part of the picture. Television has exacted a price for its patronage; some would say a very stiff price. There are those who even ask whether the various professional games—at least as we have come to know them—can survive television's embrace. Such fears may be exaggerated. They are revealing nonetheless. That the medium should in some ways threaten, while it also enriches and popularizes the professional games, goes to the heart of the television sports relationship.

The Tube of Plenty

Television has played a substantial role in the sports boom of our time. But the medium did not suddenly make us over into a sports-minded nation. Both as doers and viewers, Americans have long been a sports-oriented people. In past generations they skated and cycled, hunted, swam and hiked, played baseball and basketball. They also cheered their baseball heroes, toasted their boxing champions, and celebrated the achievements of their favorite college football players. Before World War I, Americans followed the exploits of such legendary figures as "Wee Willie" Keeler, John L. Sullivan, and Jim Thorpe. And names like Babe Ruth, Lou Gehrig, Jack Dempsey, Joe Louis, "Red" Grange, and Tom Harmon remind us of the high interest generated by spectator sports in the 1920s, 30s, and early 40s.[1]

After World War II, Americans became progressively more committed to the sporting life. They attended sporting matches in growing numbers. Between 1950 and 1970 attendance at major league baseball games rose from 17.6 million to 29 million; and over the same period football attendance went from 2 million to 9.9 million. By 1970, Americans were spending over $500 million annually on admissions to spectator sports. And attendance continued to rise in the early 1970s. At the same time, Americans increasingly participated in sports. Between 1950 and 1970 the number of golfers climbed from 3.2 million to 9.7 million. By the later 1960s, according to *Time Magazine,* one out of every five Americans was "a steady customer at the local bowling alley." Millions of people were also jogging, skiing (leading to 50,000 broken legs in the 1971–72 season), fishing, swimming, snorkeling, and playing tennis.[2] "Nowhere else in the world," Leonard Shecter observes, "is such a large portion of the population so constantly engaged in sports and games," as in the United States.[3]

Television had—and continues to have—an impressive part in this sports explosion. Naturally, people needed not only the inclination, but also the income and free time for such activities. And so spreading affluence, a declining work week, and paid vacations contributed prominently to the sports boom of the 1950s, 60s, and 70s.[4] But so, too, did TV, for the medium intensified and gave direction to the sports explosion.

Actually, the nexus between sports and TV antedated the sports boom by some years. In 1939, NBC went on the air with what is considered the first telecast of a sports event ever produced in this country.[5] On May 17, NBC's mobile unit showed the Columbia-Princeton baseball game from Baker Field. A single camera, set near the third baseline, swept back and forth across the field trying, none too successfully as it turned out, to follow the game. A reporter for the *Times* wrote of the telecast:

The players were best described by observers as appearing "like white flies" running across the screen. It was impossible for the single camera to include both the pitcher's mound and home plate at the same time. The "eye" was focused on the mound for the wind-up and quickly followed the ball to batter and catcher. Seldom were more than three players visible on the screen at one time. . . .

Those who watched the game . . . agreed that the commentator "saved the day," otherwise there would be no way to follow the play or to tell where the ball went. . . .[6]

The commentator, sportscaster Bill Stern, recalled that "I had no monitor. I had no idea where the damned thing [the camera] was pointing. I never knew whether the thing could keep up with the players or not."[7]

In August the mobile unit, using two cameras this time, telecast a doubleheader from Ebbets Field between the Brooklyn Dodgers and the Cincinnati Reds. This effort was so superior to the Columbia-Princeton telecast that a *Times* reviewer was moved to comment that baseball was "a natural for television." "Scientifically," he announced, "the baseball-television problem has been solved."[8] Equally impressive was the first football game on TV, a contest played on September 30 at Randall's Island Stadium between Fordham and Waynesburg. In the opinion of the *Times* critic, viewing the game on the screen (as perhaps some two thousand people did) was more rewarding than seeing it at the stadium![9] Events, however, abruptly short-circuited the developing connection between sports and TV. The war came, and commercial television was put aside for the duration.[10]

When the great conflict had ended, manufacturers turned to the production of television sets, and consumers were prepared to buy. By 1948 factories were producing thousands of sets a month. As for TV fare, viewers—in those days often ensconced in bars and taverns—were entertained by Milton Berle, Sid Caesar, Imogene Coca, and the vaudeville-like "Ed Sullivan Show." They also enjoyed wrestling, the Roller Derby, boxing, and baseball. In fact, as sports authority Leonard Koppett points out, the "televising of major league baseball, boxing, and college football in the nineteenforties was a key element in launching the television industry."[11]

During the late 1940s and early 1950s, however, TV still suffered from growing pains. Equipment breakdowns were common; most cities had only one station, and some had no television at all; and the lack of a national hookup ruled out coast-to-coast television.

After 1952, though, these and other problems were resolved, and television swiftly gained mass acceptance. By 1956 more than three-quarters of the homes in America had TV sets.[12]

In the meantime, the link between the medium and sports was ever more firmly forged. Whether this linkage was helpful or injurious to sports was a subject of debate at the time. On the one hand, there was a sharp falloff in attendance at sports events (especially baseball) in most television cities during the early and mid-1950s. On the other hand, some observers believed that TV was beginning to boost popular participation in golf and other sporting activities. Of more concern to the professional leagues was the fact that television, as *Business Week* remarked, had "some mighty fancy money available" for them.[13] And as the 1950s wore on, TV's "fancy money" became increasingly important to professional sports. In 1958, for example, a baseball official, testifying before a committee of Congress, admitted that "a large part of the revenue of every major league team is derived from the sale of broadcasting and television rights." By 1961, according to a witness before yet another congressional committee, television revenues had "become a vital part of every sports team budget—baseball, football, basketball."[14]

Still, these revenues were quite modest—at least when compared with what was to come. The networks were not stingy in the early 1960s, but sports' bonanza years began with the CBS-NFL deal in 1964. On January 24 of that year, the National Football League Commissioner, Pete Rozelle, opened three sealed envelopes. Each contained a bid from one of the major networks for the 1964–1965 television rights to NFL games. The winning bid was CBS's, for the then staggering sum of $28.1 million. This was more than three times the amount CBS had paid for the rights to the NFL's 1961–1963 games. It was the most lucrative contract ever agreed to for a series of sports events. Further, the money was to be shared equally among the teams of the NFL, with each garnering slightly more than $1 million per season.

CBS officials obviously believed that they had made a sound investment. Their decision reflected, in part, the growing popularity of televised football. The president of the network simply said: "We know how much these games mean to the viewing audience, our affiliated stations, and the nation's advertisers."[15]

CBS had scored a triumph over its chief competitor, NBC. A few days later the vanquished network, anxious to restore its prestige, signed a five year TV contract with the American Football League for $36 million. This deal assured the survival of the five year old AFL, a struggling—some said floundering—eight team rival of the older, more soundly based NFL. In fact the AFL was now so solidly financed that it could, and did, compete with the NFL for top-flight college players.[16] The most notable AFL coup was the signing for $400,000 of Joe Namath, a brilliant quarterback from the University of Alabama. The older league now realized that the AFL was a serious threat. Not surprisingly, the NFL agreed to a merger in June, 1966.

Like a stone tossed into a quiet pond, the CBS-NFL deal had a ripple effect on professional sports. In the first place, to change the metaphor, the deal opened up what William Johnson calls "the doors to the big money vault." Thus, by the 1970 season, professional football received an estimated $40 million—or twenty times what the sport had earned ten years earlier—for the television rights to its games. Four years later, the networks paid out $56 million for those rights.[17] Again, it would now be very difficult to exclude other sports from that "big money vault." As Baseball Commissioner Ford Frick commented on the 1964 deal: "This will boost the World Series asking price by plenty when the renewal comes up." The president of the Los Angeles baseball Angels remarked discerningly that the CBS-NFL contract "is a clear forerunner of what is likely to happen in baseball and other sports."[18]

And so it was, from such minor sports as skating and swimming on to golf, bowling, tennis, baseball, hockey and basketball. Thus the TV coverage of, and expenditures on, golf and tennis grew steadily in the bonanza years.[19] As for basketball, annual television income for that sport soared from a reported $500,000 in the later 1960s to around $5.5 million in 1970.[20] Hockey reached a comparable level of economic well-being in 1973, when NBC agreed to pay the National Hockey League around $5.5 million for television rights, a sum three times greater than that received in the previous season from CBS.[21] Professional baseball prospered, too. In that sport, the price for TV-broadcasting rights increased from $29.1 million for the 1967 season, to $43.2 in 1974.[22]

These huge sums of money served, in turn, as a powerful spur to expansion. The post-World War II redistribution of America's population, particularly the movement of people to the West Coast, was an underlying condition for expansion. But in terms of motivation, rising TV income was a financial enticement for many prospective franchise owners. For their part, the established owners charged each new buyer a healthy fee to join the league. Both groups, therefore, benefited, the new owners obtaining a share of television money, and the older ones splitting the entrance fee among themselves. By blanketing the major TV outlets, the owners also hoped to discourage the formation of rival leagues.[23] Beyond these incentives, the bull market in sports franchises made the ownership of such a franchise an attractive investment. Sports had become a growth industry. As an illustration, football teams bought in the 1950s for, say, $600,000, or in the early 1960s for $4 to $5 million, sold for $10 to $16 million by the end of the 1960s. Finally, ego gratification as well as the workings of the federal tax laws prompted businessmen to invest in major league sports.[24]

Whatever the specific reason or combination of reasons, expansion occurred at a remarkable clip in the bonanza years. As one investigator summarized the situation in 1975,

> In the four major spectator sports (baseball, football, basketball, and hockey), more than 3,500 athletes may now legally call themselves major leaguers. This is more than twice the number of players fifteen years ago. These people play for 121 major league teams, almost three times as many as fifteen years ago. . . .[25]

Another sort of expansion was also taking place during the bonanza years; that is, in the amount of sports shown on TV. Between 1960–1974, the time devoted by the networks to big-time sports a little more than doubled, from 540 to 1,100 hours. Moreover, sports events increasingly turned up during prime time. In 1970, eighty-five hours of sports were shown in prime time, and by 1975 the figure had reached almost three hundred hours.[26]

Remarkably, expanded TV coverage did not hurt major spectator sports at the gate. As we have seen, attendance at stadiums and arenas dipped for a time in the 1950s, only to rise sharply during the 1960s and early 70s. Indeed, TV attracted new fans to spectator sports. "Without the [TV] camera," said *Time Magazine*, "football would belong to the universities and the historians." "Television tends to create fans, especially among women," observed a baseball official. "Television night games may have hurt the box office a little, because of traffic and the late hour," he concluded, "but more fans are created than stay away."[27]

It is highly likely, too, that the medium encouraged people to participate in sports. Observers, as we noted earlier, first spotted such a phenomenon in the mid-1950s. It would certainly seem to be more than accidental that increased TV coverage of such activities as golf, skiing, bowling, and tennis coincided with rising popular participation in them. Watching their favorite athlete on the tube inspired viewers to emulate their hero or heroine on the golf course, ski slopes, tennis court, or at the bowling alley.[28]

Indeed, one of the more striking aspects of the bonanza years was—as it continues to be—the status that TV has bestowed upon eminent professional athletes. They have become celebrities, for the medium has given them a unique sort of exposure. As *Time Magazine* has pointed out,

> Through TV, millions of Americans have become thoroughly familiar with sports they once knew only through the often unreliable and overblown prose of sportswriters. "I'd travel around in the 1920s and tell people that pro football was a good game," says Illinois All-American Red Grange, "and they'd laugh at me. 'Did you ever see a game?' I'd ask them. 'Well, no,' they'd say." Former New York Giants Halfback Frank Gifford, who did not come into the National Football League until 1952, remembers going home to California after the season was over and having his friends ask: "Where have you been?"
> Today the big-time games and the best pros are well known at every wide spot in the road that boasts a TV receiver.... Babe Ruth may have been a hero to kids who never saw the inside of Yankee Stadium, but most of those kids never saw the Babe. Today, youngsters anywhere in the U.S. can see their heroes, and watch them play....[29]

With fame—plus interleague rivalries and business agents—has come fortune. Ten years ago only a few athletes made more than $100,000 a year. Then came the bonanza years. Today, top-flight players in football, baseball, hockey, basketball, tennis, and golf earn between $300,000 and $500,000 annually. Through collective bargaining agreements, the lesser players have also been able to improve their incomes. In 1975, the average salary in the National Football League was $42,000; in the National Hockey League, it was $85,000; and in the National Basketball Association, the average compensation was $107,000! As one further illustration, in the thirty years between 1937 and 1967, total prize money on the professional golfing tour grew from $40,000 to $4.5 million.[30]

Quite a number of athletes have also been able to bolster their incomes by hawking shaving cream, laxatives, typewriters, and other items on the tube. According to one estimate, Henry Aaron, the baseball star, has earned between $1.5 and $2 million through endorsements.[31] Moreover, some players, upon retiring from their trade, have found profitable jobs in television as sportscasters.[32] Whether athletes are overpaid or not is debatable. That many have successfully claimed their share from "the big money vault," however, seems beyond question.

The Price of Plenty

Television has enlarged and enriched the world of professional sports. To be sure, expansion, big salaries, and TV exposure have not come cheaply. The price has not been as steep, however, as some students of sports aver, and at least a few TV executives would like.

Concerned commentators believe that TV wields an immense and frequently harmful control over sports. "Television has not completely taken over sports," is the opinion of Jack R. Griffin, a Chicago sports columnist, "but already it has left deep scars." Leonard Shecter goes further, maintaining that

> Television *buys* sports. Television *supports* sports. It moves in with its money and supports sports in a style to which they had hoped to become accustomed and then, like a bought lady, sports become so used to luxurious living they cannot extricate themselves. So, slowly at first, but inevitably, television tells sports what to do. It *is* sports and it runs them the way it does most other things, more flamboyantly than honestly.

Morris K. Udall, Arizona congressman, and himself a former professional basketball player, agrees, declaring that "virtually every professional sport" in America "is now controlled, coached and managed by television." While, according to William Johnson,

> In the past 10 years sports in America has come to be the stepchild of television and, in a sense, handmaiden to the vicissitudes of Madison Avenue. . . . the impact of television in these last 10 years has produced more revolutionary—and irrevocable— changes in sports than anything since mankind began to play organized games. . . . The geography, the economics, the schedules, the esthetics, the very ethos of sports has come to depend upon television cameras and advertising monies. . . .[33]

Such assertions are inspired, in part, by the utterances of certain figures in the upper echelons of television and advertising. These individuals would very much like to mold sports to the needs of the medium. They have admitted as much. Some years ago, for example, Thomas W. Moore, the president of ABC, proposed, in a talk to the Hollywood Advertising Club, that baseball substitute for its 162 game schedule a 60-game, weekend schedule. In Moore's view, the advantages of the abridged schedule were that,

> The teams would be able to reduce their rosters, fielding only their best players. A team would need only three or four top pitchers. I believe this would increase attendance at the games, *greatly increase television audiences of baseball*, and put the games on a much sounder financial basis all over the country and not just in a few selected towns.

Moore went on to suggest further departures from traditional practices in golf, and other sports. Nothing came of these proposals. Interestingly, though, a CBS "spokesman" was reported to have said that some of Moore's suggestions were good, but that others were impractical at the present time.[34]

Over the years other plans to "improve" sports have surfaced. Thus, a public relations executive has suggested that baseball should drop the hoary four-ball-three-strike regulation, and adopt a new, three-ball-two-strike rule to "force a decision faster by the protagonists, and bring the line-up to bat more often during a game."[35] Although he had no proposal as specific as this to offer, Roone Arledge, then vice-president and executive producer of sports programs at ABC, was also eager for baseball to put aside its dawdling ways. While admitting to a certain admiration for the game, Arledge nevertheless remarked that

> As certain habits have become accepted, an awful lot of puff has been added to baseball. Most people, unless they're aggressive, have to be motivated into action; otherwise they postpone everything, beginning with getting up in the morning. So you've got the pitcher standing there with the ball in his hand because he doesn't know exactly what pitch he wants to throw, and the batter, because he's afraid to strike out, fools around and fools around before he finally steps up to the plate. People will keep doing what they've traditionally been allowed to get away with, like arguing with the umpires . . . which should have no real part in the game. . . .[36]

The fact that the tradition—ritual really—of players arguing with umpires is now over a century old apparently meant nothing to Arledge. Still, all of this is rhetoric. At most it announces intentions. But the case that Griffin, Shecter, Johnson, and others have built against television rests less on pronouncements (as revealing as they might be) than on deeds.

Network television, say the critics, has regularly manipulated sports for its own ends. Sometimes the manipulation has been, in itself, relatively harmless. Thus, to accommodate the needs of color TV, the baseball owners have agreed to Luminall Lawn-Tint infields, while the moguls of hockey have acceded to blue-painted ice.[37]

More serious, the critics insist, is the issue of commercial breaks. As viewers we have become more or less inured to them, but on occasion commercial time-outs have interfered with the progress of a game. Some years ago, for instance, player-coach Bill Russell, of the Boston Celtics, was fined $50 for refusing to call a TV-ordered time-out in the midst of a Boston rally against the Philadelphia 76ers.[38]

Another incident of this sort concerned a soccer game played in May, 1967. As *Newsweek* described the episode,

> "Down, down! Stay down!" shouted the soccer referee. Inside forward Co Prins of the Pittsburgh Phantoms stopped strugling to get up, obediently clutched his stomach and fell on the ground writhing in mock agony [an injury being the only reason for any halt in a soccer match]. "I am not hurt," admitted Hollander Prins sheepishly after the game. "The referee tells me to stay down. But I do not like what we did. It is not honest. It is not soccer."[39]

Nor has golf been immune to the commercial break. In the "World Series of Golf" a few years ago, a TV employee traveled with the golfers so that, as he explained his duties, "if a golfer looks as though he's about to get ready to hit the ball, and the mobile [TV] unit is telling me at the same time that we're just about ready to break for a commercial, I'll get the golfer's attention, and give him the signal to wait until we're back to live action."[40]

Just as troublesome as commercial breaks, in the opinion of the critics, are the time changes and rule revisions occasionally required by the networks. A rather notorious instance of the former was the delayed start of the United States Open in 1967. As the famous golfer, Jack Nicklaus, remarked testily,

> We were all bothered by the late starting time both Saturday and Sunday. It was bad for the players, the gallery, the press, and the image of golf—to say nothing of the havoc a brief rain delay would have caused. The only thing it accommodated was television, and I don't think television should rule golf.[41]

That same year, Leonard Shecter reports,

> It was television which demanded a four-o'clock starting time for baseball's 1967 All-Star game in Anaheim, California, so the

Eastern markets could be reached in prime time. The late-after-noon sun made it so difficult for the batters to see, the best hitters in baseball managed to score only three runs in fifteen innings.[42]

At times, too, the rules of a game are revised at the direction of the medium. Again, to quote Shecter: "It was television that pro-hibited red-dogging—close pursuit of the passer—in an NFL All-Star game in order to keep the game wide open and, in the opinion of television, more interesting."[43]

Golf has also revamped its rules to accommodate the medium. Since medal play (where a golfer plays the field, with the lowest score over the course winning) lends itself more readily to TV coverage, the PGA has switched from match play (where players oppose each other in a series of eliminations, the man winning the most holes being declared the winner) to medal play.[44]

This, and the other examples of network interference cited, far from exhaust the critics' case against the medium. To appreciate fully the danger that TV poses for sports, say the critics, one must look at what has happened to minor league baseball, and to boxing.

At one time minor league baseball prospered in the small cities and towns of America. In 1948 some 42 million people attended minor league games. Then came television. Without having to buy a ticket, a fan could now view major league baseball in his living room. ("When you can watch Carl Yastrzemski on TV who wants to watch Arleigh Bruge?" asked a local sports editor.) Minor league attendance plunged to 15.5 million in 1957, and dropped further to 10 million in 1969. And between 1949–1969, the number of minor league clubs fell from 488 to 155. Nor, in terms of the future of the game, was minor league baseball's loss major league baseball's gain. As major league official admitted: "Baseball can-not exist without a virile and strong minor-league organization."[45]

Perhaps the minor leagues can survive the television age. There seems less hope for boxing. Boxing was once a thriving sport, off as well as on the tube. During the 1950s, when both NBC and ABC carried the sport, there were sometimes as many as five bouts a week on TV. Boxing was so popular that Ruby Goldstein, the referee, became a national celebrity (and was even booked on the "Ed Sullivan Show"). But the pressure to provide talent was in-tense. "There always had to be a loser," remembered one fight manager, "and you couldn't bring back a loser because the sponsors wouldn't take him." Moreover, the local boxing clubs—the training ground for new young fighters—were being ignored by the TV-absorbed fight fans. Between 1952 and 1959 about 250 of the 300 boxing clubs in this country closed down. "With its sources dried up at the small club," writes Jack Griffin, "boxing began to decline and was kept alive only by the plasma of television money." "And then one day," he adds, "boxing had no more viewer attraction, no more sponsor appeal." In 1964, after twenty years on the tube, TV dropped boxing. The ratings had slumped badly.[46]

To the critics, the lingering demise of boxing should stand as a grim warning to all of sports. Television exploited boxing. At the same time, the sport allowed itself to become dangerously dependent on TV money. And then, when it had been overexposed on the tube and had lost drawing power, television discarded boxing.

The critics maintain that a parallel situation has developed throughout the realm of sports. In the first place, the games have become too reliant on TV revenues. Sports officials themselves acknowledge the dependency. "Without our television fees," admitted Pete Rozelle, "we would not be able to attract some fine college athletes. They'd be working for General Electric—and we'd be out some of the better players in our league." "There is no way we could survive without television," conceded William Ford, owner of the Detroit Lions. Michael Burke, president of the New York Knickerbockers, said summarily: "If sports lost those [TV] revenues, we'd all be out of business."[47] While sports world officials made these admissions, media and advertising personages circulated complaints about the rising cost of TV sports—particularly of pro football. "Frankly," remarked one network sports chief, "just about everybody I know in this business is getting jumpy about the spiraling costs. . . . Maybe it's cliché, but where will it end?" And a television executive, worried about the high cost of football rights, said "We have a vague feeling that TV may kill football just as it did some years ago with boxing."[48]

Secondly, the critics warn that television has overexposed sports. Even some noncritics agree with this proposition. Russell Baker, a *New York Times* columnist, complains that "there was just too much of it [sports] for any of it to be engaging anymore. . . . It was like having a banana split with every meal. It just quit being fun." Sports seasons also increasingly overlap. The National Basketball Association, for instance, started its 1975–1976 season in mid-October, and ended it in early June. It has become possible to watch baseball, football, tennis, golf, basketball, and hockey all on the same day (most likely in October). In Leonard Koppett's words, each sport has extended its time period "like a fungus gone wild."[49]

The peril of overexposure is, of course, boredom. But worse than the jaded is the alienated fan. Together, expansion, the concomitant moving about of franchises from city to city, and the high salaries of athletes have, according to some reports, begun to erode the loyalty of the fans. As one such fan lamented,

> For the first time in 20 years, I don't even read the sports pages. You can't keep track of all the teams, everybody's fighting with one another, and it's just a confusing mess. How can you follow a favorite team when the teams and players switch every other week? They've ruined it for me.[50]

Even a few athletes have expressed concern over the commercialization of sports. "There is too much big money in television," said Dizzy Dean, ex-St. Louis Cardinals pitcher, "it is changing sports all around. Instead of learning the fundamentals, kids in the Little League are all thinking of that half-million-dollar price tag."[51] Basketball player Tom Meschery became so disillusioned he quit the game he loved. As he explained,

> There is sickness there. It is in basketball, and it is in sports in general. . . . Integrity is disappearing. Contracts mean nothing; not between owner or player, or owner and fan. Players jump teams. Teams jump cities. And all the while the money flows as from a cornucopia.[52]

The critics have put together a strong but selective case against television. That the medium has strongly influenced "the geography, the economics, and the schedules" of the world of sports is undeniable. Moreover, through the insertion of numerous commercial breaks and insistence on certain rule changes, network officials have impinged on the autonomy of sports.

On the other hand, the nabobs of the sports world have minds (and power bases) of their own. Like the businessmen they are, club owners and promoters have made adjustments in their games to improve the "product" they are offering to the public.[53] They instituted rules, and other changes, long before the television era (such as, in baseball, banning the spitball in 1920 and introducing the lively ball shortly thereafter). And some of the post–World War II adjustments, like the adoption by the National Basketball Association in 1954 of the 24-second clock, have owed little to pressure from the medium.[54] At other times, such as in the agreement in 1973 on baseball's designated hitter rule, television was certainly an important, but not the only concern.[55] If there is a lesson here, it is that change, as much as tradition, has been an integral part of the history of American sports.

Club owners have also at times resisted the wishes of TV executives. When, for example, ABC once wanted to use Bill Veeck as a baseball commentator, "the owners wouldn't let us," Roone Arledge declared peevishly. Again, because ABC refused to give the NBA directors control of the game on the tube, they switched to the more amenable CBS. And Pete Rozelle, with the support of the NFL owners and against the combined opposition of NBC and CBS, succeeded in his campaign to have football televised on Monday evenings.[56]

It is well to remember, too, that there is more to the story of sports even in this age of the medium than television. Thus, basic economic and social factors should be included in any account of the deterioration of minor league baseball, or of boxing. The decline of small town civic pride (and hence small town rivalries), the emergence of other, competing diversions (bowling, boating, drive-in theaters, and so forth), and the widespread ownership of the automobile (allowing people to seek out those diversions) have all adversely affected minor league baseball.[57] As for boxing, lower class ethnics, who once used the ring as a way to climb out of the ghetto, found more attractive vocational opportunities in prosperous postwar America. And when blacks and Hispanics took the place of Jewish, Irish, and Italian fighters, white fans lost interest in boxing.[58]

TV's impact on minor league baseball and boxing, then, though considerable, has often been overstressed. But what can be said of the threefold dangers of overexposure, commercialism, and dependency? It is possible that there is too much sports on TV. At the present time, though, the ratings do not appear to confirm the complaint.[59] This is really a question of public taste, and a considerable portion of the American people would seem to have a very large appetite for televised sports. To quote Pete Axthelm, the author of *The City Game*:

> Perhaps the saturation issue was best summarized by an acquaintance who once watched fourteen hours of sports in a single weekend. "How can they do this to us?" he screamed when the vigil ended. "They're not showing the hockey game from the West Coast!"[60]

If, however, the fans really are alienated by the so-called commercialization of sports, they might well turn away from the professional games. Is this a genuine threat? Overall attendance figures suggest otherwise.[61] Professional sports have, of course, been commercial enterprises for decades, and it seems likely that most fans realize this fact. In the words of sportswriter Roger Kahn,

> Why aren't things the way they were? But in most ways they *are* the way they were. It is mostly the appearance of things that has changed. Jack Dempsey's super gates stirred people fifty years ago as much as Muhammed Ali's super gates arouse cupidity today. Contract negotiations have grabbed headlines ever since some baseball writer invented the word "holdout." Sports have always drawn hustlers, con men. . . . I can remember being presented a Little Dizzy Dean baseball suit during the late 1930's. Dean got his royalty; the suit lasted for three games, or one washing. . . . Emphasis shifts. The faces are new. The hustlers are slicker. But anyone who wants to weep for the carefree days, when sports and money were distinct, will have to weep alone.[62]

One suspects that there are few who will weep alone.

Though overexposure and commercialization are, at present, indistinct and basically unverifiable trends, the same cannot be said of the strong drift towards dependency. A third or more of the gross income from all major league sports comes from TV and radio. With the apparent exception of the teams in the National Hockey League, the large majority of major league franchises would be operating at a loss without TV revenues.[63] Furthermore, if the chief sponsors lost interest and consequently the revenues from a televised sport fell sharply, or if the television establishment decided that the price of a sport's rights had gotten completely out of hand, the networks might well cut back or even unload that sport. Given the current economic dependency on TV, this would, at the very least, be a severe blow to the affected sport. Players would be cut, salaries slashed, and the weaker teams would fold. If the sport managed to survive, it would do so as a sad relic of the bonanza years.

This is not to suggest that the dropping of, say, football or basketball would be an easy decision for the sponsors or the networks. The advertisers, who spend well over a billion dollars a year on sports programs, complain of the high charges for television time. Yet they also admit the value of sponsoring the professional games. "It remains our belief," said the president of the Pabst

Brewing Company, "that sports are still the most wholesome attraction available to the television medium." A spokesman for the Gillette Company felt "that sports broadcasts are an ideal medium for our advertising message. Network sports attract the large male audience we want." And an executive of Chrysler Corporation explained,

> Sports offers Chrysler a selective audience of males. We can reach the 18-to-49 age group, the family-oriented man, the young-minded man. There is prestige for Chrysler in having the product associated with these events. . . . Sports is a wholesome, clean, healthy setting for our product.[64]

Nor would the television establishment lightly part with football, or one of the other major league sports. Television executives grumble about the costs. They claim that sport "is a bad investment," and that the networks actually lose money on football.[65] But they must balance these asserted financial losses against other kinds of considerations. According to Roone Arledge, the image of a network is built on sports and news. Sports have attracted sponsors, and have even brought to the medium companies which had never before advertised on television. The affiliated stations also clamor for sports programming, and their interests cannot be ignored. Moreover, TV requires vast quantities of material to fill up the time between commercials. And here sports offer the medium not only hundreds of hours of ready-made entertainment, but also "an escape from the deluge of taped and filmed TV and a return to the sense of immediacy which has always been the medium's basic fascination." In sum, television seems to need sports almost as much as sports need television.[66]

There is one final point that television executives must ponder carefully: the coming of pay TV. If the commercial networks ever abandoned a major sport, they might never reclaim it. In fact, there are promoters in the sports realm who—wisely or otherwise—look to the day when, as one analyst remarks, "it will be logical to spurn the advertiser's money and telecast *all* games via pay TV. And not just in the U.S. either."[67]

All in all, the present sometimes strained and certainly complex relationship between commercial television and the sports world would seem relatively stable. But one would be rash to assume that it will always remain so. There are many imponderables, ranging from the state of the economy and the future of pay TV, to the restless minds and eyes of millions of television viewers.

The Vicarious Experience and the TV Viewer

For over a century, technology has left its impression on sports, as it has on most other institutions of our culture. For instance, the railroad first made regular intercity team competition feasible; the sewing machine and related technologies standardized sporting equipment; the electric light allowed athletic events to be played at night; the jet aircraft has made coast-to-coast rivalries a commonplace of the sports scene; and the computer is now being used to assess the abilities and accomplishments of athletes.[68]

In one sense, television, like many of these technological innovations, has helped to expand and nationalize American sports. The medium, though, has also done something else; it has altered the way we perceive and enjoy sports.

At one time Americans took their spectator sports in ball parks, or arenas. For those open to its various nuances, it was (and of course remains) a special time. "There was a magic going to a ball park," recalls Roger Kahn, "leaving the house, the trip to the field, being there." Being there was, in part, a shared set of experiences. For a few hours a community had been formed, and its members shared not only the game, but also the noise, food, tension, brawls, and weather. One was, too, part of a visible audience, and as the historian Daniel Boorstin reminds us, "the audience was half the fun."[69]

Being there involved another experience. One saw what one chose to see—whether the whole event, or particular segments thereof. Sport on television, however, is a private affair. The living room replaces the stadium, or arena. "The once warmly enveloping community of those physically present," remarks Boorstin, is "displaced by a world of unseen fellow TV watchers."[70]

We also witness only what the tube shows us. Occasionally, such as with a golf match, watching in the living room can, in some ways, surpass being at the event. The gallery on a golf course can only follow the progress of a few players. The TV viewer, assisted by a score or so of strategically located cameras, is able to see a great deal more of the action. Today, even golf writers cover a tournament on TV.[71]

More often, though, televised sport is a restrictive experience. For all the zoom lenses, split screens, and instant replays, we are missing much in our living rooms. Patterns of play in football and the rhythms of a baseball game frequently elude us. In basketball, the tube manages to level out differences in players' size, and in hockey the camera sometimes cannot take in all of the swift-paced action. Television, as critic Michael J. Arlen observes, "filters out the senses," and "places us finally in the position of watching, with a peculiarly modern sort of bland, detached excitement, the leaps and strains and prowess of modern athletes as if from the other side of a pane of glass." In short, what we know of a game—or think we know—comes from the vicarious experience of the tube.[72] Technical improvements can, and doubtless will be made in TV's presentation of sports. More, and better situated, cameras, for example, would enhance our enjoyment of televised basketball.[73] Whatever the changes, though, sports on the tube and at the ball park will remain two different experiences.

There is a further consideration. Millions of people have first learned to appreciate their sports from the tube, rather than at the event itself. What does this imply for the future of American sports? This is one possibility that no affectionate student of traditional sports can dismiss.[74] That is, that several generations of Americans, reared on TV sports, will come to prefer the second-hand experience to the real thing. In that event, games will come to be staged in stadiums and arenas which are empty of people, save, ironically, for TV personnel. Teams will find themselves deprived of what Pete Rozelle has referred to as "the electricity of the crowd."[75] Sports will inevitably become appendages of the medium. Eventually, one or more of the traditional games—baseball being a likely candidate—may wither and fade away.[76] Television, meanwhile, will fabricate new sporting ventures, tailored to its own requirements. (ABC's "Superstar" series is one likely prototype.)

On the basis of present trends however, the more likely scenario over the next decade, at any rate, is for a continuation of the bonanza years. People will still flock to the coliseums, as well as watch more and more sports on TV; leagues will expand further (migrating perhaps to Latin America, Europe, and the Orient); franchises will grow in value; and athletes' salaries will climb, though at a much more moderate rate than in the 1960s and early 70s.[77]

Over a decade ago, a thoughtful critic of the American sporting scene asked: "Is TV a benevolent Sugar Daddy of sports ... or a greedy ogre ... ?"[78] From our present vantage point we can answer: assuredly more of a Sugar Daddy than an ogre.

The past generation has been a golden age of sports in America.

The professional games have, of course, gained from the general prosperity and the leisure boom. But they have also benefited enormously from television exposure, and the opening of the doors to TV's "big money vault." The leagues have grown greatly, as have the values of franchises and the celebrity status and salaries of athletes. Nor should we forget that television has encouraged popular participation in a variety of sporting activities.

Sports, it is true, have lost some autonomy. Moreover, there exist several potential hazards. Overexposure is one.[79] Far more serious, though, is the danger of domination by the medium, and the subsequent transformation of our traditional professional games. But the near future, at least, would seem to promise further evolution, rather than any kind of revolutionary change in the world of American sports.

Notes

1. For background see Foster Rhea Dulles, *A History of Recreation* (New York, 1965) and John Rickards Betts, *America's Sporting Heritage: 1850–1950* (Reading, Massachusetts, 1974).
2. *Statistical Abstract of the United States* (1966), p. 210; *Statistical Abstract of the United States* (1973), pp. 208, 209; "Upheaval In Pro Sports," *U.S. News & World Report*, 77 (12 August 1974), p. 52; "The Golden Age Of Sports," *Time Magazine*, 89 (2 June 1967), p. 18; *New York Times*, 31 December 1972, V, p. 14. Between 1940–1970, according to the *Statistical Abstract*, expenditures for recreation, including sports, rose from $3.7 billion to $40.1 billion.
3. Leonard Shecter, *The Jocks* (Indianapolis, 1969), p. 3.
4. Fessenden S. Blanchard, "The Revolution In Sports," *Harper's Magazine*, 212 (May, 1956), pp. 77–79; Carl N. Degler, *Affluence and Anxiety: America Since 1945*, 2nd ed. (Glenview, Illinois, 1975), p. 180. In the quarter of a century since 1950, average hours of work declined more than 25 percent, while the discretionary part of income of the typical American family now approaches 40 percent.
5. William Johnson, "TV Made It All A New Game," *Sports Illustrated*, 31 (22 December 1969), p. 89.
6. *New York Times*, 18 May 1939, p. 29.
7. Johnson, "TV Made It All A New Game," p. 89.
8. *New York Times*, 27 August 1939, V, p. 4; 3 September 1939, IX, p. 10.
9. Ibid., 15 October 1939, IX, p. 12; *Broadcasting*, 77 (28 July 1969), p. 38.
10. Eric Barnouw, *Tube Of Plenty: The Evolution Of American Television* (New York, 1975), pp. 92–93.
11. Barnouw, *Tube Of Plenty*, pp. 99–102, 114, 117; *New York Times*, 23 July 1973, V, p. 23.
12. Johnson, "TV Made It All A New Game," p. 101; Barnouw, *Tube Of Plenty*, pp. 112–13, 151; *Sponsor*, 20 (7 March 1966), p. 28; *The Statistical History of the United States, From Colonial Times to the Present*, rev. ed. (New York, 1965), p. 488.
13. Barnouw, *Tube Of Plenty*, p. 114; *U.S. News & World Report*, 39 (2 September 1955), p. 43; *Business Week*, 27 September 1952, p. 42.
14. U.S. Congress, Senate, *Organized Professional Team Sports*, Hearings Before the Subcommittee On Antitrust And Monopoly Of The Committee On the Judiciary, U.S. Senate, 85th Cong., 2nd Sess. (1958), p. 78; U.S. Congress, House, *Telecasting of Professional Sports Contests*, Hearings Before the Antitrust Subcommittee Of the Committee on the Judiciary, U.S. House, 87th Cong., 1st Sess. (1961) p. 72.
15. William Legget, "The 28-Million-Dollar Deal," *Sports Illustrated*, 20

(February 3, 1964), pp. 16–17; *New York Times*, 25 January 1964, p. 1; *Business Week*, 1 February 1964, p. 23.

16. William Johnson, "After TV Accepted The Call Sunday Was Never The Same," *Sports Illustrated*, 32 (5 January 1970), pp. 27–29: *New York Times*, 30 January 1964, p. 59: *U.S. News & World Report*, 58 (18 January 1965), pp. 64–65.

17. Johnson, "After TV Accepted The Call . . . ," pp. 27, 23; *Broadcasting*, 86 (May 6, 1974), p. 39.

18. *Advertising Age*, 35 (3 February 1964), p. 20; Leggett, "The 28-Million-Dollar Deal," p. 17.

19. *Advertising Age*, 35 (20 December 1965), p. 86, 41 (November 23, 1970), p. 1, 42 (27 December 1971), p. 42, 45 (6 May 1974), p. 3, 46 (21 July 1975), p. 2.

20. *Advertising Age*, 38 (13 November 1967), p. 38; *Broadcasting*, 78 (23 February 1970), p. 63.

21. *Business Week*, 6 January 1973, p. 22.

22. *Broadcasting*, 72 (20 February 1967), p. 36; 86 (25 February 1974), p. 37.

23. *New York Times*, 13 February 1966, V, pp. 1, 3; "The Sports Boom Is Going Bust . . ." *Forbes*, 115 (15 February 1975), p. 25.

24. "Pro Football's Boom," *U.S. News & World Report*, 67 (22 September 1969), pp. 82–84; *Wall Street Journal*, 9 September 1969, p. 1; *Business Week*, 12 January 1974, p. 63. In brief, tax laws allow an owner to depreciate, over three to seven years, his team's "assets"—which principally consist of his players. (Consult Benjamin A. Okner, "Taxation and Sports Enterprises," in *Government and the Sports Business* ed. Roger G. Noll, [The Brookings Institution, 1974], pp. 159–83.) A recent federal district court decision, however, has reduced the amount an owner can write off. We can only wait to see the effect of this decision.

25. Randall Poe, "The Angry Fan," *Harper's Magazine*, 25, (November 1975), p. 88.

26. *Advertising Age*, 44 (22 October 1973), p. 124, 45 (2 September 1974), p. 25; Poe, "Angry Fan," p. 86.

27. Stephen Mahoney, "Pro Football's Profit Explosion," *Fortune*, 70 (November, 1964), p. 155; "Good Sports All," *Newsweek*, 81 (7 May 1973), p. 74; "Football: Show Business With A Kick," *Time Magazine*, 102 (8 October 1973), p. 57: *Broadcasting*, 78 (9 February 1970), p. 27.

28. *New York Times*, 5 February 1966, p. 39. For a brief but relevant analysis of TV and golf, see *The Economist*, 236 (11 July 1970), pp. 50–51.

29. "Golden Age Of Sports," p. 18.

30. Leonard Kopett, "Have Athletes' Salaries Hit Ceiling?" *New York Times*, 4 May 1976. pp. 49–50; *Business Week*, 2 September 1967, p. 28. The effects of interleague competition on the salaries of basketball players are examined in Lacy C. Banks, "Take The Money And Run," *Ebony*, February 1972, pp. 99–104.

31. *New York Times*, 30 April 1973, p. 36; *Advertising Age*, 44 (22 October 1973), p. 32.

32. *Newsweek 66*, (13 September 1965), pp. 88B–89. For an evaluation of athletes as sportscasters, see Richard L. Tobin, "When Sports Stars Broadcast," *Saturday Review*, 52 (13 September 1969), pp. 107–8.
33. Jack R. Griffin, "TV Kidnaps Sports," *Nation*, 200 (29 March 1965), p. 336; Shecter, *The Jocks*, p. 68; *New York Times*, 29 March 1971, p. 44; Johnson, "TV Made It All a New Game," p. 88. For similar views, see: Poe, "Angry Fan"; Albert Hunt, "TV and Sports," *The Wall Street Journal*, 22 April 1966, pp. 1, 18; John R. Tunis, "Laugh Off $11 Million?" *New Republic*, 152 (2 January 1965), pp. 11–12; Michael J. Arlen, "The Bodiless Tackle, The Second-Hand Thud," *The New Yorker*, 43 (29 April 1967), pp. 159–64.
34. *Broadcasting*, 66 (27 April 1964), p. 78 (my italics).
35. *New York Times*, 14 July 1972, p. 31.
36. Roone Arledge and Gilbert Rogin, "It's Sports . . . It's Money . . . It's TV," *Sports Illustrated*, 24 (24 April 1966), p. 100.
37. Hunt, "TV and Sports," p. 18; *Newsweek*, 69 (5 June 1967), p. 66.
38. Ibid.
39. Ibid. Derek Morgan in, " 'I Want My Bloody Game Back'," *Sports Illustrated*, 27 (28 August 1967), pp. 52–54, has some observations on the damage he believes TV has done to soccer.
40. *Broadcasting*, 82 (5 June 1972), p. 45.
41. Shecter, *The Jocks*, p. 75.
42. Ibid.
43. Ibid. For other examples, see Bernie Parrish, *They Call It a Game* (New York, 1971), pp. 126–27.
44. Hunt, "TV and Sports," p. 18.
45. Johnson, "TV Made It All a New Game," pp. 101–2; J. Anthony Lukas, "Down and Out in the Minor Leagues," *Harper's Magazine*, 236 (June 1968) p. 74; *Organized Professional Team Sports*, Senate Hearings (1958), pp. 96, 151.
46. *Sports Illustrated*, 43 (8 September 1975), p. 76; Johnson, "TV Made It All a New Game," p. 101; Griffin, "TV Kidnaps Sports," p. 337; *Newsweek* 36 (6 January 1964), p. 41.
47. "Football: Show Business With A Kick," p. 54; Johnson, "After TV Accepted the Call . . . ," p. 25; "The Sports Boom Is Going Bust . . . ," p. 25.
48. Eugene Feehan, "The Economics of $P000,000,000RTS," *Television Magazine*, 24 (April 1967), pp. 44, 51.
49. Shecter, *The Jocks*, p. 72; Russell Baker, "Please Turn Off the Sports," *New York Times*, 20 April 1975, p. 31; Leonard Koppett, "Sports Overlap Makes It June in January," Ibid., 22 August 1975, p. 23.
50. "Upheaval in Pro Sports," p. 52. See also, Poe, "Angry Fan," pp. 90, 94–95, and Bill Surface, "In Pro Sports, the Dollar Is King," *Reader's Digest*, March 1972, pp. 146–49.
51. "The Golden Age Of Sports," p. 19.
52. Tom Meschery, " 'There Is a Disease in Sports Now . . .'," *Sports Illustrated*, 37 (October 7, 1972), pp. 56–59.
53. Leonard Koppett, "The Sports Game," *New York Times*, 9 January 1972, III, p. 1.

54. Leonard Koppett, *24 Seconds To Shoot: An Informal History of the National Basketball Association* (New York, 1968), pp. 2, 86.

55. *New York Times*, 12 January, pp. 1, 25, 14 January, IV, p. 5, 31 January 1973, p. 73. In the American League (the National League rejected the change), many clubs were doing poorly at the gate, and the hope was that the designated hitter would enliven the game, both for spectators and TV viewers. For the rules changes made in 1974 by the National Football League see Tex Maule, "The Pro Football Revolution," *Sports Illustrated*, 40 (6 May 1974), pp. 21–23, and *Advertising Age*, 45 (6 May 1974), p. 84.

56. Arledge and Rogin, "It's Sports . . . It's Money . . . It's TV," p. 94; Sol Yurick, "That Wonderful Person Who Brought You Howard Cosell," *Esquire*, 82 (October 1974), p. 244: Johnson, "After TV Accepted the Call . . . ," p. 29.

57. *Organized Professional Team Sports*, Senate Hearings (1958), p. 186; U.S. Congress, Senate, *Professional Sports Antitrust Bill— 1964*, Hearings Before the Subcommittee On Antitrust and Monopoly of the Committee On the Judiciary, U.S. Senate, 88th Cong., 2nd Sess. (1964), pp. 31, 44: Lukas, "Down and Out in the Minor Leagues," p. 73.

58. Robert Lipsyte, *Sports World: An American Dreamland* (New York, 1975), pp. 103–4.

59. The ratings for that bellwether sport, professional football, dipped in 1973–74, but rebounded in 1975. *Time Magazine*, 104 (December 9, 1974), p. 98: *New York Times*, 4 July 1976, V, p. 3.

60. Pete Axthelm. "The Masochists," *Newsweek*, 85 (5 May 1975), p. 57.

61. Ron Fimrite, "Grand New Game," *Sports Illustrated*, 43 (August 11, 1975), pp. 10–13; Roger Kahn, "Can Sports Survive Money?" *Esquire*, 84 (October, 1975), p. 108.

62. Kahn, "Can Sports Survive Money?" p. 106 (his italics).

63. *New York Times*, July 23, 1972, V, p. 23; Ira Horowitz, "Sports Broadcasting," in *Government and the Sports Business*, p. 290.

64. *Broadcasting* 70 (February 7, 1966), p. 40, and 68 (June 7, 1965), pp. 48, 52; William Johnson, " 'You Know You're Not Getting Maudie Frickert,' " *Sports Illustrated*, 32 (January 6, 1970), p. 35. For a fuller discussion of sports, advertising, and TV, see Horowitz, "Sports Broadcasting," in *Government and the Sports Business*, pp. 310–19.

65. Johnson, "TV Made It All A New Game," p. 97; Feehan, "The Economics Of $P000,000,000RTS," pp. 44ff; Kay Gardella, "Does Pro Football Pay? In Prestige, CBS Says," *New York Daily News*, 25 December 1975, p. 44. Other reports claim, however, that the networks do make a profit. See, for instance, *Broadcasting*, 86 (6 May 1974), p. 39.

66. Arledge and Rogin, "It's Sports . . . It's Money . . . It's TV," p. 98; Frank Reysen, "The Cluttered World Of Sports And Media," *Media-Scope*, 13 (December 1969), p. 42: Johnson, "After TV Accepted the Call . . . ," p. 25; *New York Times*, 16 February 1964, II, p. 17; Paul Hoch, *Rip Off: The Big Game* (Anchor Books, 1972), p. 145.

67. Mahoney, "Pro Football's Profit Explosion," p. 230 (his italics). On

the coming of pay TV see also, *New York Times,* 14 September 1971, p. 51, 23 July 1972, p. 23, and *Broadcasting,* 89 (10 May 1976), p. 58. Of relevance here, the Federal Communications Commission has prohibited the cable TV broadcast of sports events that have been on commercial television during the previous two years. *Advertising Age,* 44 (17 September 1973), p. 79.

68. The pioneer treatment of this subject is, John Rickards Betts, "The Technological Revolution and the Rise of Sport, 1850–1900," *Mississippi Valley Historical Review,* 40 (September 1953), pp. 231–56.

69. Roger Kahn, "Where Have All Our Heroes Gone?" *Esquire,* 82 (October 1974), p. 387; Daniel J. Boorstin, *The Americans: The Democratic Experience* (Vintage Books, 1974), p. 393.

70. Ibid.

71. *Broadcasting,* 82 (19 June 1972), pp. 47-48; *Time Magazine,* 90 (20 October 1967), p. 73.

72. Arlen, "The Bodiless Tackle, the Second-Hand Thud," p. 164; Martin Mayer, "What to Do About Television," *Commentary,* 53 (May 1972), p. 66.

73. Neil D. Isaacs, "Basketball's Beauty Tends to Fade Before TV Techniques," *New York Times,* 4 January 1976, V, p. 2.

74. We are concerned here only with sports and TV. For a variety of sports studies based on demographic and social trends, see William O. Johnson, "From Here To 2000," *Sports Illustrated,* 41 (23 December 1974), pp. 73–83.

75. Jerry Kirshenbaum, "Chirp-Chirp, Crunch-Crunch," *Sports Illustrated,* 39 (1 October 1973), p. 40.

76. Among those pessimistic about the future of baseball in the TV era is Roger Angell, *The Summer Game* (Popular Library, 1972), p. 113.

77. See the predictions in the *New York Times,* 4 January 1970, V, p. 4.

78. Hunt, "TV And Sports," p. 1.

79. See the comments by Howard Cosell, in his *Like It Is* (Pocket Books, 1975), pp. 252–53.

Bibliography

As the notes indicate, the most valuable sources for this paper were *The New York Times* (especially the articles by Leonard Koppett and others on its superb staff of sportswriters), *Sports Illustrated* (particularly the provocative series of essays by William Johnson on sports and TV), and *Broadcasting* (which magazine offered insights into the television industry's point of view). Useful, too, were *Advertising Age, Time Magazine, Newsweek, Business Week*, and *U.S. News & World Report*. Roger Kahn's essays in *Esquire* were also quite helpful. Congressional hearings, unfortunately, proved of only limited value for the purposes of this study.

There is a large and growing literature on American sports. Sportswriters, athletes, and academics have all made their contributions. Of the recent volumes by sportswriters, perhaps the best is *The Jocks* (Indianapolis, 1969), by Leonard Shecter. It is a sharp, witty, debunking, and opinionated book. Like most sportswriters (and for an obvious reason), Shecter overemphasizes the baneful effects of TV on sports.

Athletes and ex-athletes have also had their say. But few have much to add to the debate about TV and sports. One of the few is Bernie Parrish, whose *They Call It a Game* (New York, 1971), has an interesting chapter on television and football from the player's point of view.

Of the recent contributions by the academic community, the most valuable is Roger G. Noll, ed., *Government and the Sports Business* (the Brookings Institution, 1974). Among the book's achievements is that it sheds some light on the profitability of professional sports. Now if we could only discover whether the TV networks make or lose money on sports broadcasting, we would have a more rounded picture of the sports industry.

Mention should also be made of James A. Michener's delightful and highly personal, *Sports in America* (New York, 1976). The book, which came to hand after this paper was completed, has a well-balanced chapter on sports and the medium. Michener really falls into none of the categories of sportswriter, athlete (though an avid tennis player), or academic. But he is a close student of American sports, and he has an apt piece of advice for the sports world. "The guardians of each [professional] game," he warns, "will have to keep close watch on the concessions required by television."

Other volumes—most of them previously cited—which were useful in the preparation of this paper include: Roger Angell, *The Summer Game* (Popular Library, 1972); Eric Barnouw, *The Tube of Plenty: The Evolution of American Television* (New York, 1975); John Rickards Betts, *America's Sporting Heritage: 1850–1950* (Reading, Massachusetts,

1974); Daniel J. Boorstin, *The Americans: The Democratic Experience* (Vintage Books, 1974); Howard Cosell, *Like It Is* (Pocket Books, 1975); Foster Rhea Dulles, *A History of Recreation* (New York, 1965); Paul Gardner, *Nice Guys Finish Last: Sport and American Life* (New York, 1975); Paul Hoch, *Rip Off: The Big Game* (Anchor Books, 1975); Leonard Koppett, *24 Second to Shoot: An Informal History of the American Basketball Association* (New York, 1968); William Lineberry, ed., *The Business of Sports* (New York, 1973); Robert Lipsyte, *Sports World: An American Dreamland* (New York, 1975); and David Quentin Voigt, *American Baseball: From the Commissioners to Continental Expansion* (Norman, Oklahoma, 1970).

5. Education in the Video Age: Learning Via Television

Bryce Perkins
University College
Garbone, Botswana

Ever since the Mayflower lowered her sails and the Pilgrims disembarked at Plymouth Rock, Americans have lived with change. With some exceptions, they have been anxious to leave the old ways behind and eager to strike out into the unknown. Our great heroes from Daniel Boone to Neil Armstrong have been men famous for the regions they have explored and the distances they have covered. America has produced heroes and leaders in every field of endeavor, who have inspired countless numbers of their fellow Americans to explore new ways to improve the human condition. But there has also been mounting resistance to change as it occurs with bewildering rapidity. Adjustments to one discovery are barely made before a new one has replaced it. Nowhere in American society is the dichotomy more prevalent than in the field of education and in no field are these two conditions—desire for and resistance to change—more controversial. In the face of skepticism and negative criticism, educational values endure and the search goes on for new and different ways to enhance the work of the classroom teacher.

An important innovation in the area of educational technology has been the use of television. Its potential to improve education has been a subject of considerable speculation—whether its advantages outweigh its dangers. It is important to note that the momentum of this invention has outpaced the study of its impact on education.

It is well known that education occurs not only in schools, and also that many school age children spend more time in front of the television set than they do in a formal classroom setting. It would be impossible here to examine all the many ways television affects education in or out of school This essay, therefore, will briefly describe the climate for educational change since television became part of the mass media; distinguish among the types of television and the implications for their use in a formal classroom setting; and discuss the results thus far and the need for further research on the impact of television on school achievement.

It is important to understand the three types of television which affect education. One type is instructional television, which is directed at students in a formalized educational setting. Public television is also instructional television, but is often directed at the general community. Commercial television provides education but the difference is that it seeks to capture a large audience whose desire is to relax and be entertained. Of the three types, commercial television seeems to have the greatest impact on education. It is therefore considered in greater depth than either instructional television or public television.

Climate for Change

In the 1950s when the writer was an elementary school principal in a Connecticut school system, the country was experiencing a severe shortage of classroom teachers. In order to overcome this difficulty, educators in public and private schools as well as in the universities began to reexamine school organization; the utilization of talented teachers, school facilities, and financial resources; and teaching technology. The pioneer work in team teaching in Connecticut and Massachusetts, in association with Harvard University, touched on all these areas. The use of teacher aides in the schools, which had its most noteworthy beginning in Michigan, received great impetus in connection with team teaching programs and spread rapidly throughout the United States. These developments are mentioned because it is within this framework of innovation and change that the possibilities of educational television as a new instructional technology were considered. Ways had to be found to make the best use of teaching talent across as broad a spectrum as possible. In its broadest sense, the uses to which television could be put were staggering to the imagination.

Even though there is no longer a shortage of classroom teachers in the United States and the need for expending large sums of money on closed circuit and other forms of instructional television has been minimized, commercial television is apparently here for a long time to come. In its report on educational television, the Carnegie Commission recognized that the great power of television whether commercial or noncommercial was that it continues to educate us long after we leave the classroom. It provides us with information; it stimulates us; it challenges us; and it affects our judgments. In this way it is not different from life itself. Life, in a broad sense, is education without a formal syllabus to which we make reference in order to measure what we have learned.[1] In 1974 Peggy Charren, writing in the December issue of *Signature Magazine,* reported that "television's power to affect the thoughts, dreams, attitudes and behavior patterns of developing children is an unknown variable yet to be adequately measured."[2]

Instructional Television

Extravagant claims are made for television as a teaching medium. Bernard Friedlander states matter-of-factly that no other medium can perform as well or as flexibly as television in making the world of information and reality accessible to the thought processes of the young child. He states that no other medium can manipulate action, object, and speech in virtually any imaginable visual and auditory combination, and that no other medium can as readily combine any visual event with any verbal description, make any conceivable transformation, alternative, or accompaniment, or offer limitless repetitions of these elements in pursuing limitless instructional goals. He has, however, enumerated some difficulties that must be resolved before television in the primary school can realize its enormous potential.[3]

One of these difficulties, at least in this writer's view, is a serious question as to whether television is in fact the most effective teaching medium. The lack of adequate knowledge of primary-level children's visual and auditory comprehension makes it difficult to draw comparisons. Problems in the implementation of instructional television, including cost factors, are less significant. Refinements in technology are also needed, but they are more easily achieved. Among these refinements is the need to develop systematized techniques for the pupils' active participation in TV presentations and the need to develop techniques for integrating TV presentations with other media.

Friedlander has pointed out that it is debatable whether children understand adult-oriented presentation of new information on television. Children retain large amounts of commercial jingles and alphabet songs, as the result of rote learning which comes about with endless repetition. The producers of "Sesame Street" and "The Electric Company" based their programs pretty much on the notion that young children can learn from cartoons, dramas, and commercials. There is apparently no conflict between those observations and the fact that the same children often fail to absorb the kinds of information presented in unsystematized nonrepetitive instructional programs.

In a thought-provoking analogy Friedlander compares instructional TV programming to contemporary medical practice. Medical experts have become alert to the danger that the pursuit of one effect, by means of medication, may induce unwanted and seriously counter-productive side effects. Similarly, the fast pace and frequent scene changes on television may be highly suited to gaining children's attention. On the other hand such techniques may impede comprehension. A shortcoming of television as an instructional medium is that its pace and forward movement is not subject to control and review by the learner.

In a report published in 1962 by the Institute for Communication Research, Stanford University, Wilbur Schramm addressed himself to what was known about learning from instructional television. In summing up the results of 393 cases in which instructional television had been compared with other classroom teaching, the Institute found that instructional television was at least as effective as ordinary classroom instruction when the results were measured by the usual final examinations or by standardized tests. In 65 percent of the cases, there were no significant differences. In 21 percent, students learned significantly more and in 14 percent, they learned significantly less from television.[4]

Some other interesting data came from this study. It was clear that televised instruction had been used with greater success in the elementary school than in high school or college. In 33 percent of the elementary school cases, TV was more effective. In high school, its greater effectiveness dropped to 13 percent and in college to 3 percent. Some subject-matter areas had been taught more effectively than others. Mathematics and science headed the list with social studies following closely. History, humanities, and literature were less successful. Language skills and health and safety were in the middle range.

These results are not surprising to anyone who has experienced change and innovation across the broad spectrum of elementary, secondary, and post-secondary education. Elementary teachers have historically been under greater pressure to change their methods and approaches than any other segment of the profession. There are several reasons for this pressure. Among them is the necessity to provide the tool skills required by pupils to gain the advanced knowledge dispensed in upper division schools. The pressure has come from the public as well as secondary and post-secondary schools. Another reason is that elementary teachers see fewer pupils, and spend more time with them, than do secondary school teachers. Elementary teachers are more geared to changes in technology and begin their careers in a climate where change and innovation are more acceptable than in secondary schools or colleges.

Elementary teachers have long been aware of the entertainment value in their teaching. Reading and telling stories have often been accompanied by drama and illustration. Anything which would arouse the interest and enthusiasm of their pupils has always been used. Team teaching, the use of teacher aides, and the use of audio-visual devices had their beginning in elementary schools. Because of its entertainment value, television provides competition to the classroom teacher. The odds are in favor of the teacher however. It is the teacher who can sense the needs of the pupils and can individualize pupil programs. The teacher can use television to enhance instruction.

Eight years after Wilbur Schramm made his report, George Gordon described what he considered to be the state of instructional television research at that time. A chapter in his book, *Educational Television,* with the novel title "Research and the Wonder Drug: NSD," presents no further evidence that courses taught over television and equivalent courses taught by some other method show any significant differences. N.S.D. (no significant differences) is a phrase heard ad nauseam in general. It is confined not only to research into the effects of instructional television but permeates the whole field of educational research.[5]

The terms educational television and instructional television are used synonymously. The letters ETV are often used to connote the same meaning. Large-scale efforts to promote the use of ETV as an instructional medium in the late fifties and early sixties were financed by the Ford Foundation and were centered in Hagerstown, Maryland, and in the midwest. The primary purpose of ETV was to make the best use of teaching talent and to spread it as widely as possible in order to counteract the severe shortage of classroom teachers. Other advantages were discovered as experimentation continued.

In the summer of 1961, the writer taught a course in the organization and administration of team teaching programs at the University of Hawaii. Part of the course was devoted to the study of the usefulness of various audio-visual devices in large-group instruction. Some of the students who were members of the faculty and administration of the Punahao School in Honolulu invited the rest of the class to the school to observe the use of ETV. One of the advantages was aptly demonstrated when a science experiment was performed and magnified so that a large number of students could see it at one time.

Fifteen years later in the summer 1976 issue of the *Delta Kappa Gamma* bulletin, Marjorie McGilvrey describes a recent visit to Punahao School and reports that it now has a $400,000 annual budget for audio-visual aids. She does not state how much of that amount is spent on television, but she does mention several other school systems throughout the United States where the uses of ETV are impressive.[6]

Much of the research done on the contribution of television to learning has been concerned with establishing the effectiveness of television relative to some other method of instruction for various subjects at different age levels. In most of these studies, the results of examinations of students who use television are compared with the performances of students who are taught face to face by a teacher. Other studies have evaluated the effectiveness of instructional television on the basis of student performance on nationally administered standardized tests. As is so often the case in measuring innovations in education, no significant difference has been found. When the tests do reveal a difference it has been more frequently slightly in favor of television. From a human as well as an intellectual standpoint, learning via television is, as yet, in a primarily experimental stage. This lack of knowledge about instructional television is not unique; it holds for all instruction as well.

The implications for instructional television are clear. The subject matter specialists and the television teachers need to learn about television production. Television producers need to learn a lot about education. People who are skilled both in education and in television production are in short supply. The lack of conclusive research on instructional technology is often the result of the caution and evasive language that has surrounded so much educational research. Most of the research in teaching uses of television concludes that there is no significant difference. Often some writers conclude that a project is successful while others conclude that it is a failure.

There has been some teacher resistance to instructional television. In some instances this may have included a component of common sense concerning the learning effectiveness and the classroom effectiveness of the instructional television offered them. There are also practical problems in the classroom, one of which is the problem of previewing television material. Considerable viewing time is necessary to sample the program. The previewing problem is compounded in a school situation where television programs stored in videocassettes play a large part in individualized instruction. For the teacher to find the time to ascertain the contents of all the cassettes would be a virtual impossibility. A written description is often not useful because the visual nature of a television program supplies its particular character. Other practical problems relate to the storage of television programs, educational effectiveness, space, and cost.

There are many books and articles on the effects of or impact of television on the education of preschool and school-age children. Our educational researchers, those who are skilled in research design and statistical analysis along with the less-skilled practitioners and students of research upon whom they frown, are quite unanimous in most of their findings or results of their studies. "There seems to be" or "there appears to be" or "the studies seem to indicate" are frequently heard phrases. In large scale innovative projects where comparisons of the new methods have been made with standard procedures in education, statistical analyses usually show no significant differences in the achievement of students.

The key to educational research is in the hands of the classroom teacher. It has been shown over and over again that it is the preference of the teacher for the method and the success she or he has with it that makes the difference. When competent teachers are measured against competent teachers, the only variable is teaching style. The differences in the results they get are not significant. When there are differences in the results teachers get from their own teaching, it is because of their positive attitude towards the new or different approach. This writer's experience has been that dedicated teachers are willing to try new methods if they feel it will make them more effective in their own teaching.

Commercial Television

Children's viewing of commercial television may be compared to informal education in its worst aspects—a potpourri of possibilities without any central and unifying theme. Television viewing can become more formalized when the central purposes of the particular program are identified in advance and then evaluated at its conclusion. There are some programs which measure up to the second standard, but children spend more time watching programs that do not. Informal education versus formal education has been the center of controversy in educational circles for decades. No attempt is made here to define the difference but a report on a recent book about education in England may be helpful in illustrating the difference.

In an informative advertisement sponsored by Local 2 of the United Federation of Teachers, Albert Shanker describes *Teaching Styles and Pupil Progress,* by Neville Bennett. The study described in this book isolated various characteristics which differentiate traditional teachers and progressive teachers. Teachers selected for the study were grouped and identified as formal, informal and mixed. Their classes were tested at the beginning of the school year and again at the end.[7]

Research showed that in English and mathematics the best results came from formal instruction. In reading, the mixed approach was best, followed by the formal, with the informal far less effective. The research also showed that while students in informal classes tended to view school more favorably, there was also more anxiety in informal classes because of the lack of structure. Bennett has concluded that formal teaching is able to fulfill its academic aims without detriment to the social and emotional development of pupils whereas informal teaching only partially fulfills its aims in the latter area as well as engendering comparatively poorer outcomes in academic development.

However, Bennett did find one teacher who used informal approaches and whose students did as well as those in any formal classroom. A possible reason is that the time spent on mathematics and English in this particular class was equal to or in excess of that spent by many formal classes. Some of the implications of

Bennett's study are that the more time that is spent studying a subject the better the results and that the more careful the teacher is in structuring and sequencing the curriculum, the more students will understand.

Some attempts have been made to formalize education via commercial television. Its importance in the life of children has been amply demonstrated in a study made of a group of approximately 500 students in Atlanta, Boston, Hartford, Los Angeles County, and Oklahoma City.[8] The evaluation staff of the Education Development Center in Newton, Massachusetts made a survey of the television viewing habits of the 8 to 11 age group in those areas. The children were asked: What do you do (1) when someone has made you angry? (2) when you feel lonely? (3) when you want to relax? (4) when someone has hurt your feelings? (5) when you want to be entertained? Would you choose to (1) watch television? (2) listen to music? (3) go to the movies? (4) go off by yourself? (5) play a game or sport? (6) talk to somebody? The first choice by most children in all situations was to watch television except when they felt hurt or angry, in which cases they indicated a preference to go off by themselves.

Mathematics

Jerrold Zacharias, a former member of the President's Science Advisory Committee, has been working with the Center in Newton. He has long been concerned with the problem that most Americans at all educational levels and in all walks of life don't do well in mathematics. He feels the source of the problem is fear. This fear is a result of the confused identification of mathematics with arithmetic, which comes about because the first six or eight years in school are devoted to arithmetic. It is easy to make mistakes in arithmetic, which relates to mathematics in the same way as drills and scales relate to music.

"Infinity Factory" is a new TV series put together by Zacharias and his associates in an effort to change attitudes toward mathematics. Other goals of the series are to advance ethnic and cultural perspectives to show mathematics in real situations; present some basic and simple mathematics tools to help the audience cope with real problems; provide help in thinking analytically, reasoning clearly, and solving problems; and encourage self-confidence and ethnic pride in the audience to help them deal with the world around them.

The program is geared to children in the 8–11 age group, particularly those from black or Spanish-speaking backgrounds, and emphasizes realistic uses of mathematics in ethnic settings. Mathematics is not treated as an abstract skill but as a part of the life and the world black and Hispanic children know. The mathematical concepts developed, however, are universally applicable to all children. These concepts include estimation, mapping and scaling, measurement, grouping, and the decimal number system—all necessary for full participation in today's society.

In an article describing this program Fred M. Hechinger says that Zacharias hopes to make the uses of mathematics so clearly evident and its application so interesting that "Mathophobia—the traditional fear of Math.—and boredom—a yawn in the face of an equation will be things of the past."[9] This program, very likely inspired by Children's Television Workshop (producers of "Sesame Street" and "The Electric Company") is aimed at 8–11 year olds but will also try to convert their parents to the view that mathematics can be fun and that they can understand what their children learn. The program also is planned to avoid the criticism sometimes leveled against "Sesame Street," that televised instruction tends to encourage passivity in children.

Bilingual Education

As a result of legislation requiring bilingual education in the schools and federal money to promote it, curriculum specialists and other educators have been searching for ways to implement programs. One of the media used has been television.

The first bilingual education TV series in the country was produced at station KLRN-TV in Austin, Texas, and was aired during the 1971-1972 school year in Austin and San Antonio, Texas.[10] Although classroom viewing with follow-up was encouraged, most of the children ages six to eight turned to the programs at home since they were repeated after school hours. The central purpose of this program, entitled "Carrascolendas" was to improve the self-concept of children of Hispanic cultural background. Because they are expected to function exclusively in a language and culture that is not their own, they experience many learning difficulties. Initially subjects such as mathematics, science, language skills, history and cultural insights were laced into the "Carrascolendas" programs in a somewhat fragmented way with unrelated riddles, games and songs. It has now evolved into more sophisticated fare with complete and integrated stories, each with a plot developed around a central theme.

Research studies indicated, even in the first year, that parents noticed increased Spanish language skills in children who watched the series and that teachers believed that the program was already meeting its long-range objectives, including the development of language skills in both Spanish and English and improvement of self-concept and cultural pride for the target area children.

"Sesame Street"

There are many lessons to be learned from "Sesame Street," a program designed for preschool youngsters. Those lessons are aptly described in Gerald S. Lesser's book, *Children and Television*. Lesser has two different interpretations for the program's success. The first has to do with the ingredients of the operational model. Briefly, they were (1) the assumption that entertainment could be a useful vehicle for education; (2) the high degree of media literacy to television viewing, such as wide exposure to live action film, animation, game formats, music puppets, and various camera techniques; and (3) the teamwork of educators and production staff working together to design the instructional content with continuous self-correction based upon the observations of children. The second interpretation is that the success of "Sesame Street" can be attributed to the skillful implementation of a novel idea, financial backing, and the social and political climate of the times —"along with doses of pure luck."[11]

The founders of the program do not feel they know which view is right. It is quite likely that both views or a combination of the two are right. Much can be said for a propitious social and political climate which lent great impetus to innovation in education. Many educators will agree, however, that a measure of its success is that "Sesame Street" has shown that children can learn certain language skills and number competence through television. Another thing to the producer's credit is in the advertising for "Sesame Street."

> Nobody gets killed on Sesame Street. There's room in this world for children's TV where nobody gets clubbed for fun. There's room on TV for something that holds a child like a circus on the Fourth of July or a Sunday picnic. A year's research with kids three to eight years old and eight million dollars guarantees it.

"Sesame Street" has reached millions of homes. Untold numbers of children who came from such diverse places as the inner cities, the remote hills and the farms; and from the families of the poor, the black and the Spanish-speaking are coming to school better prepared than they might have been had they never been exposed to the program.

"The Electric Company"

Another series developed by the Children's Workshop is "The Electric Company." TEC was designed to help teach basic reading skills to seven-to-ten year olds either at home or in school.[12] Since the first show was aired in October, 1971, research has indicated highly positive results for TEC, in terms of pupil interest and teacher willingness to use it. A survey conducted among teachers after the first year showed that 28 percent of them noted a great improvement in their pupils' ability to decode words; 21 percent noted great improvement in spelling; and 33 percent found great improvement in basic sight vocabulary.

Some lessons learned by producers of TEC are similar to those learned by other educators in overcoming the resistance to adoption of other innovations in education. One is that school staff need to be informed about the availability and utility of the innovation. Another lesson is that teachers need to have access to the resources that give them technical capability to implement a new approach. A third is that teachers have to be convinced that the innovation is a desirable adjunct to their educational program or at least is worth an experiment.

Television Commercials

An area of interest to educators is the impact of television commercials on the education of young people. Two research studies described here should be of concern to business people as well as educators.

Clara Ferguson, associate professor of marketing at the University of Arkansas at Little Rock, has published the result of her research on the attitudes of preadolescent children to television commercials.[13] She has found that a significant proportion of the children doubt the validity and truthfulness of commercials. The predominant reason they give for believing that television commercials generally do not tell the truth was "Products are not like the commercials say they are." The reasons for liking and disliking television commercials are essentially the same reasons mentioned by adolescent children in other research studies. These reasons are predominantly concerned with entertainment values. Children also dislike commercials that are not in tune with reality and that are shown too frequently.

Dr. Ferguson's findings have important implications for commercial advertisers and for television networks. Children are active viewers of television during all nonschool hours and are being exposed to advertising for all products typically found in the marketplace. They are forming attitudes about the products being advertised as well as the commercial content. Children represent a potential market that must be carefully cultivated. If commercial advertisers do not take appropriate action to nullify negative attitudes that are prevalent among preadolescent children, sales volume will eventually decline and the value of television advertising and the resulting loss of revenue could adversely affect commercial television.

In their study on television commercials reported in *The Harvard Business Review* in November of 1975, the authors of "Young Viewers' Troubling Response to TV Ads," found that ten-year-olds considered them to be all lies.[14] Applying the theories of Jean Piaget, an authority on elementary and early childhood education, the authors talked with children aged five to twelve and found surprising trends in the development of their attitudes toward advertising. Children's skill in acquiring an impression from advertising exceeds their skill in understanding them logically. Young children do not seem to be uncomfortable with the disparity between these skills and are not upset if advertising is misleading. By middle childhood, however, the conflict is so frustrating to children that they decide all advertising is a sham. Children are then ready to believe that, like advertising, business and other social institutions are riddled with hypocrisy.

There are fifty million children under the age of thirteen in the United States. They constitute a quarter of our population and spend more time watching television than they spend in school. Three-fifths of this viewing time is taken up by commercials. All of this raises some very serious questions. They are important enough to be listed here:

1. What information-processing skills do children develop at different age levels?
2. Do these skills enable children to evaluate information from television commercials properly?

3. Is there any age at which children are so unskilled at processing information that they can be exploited by irresponsible advertisers?

4. Do television advertising and learning to deal with it have any harmful effects on children's attitudes toward business and society?

In order to answer these questions a series of interviews was conducted with 48 children ages five to twelve grouped in two-year intervals. These groups were composed of a cross-section of middle and working-class families in northern New Jersey. There were six boys and six girls in each two-year age group. Questions were asked in the areas of morality, fantasy and economics.

An important question arose from the fact the television advertising is a commercial medium based on adult conversational and perceptual habits but is massively presented to young children. According to Jean Piaget, a child develops different representations of reality as he matures. How do children react to this adult medium and to the fact it may mislead them?

Of all groups tested, the seven- to ten-year age group was most vulnerable to the manipulation of television advertisers. The ten-year-olds displayed the most tension in dealing with questions about morality, fantasy and economics. They were able to give reasons for distinguishing between "make-believe" and lying. They evidenced much skepticism toward authority figures. They believe that telling the truth is important and lying is harmful although they have a conviction that lying is acceptable under certain circumstances. They are aware that adults sometimes lie and are critical of adult hypocrisy. The ten-year-olds' anger toward misleading advertising as well as the eleven- and twelve-year-olds' increased tolerance of social hypocrisy raise serious questions about the role of television advertising in the socialization of children. It seems that both parents and educators have an obligation to help children learn how to deal with social hypocrisy and institutionalized lying. The evidence of this study is that television advertising stimulates children to think about socially accepted hypocrisy and distorts their views of morality, society, and business.

Of course television advertising is only one way in which society affects the child's growth but the nagging and recurring question remains. How can current practice be modified to reduce the conflicts that television advertising appears to arouse in children? In spite of some of its more adverse effects, it is extremely unlikely that advertising on commercial television will be abandoned at least in the near future.

Classroom Use of Commercial Television

One English teacher has made good use of commercials in his teaching. He feels that for a teacher interested in dealing with the function of language, television commercials offer a wealth of possibilities. Each advertisement presents a unique selling proposition. It describes a quality of the product which distinguishes it from all others, even though many of the propositions are semantically empty or so abstract as to mean almost anything.[15]

There are other aspects of television which merit study in English classes. Among them, in addition to program content, are the development, scheduling, and selection of television programs. One way to begin examining program content is to conduct a survey of students' viewing habits on each night of the week. In order to make good program choices students should understand what they are watching and consider why. Television is fundamental to the dynamics of modern communication. Teachers of English who wish to succeed in improving their students' understanding of language and the communication world in which they are living must include television in the curriculum.

Another writer suggests that one area of the impact of television that should be explored is the sort of images that are projected on the screen by various programs. Classes might consider alternative ways of presenting professions, roles and ethnic groups.[16] In addition to discussions of roles of policemen, lawyers, doctors, and private detectives, consideration can be given to the attitudes toward them and to others such as parents and other relatives. The processes of law enforcement, psychologist-patient relationship, and the nature of friendship are areas for study. The list is endless. Television programs provide gold mines for teachers wishing to develop critical attitudes toward contemporary values.

An organization known as ACT (Action for Children's Television) has been working since 1968 to upgrade the content of children's television programs. The problem was primarily with Saturday morning programming, which was monotonously centered around animated characters who often were violent and stereotyped in adult situation comedies. The founder of ACT, Peggy

Charren, has reported a promising trend in the diversification of the Saturday morning schedule but feels there are many unexplored topics waiting for creative television producers.[17]

ACT has also been working to overcome the worst abuses of commercial messages in advertising. Among these abuses is the promotional bombardment of products which are not recommended by nutritionists, dentists, teachers, and parents. Ads for heavily-sugared cereals and snack foods, vitamins and over-the-counter drugs, are in disfavor with both the American Dental Association and the American Pharmaceutical Association.

While public pressure to reduce violence may be helpful, full use of television may require a skillful teacher who is aware of the programs that children watch, and who can use them to teach children to take another person's point of view, to take turns, share tasks, and to understand rules of justice and fair play. In teaching value behavior through television it would be desirable to involve the whole family.

Educators have always been critical of standardized tests. One reason is the claim that they are culturally biased; that they ask children questions about things they have never seen and people and ideas that are not within their imagination. Television has weakened this argument. Whatever its faults television can show children what goes on in the world and how to think about it. Television makes no distinction in its audience. The same program is seen by children from all walks of life.

While organizations such as ACT are helpful in trying to improve the quality of television, teachers, by sheer force of numbers, are in a better position to nullify its more harmful effects. According to *Christian Century* magazine, the track record for the FCC (Federal Communications Commission), which was created to represent the public interest, has not been meritorious in the improvement of children's television. The FCC has demonstrated that it is more responsive to the desires of the industry it is supposed to regulate than to the needs of the public it is supposed to represent.[18]

One of the reasons given for the apparent inability of the FCC to truly represent the public interest is the power of the broadcasting industry over the Congress which funds regulatory agencies like the FCC. In 1972, a study conducted by FCC consultant Alan Pearce revealed that the networks and their stations regularly realize more than $200 million annually in profits. If this is true the question is raised: Why should profits be placed ahead of program service in the use of the public's airwaves? Another question is, why are commercials necessary on children's television?

Violence on Television

Another area worth mentioning and which is of great concern to educators as well as parents is violence in television programming. Edward Keister, Jr. writing in *Better Homes and Gardens* magazine, reports that your child, if he is typical, will watch 13,000 people die on television before he is 15 years old. If he were to see every show on network prime time this year, he would witness murders, beatings, rapes, muggings and robberies at the rate of eight an hour, with three out of four programs featuring violence.[19]

Keister suggests some measures parents can take to offset TV violence. He feels that even though many parents set viewing rules for children, they do it only in terms of time, not content. If parents watch shows with their children they can discuss the content. Parents can preview programs and schedules and call attention to worthwhile shows coming up. They can call or write stations, networks, congressmen, and sponsors, protesting shows they find objectionable. Children can be lured away from television when offered more interesting pastimes. Does anyone ever read aloud to their children anymore? Even though it is going to cost them time and effort, at least for the time being control of the channel selection switch and the on-off switch is in the hands of the parents.

In October of 1975 the Opinion Research Corporation of Princeton, New Jersey, conducted a national poll for *TV Guide* on the subject of family viewing time (FVT).[20] Telephone interviews were held with a sample of 1,024 Americans (512 men, 512 women), all 18 or older and living in private households. On the basis of that poll, more than seven out of ten Americans seemed convinced that television programs were much too violent. Nonetheless most Americans were against stricter government controls of TV entertainment, and believed that each family should decide for itself what it will or will not watch on television.

Beginning with the 1975–1976 television season, the industry began operating under the new family viewing time rules that had been written into the National Association of Broadcaster's Television Code. It states that between the hours of seven and nine P.M. (seven to eight P.M. in the central time zone) no program deemed "inappropriate for viewing by a general family audience" would be aired.

The debate that ensued was one of the most contentious in TV history. TV producers and writers, some segments of the press and various industry watchdogs accused Congress of employing pressure tactics on members of the FCC, who in turn pressured TV networks for some action that would take the heat off them. These commentators asserted that censorship and government meddling were not to be tolerated. The rule's defenders were equally convinced that family viewing time was a tangible expression of the industry's desire to correct a problem that had plagued it for years.

Three industry trade unions—The Writer's Guild of America, The Director's Guild of America, and the Screen Actor's Guild brought suit against the FCC, the NAB and the three commercial networks to end family viewing time on the grounds it was the product of political coercion. At the end of 1976 Federal judge Warren Ferguson, in a 223 page opinion, decided that censorship by government or privately created review boards cannot be tolerated, thereby pulling the plug on television's controversial family hour.

It was against this background that *TV Guide* commissioned its national poll on public attitudes toward family viewing time. As indicated, the results showed that Americans were overwhelmingly in favor of it. Among advantages listed were relieving the parents of the task of screening out programs they would not want their children to see, absence of violence, and the possibility of bringing the family together. Only one person in five could think of any shortcomings of the FVT rule. The poll clearly established that public dismay over televised scenes of violence was stronger than ever; that Americans in overwhelming numbers were certain that a need exists for some such device as FVT to reduce the amount of violence on American television screens; and that the new rule met with the approval of eight out of ten United States adults.

A recent and significant voice that has been added to the clamor protesting violence on television is that of the advertising agency.[21] J. Walter Thompson, one of the biggest agencies in the United States, conducted a research study which found that as many as 10 percent of the viewers who had watched a violent show reported that they had considered not buying the sponsor's product. Even more significantly, eight percent said they actually had not bought something because it had been advertised on a violent show.

This agency is counselling its client advertisers to consider the possible negative effects in buying commercial time on violent programs. The agency plans to continue to speak out on programming that exploits violence. It feels that if young children are constantly given models of violent behavior their behavior will probably become violent. The agency also feels that excessive doses of violence tend to desensitize even stable adults and they become indifferent to the suffering of others. General Foods, a large advertiser, earlier announced it would not buy advertising in violent programs. Unfortunately other agencies and advertisers seemingly are impressed by the number of viewers who enjoy physical combat, the frenetic pace of action shows, and screaming car chases.

It is difficult to determine who is responsible for all the violence on television but certainly the viewers must share the blame. Despite the dissatisfaction expressed in opinion polls, surveys, and letters of complaint, viewers continue to make violent programs among the most popular ones on the air. Perhaps when more viewers become satiated with violence or indignant about it the networks will respond quite promptly with programs of a different sort.

Models of behavior presented on television have important implications for classroom behavior. How far can educators go to protect school age children from the images of people portrayed through the medium of television? Is the best way to stamp out violence to keep people from seeing its effects or the reality of its existence? Do people learn best when they are denied access to information about life as it really is? The answers to these questions are highly speculative and varied. Obviously some parents and teachers will agree that children should have access to any information that they can handle. It is clear there can be no blanket rule for what children can handle.

Priorities for Research

In spite of more or less good-natured gibes against the Ford Foundation, it has moved significantly from mere support of projects on the improved use of television, to considering support for new research, and finally to organizing a conference which reflected increasing concern among many public and private groups about the role of television in the lives of the young. This conference, cosponsored by the Ford Foundation, the National Science Foundation, and the John and Mary R. Markel Foundation, was held in Reston, Virginia in November of 1975.[22]

One of the objectives of the conference was to bring together a

broad range of people to consider the directions future research on
television and children might take and to produce from these possibilities a set of guidelines for the benefit of researchers and sponsors of research. The second objective was to frame the guidelines
in such a way that those responsible for formulating television
policies might be aided by social science research. As a result of
this conference, which came up with a series of recommendations
concerning questions that face hard reality, the Ford Foundation
has dispelled once and for all the notion advanced by one critic that
it lives in a hothouse—"in the most stunning piece of architectural
symbolism in America—but everyone else must live in a cold hard
world."[23]

Two examples of the impact of advertising on children have already been given in this chapter but further research studies are
recommended. Such studies would focus on children's cognitive
and behavioral responses to television advertising and would include research on processes by which children learn to select, evaluate, and use information from television advertising as well as
related information from other sources. Critical variables in these
research projects that ought to be considered are the age of the
television viewers as well as the ethnic, cultural and socioeconomic
backgrounds as each affects the television experience of each child.
Complex questions need to be answered as to whether and how commercial pressure through repeated advertising tends to develop
cynicism and distrust of the advertising message by the child
viewer.

More knowledge is necessary about how children process information received from television. Of concern is their response to
program material involving violence, deceptive behavior as a means
of problem solving, and sexually oriented subject matter. What
children perceive when they watch television programming and
how their perception differs from adult perception is basic to the
study of the impact of television on children. The research should
contribute to a better understanding of the degree to which the
child perceives television as representing reality and the extent to
which some children imitate behavior they perceive on television.

A third priority for research is the contribution of television to
the formation of children's attitudes and values as well as to their
acquisition of basic cognitive skills. Through analysis of these
studies, guidelines could be developed which might help parents

to make decisions with regard to their own children's viewing habits.

While there is need to know more about television's damaging effects on children and how these effects can be controlled, more information is also needed on the constructive uses of television and the ways in which they can be promoted and enhanced. There is an important need for improved instruction about the mass media in the public schools. Literacy of young persons in regard to the mass media is the proper concern for educational institutions just as is language literacy. A large-scale research effort must be mounted to develop and introduce mass media instruction into the curriculum, to train teachers to teach it well, and to evaluate its effectiveness.

The curriculum could include such subjects as analysis of media appeals, the character and role of nonverbal cues, overview of the history and structure of the broadcasting industry, the economic basis for television, analysis of typical formats for entertainment programming, major concerns about negative effects of programming, analysis of the values portrayed in television content, standards for criticism of television content, and, if possible, some direct experience with television equipment. Producing messages, it is believed, will be helpful in attaining media literacy just as speaking and writing are useful to the skill of reading.

Conclusion

In an intensely pragmatic society we can dream about what television ought to be. However, unless someone can convince the sponsors of commercial television to change their programming our dreams will remain exactly that. The costs of research, development, production and broadcast are phenomenal. Therefore, it does not seem that educational and public television will ever have the resources to provide any serious competition to commercial television. Given these facts, ways must be found to make quality programs on commercial television available to children.

One of the negative criticisms of television is that its programs emphasize the bizarre and dramatic. The same criticism can be applied to the daily newspaper in which more space is often given to the catastrophic, the unhappy, and the sick than to other things that are important but pleasant and more ordinary in our lives. The challenge for television is to show the world as it really is, including both its triumphs and failures, and for educators to learn how to use it to enhance rather than to interfere with the educational process. As Martin Mayer says, television will not go away; "it is embedded in the culture now, like frozen lasagna, golf carts and sociology departments."[23]

Notes

1. L. C. Carnegie Commission on Educational Television, *Public Television: A Program for Action* (New York, Bantam Books, 1967).
2. Peggy Charren, "Children's Television: Some Improvement—Much More Needed." *Signature* (December 1974).
3. Bernard E. Friedlander, "Instruction Television in the Primary School Classroom: New Horizons, Or Another Wasteland?" Hartford University, West Hartford, Connecticut. Infant/Child Language Research Laboratory (January, 1973).
4. Stanford University Institute for Communication Research, *Educational Television, the Next 10 years.* A report and summary of major studies on the problems and potential of educational television conducted under the auspices of the U.S. Office of Education. Studies by Asheim and others. (Stanford, 1962).
5. George N. Gordon, *Educational Television* (New York: Center for Applied Research in Education, 1965).
6. Marjorie McGilvrey, "Educational Television in America," *Delta Kappa Gamma* (Summer 1976).
7. Albert Shanker, "British Study Gives First Hard Data." Advertisement entitled "Where We Stand" appears every Sunday in the *New York Times* and is paid for by the United Federation of Teachers, Local 2, of which Mr. Shanker is president.
8. "Story of Math: Infinity Factory," *American Education* 11 (December, 1975): 16–17.
9. F. M. Hechinger, "Ventures in Videomedia: Count Us In," *Saturday Review* (28 June 1975).
10. L. Montgomery, "Carnival of Bilingual Learning: Carrascolendas," *American Education* 10 (August 1974): 34–7.
11. Gerald Lesser, *Children and Television* (New York: Random House, 1974)
12. Robert E. Herriot and Roland J. Libert, "The Electric Company" In School Utilization Study. Children's Television Workshop, New York. 15 August 1972.
13. Clara P. Ferguson, "Preadolescent Children's Attitudes Toward Television Commercials." Bureau of Business Research, Graduate School of Business, University of Texas at Austin, 1975.
14. T. G. Bever, M. L. Smith, B. Bergen, and T. G. Johnson, "Young Viewers' Troubling Response to TV Ads." *Harvard Business Review* 53 (November 1975): 109–20.
15. R. A. Lucking, "Teaching the Message and the Massage," *English Journal* 63 (October, 1974): 74–6.

16. Patrick D. Hazard, *TV as Art. Some Essays in Criticism.* Champaign, Illinois, National Council of Teachers of English, 1966.
17. Peggy Charren is president of Action for Children's Television, 46 Austin Street, Newtonville, Mass. 02160. This is one of the most effective citizen's organizations lobbying for improvement in children's television.
18. W. F. Fore, "FCC Cops out on Children's TV," *Christian Century* 91 (20 November 1974): 1084–85.
19. Edward Kiester, Jr., "TV Violence: What Can Parents Do?" *Better Homes and Gardens* (September 1975).
20. Neil Hickey, "Does America Want Family Viewing Time?" *TV Guide*, 6 December 1975.
21. Charlotte Montgomery, "Speaker for the House," *Good Housekeeping* (September 1976).
22. *Television and Children: Priorities for Research.* Report of a conference at Reston, Virginia, November 5–7, 1975. Copies of this report may be obtained from the Ford Foundation, Office of Reports, 320 East 43rd Street, New York, N.Y. 10017.
23. Martin Mayer, *About Television* (New York: Harper and Row, 1976), p. 389.

Bibliography

Bever, T. G., Smith, M. L., Bergen, B., Johnson, T. G. "Young Viewers' Troubling Response to TV Ads," *Harvard Business Review* 53:109–20. November, 1975.

A report of a study on television advertising which attempts to explain one way in which society affects a child's growth and development. The results of the study are compared to Jean Piaget's theory of child perceptions of reality which change as he matures.

Charren, Peggy. "Children's Television: Some Improvement—Much More Needed." *Signature* (December 1974).

Peggy Charren is president of Action for Children's Television, 46 Austin Street, Newtonville, Mass. 02160. This is one of the most effective citizen's organizations lobbying for improvement in children's television. Leaflets and reprints are available and membership in the organization is encouraged.

Ferguson, Clara P. "Preadolescent Children's Attitudes Toward Television Commercials." Bureau of Business Research, Graduate School of Business, University of Texas at Austin, 1975.

This report is a dire warning that misrepresentations of the worth of advertised products cause negative attitudes among preadolescent children. These attitudes will eventually adversely affect sales volume as well as revenue for commercial television.

Fore, W. F. "FCC Cops out on Children's TV." *Christian Century* 91: 1084–5, November 20, 1974.

Discusses the responsibilities of the Federal Communications Commission for the improvement of children's television and some reasons for its apparent failure.

Friedlander, Bernard E. "Instruction Television in the Primary School Classroom: New Horizons, Or Another Wasteland?" Hartford University, West Hartford, Connecticut. Infant/Child Language Research Lab. (January, 1973).

The author discusses five major problems concerning instructional television. They are related to lack of precise information about the communicative effectiveness of instructional presentations in appropriate time frames. It is suggested that these problems might be solved with careful research and a proposal is made for implementing such a program.

Gordon, George N. *Educational Television.* New York: Center for Applied Research in Education, 1965.

Research described supports findings in an earlier study by the Stanford University Institute for Communication Research which show little significant difference in the effectiveness of instructional television as compared to ordinary classroom instruction.

Hazard, Patrick D. *TV as Art. Some Essays in Criticism.* Champaign, Illinois: National Council of Teachers of English, 1966. Helpful for those who wish to succeed in improving their students' understanding of language and the communication world.

Hechinger, F. M. "Ventures in Videomedia: Count Us In." *Saturday Review* (p. 48, June 28, 1975).

Describes an instructional television program emphasizing realistic uses of mathematics in ethnic settings. The mathematical concepts developed are universally applicable to all children.

Herriot, Robert E. and Liebert, Roland J. "The Electric Company in School Utilization Study." Children's Television Workshop, New York. 15 August 1972.

This report describes two in-school audience surveys of TEC utilization—a Fall, 1971 survey of elementary school principals which provides national estimates of utilization levels by different types of schools and pupils, and a Spring, 1972 survey of teachers who were using TEC which provides data on the conditions under which pupils were actually viewing the program.

Hickey, Neil. "Does America Want Family Viewing Time?" *TV Guide,* 6 December 1975.

The article is a comprehensive report of the results of a national poll conducted by the Opinion Research Corporation of Princeton, New Jersey, during the period October 10–12, 1975. It shows a picture of changing American attitudes toward television programming and "family viewing time."

Kiester, Edward, Jr. "TV Violence: What Can Parents Do?" *Better Homes and Gardens.* September. 1975.

Beginning with this issue *Better Homes and Gardens* magazine offered a two-part series to assist parents in deciding what television is suitable for their child to watch. In this issue the effects on children of a steady diet of televised violence are reviewed, with guidelines for minimizing the amount to which a child is exposed. The October issue featured a parents' guide to television viewing.

L. C. Carnegie Commission on Education Television. *Public Television: A Program for Action.* New York, Bantam Books, 1967.

For those who are interested in the history of societal pressures and some of the more technical aspects of public television production, the book provides an important source of information.

Lesser, Gerald. *Children and Television.* New York, Random House, 1974.

The author discusses in detail factors in child growth and development which may be influenced by television viewing. He considers the possibilities of the harmful effects of television as well as distinctive benefits.

Lucking, R. A. "Teaching the Message and the Massage" *English Journal* 63:74–6 October 1974.

Describes positive ways in which English teachers can make good use of television commercials particularly when dealing with the function of language.

Mayer, Martin. *About Television.* New York. Harper and Row, 1970.

A commentary on the social impact of television and the possibility of meliorating that impact by government actions. That and economic overtones discussed may be useful reading for researchers on children's television.

McGilvrey, Marjorie. "Educational Television in America." *Delta Kappa Gamma* bulletin, Austin, Texas. Summer, 1976.

The article reflects what the author, in a six month tour of the United States and Canada, observed in the uses of television in education.

Montgomery, L. "Carnival of Bilingual Learning: Carrascolendas." *American Education* 10:34–7. August, 1974.

Describes a bilingual education TV series which was the first in the U.S.A. The central purpose of this particular series was to improve the self-concept of children of Latin culture.

Stanford University Institute for Communication Research. *Educational Television, The Next 10 Years.* A report and summary of major studies on the problems and potential of educational television conducted under the auspices of the U.S. Office of Education. (Studies by Asheim and others. Stanford, 1962)

Although this report is dated it is one of the most comprehensive available on the effects of instructional television as compared to ordinary classroom instruction.

"Story of Math: Infinity Factory," *American Education* 11:16–17 December, 1975.

Describes the results of a study of the television viewing habits of 500 students in the eight to eleven year age group in Atlanta, Boston, Hartford, Los Angeles County and Oklahoma City.

Television and Children: Priorities for Research. Report of a Conference at Reston, Virginia. November 5–7, 1975. Copies of this report may be obtained from the Ford Foundation, Office of Reports, 320 East 43rd Street, New York, N.Y. 10017.

This conference, which was organized by the Ford Foundation, reflected increasing concern among many public and private groups about the role of television in the lives of the young. In addition to the Ford Foundation, the workshop was cosponsored by the National Science Foundation and the John and Mary R. Markle Foundation. Priorities for new research on television and children were proposed.

6. The Influence of Television On Social Relations: Some Personal Reflections

Winston L. Kirby
Director of Television Center and
Adjunct Professor of Mass Communications
St. John's University

Television viewing time rose dramatically in the three decades following World War II. By the mid 1970s the American housewife spent approximately one quarter of her leisure time before the tube and her husband not much less. This essay provides some personal reflections upon the consequences of such addiction to television, including the impact upon family relations, social vitality, human interaction, and basic values and interests. It also offers an individual assessment of what protracted viewing of this medium, which more than any other seeks to define the physical and social world, has done to viewer interests, individual initiative, and the use of leisure. At the same time it maintains that television, which originally created a sense of community, has contributed to the sense of alienation so prevalent in much of the United States. Finally, the essay speculates upon the social consequences of some recent changes in American television.

Long involvement with television in a professional capacity like the author's is not needed to recall the excitement and sociability of the early days of television. Initially, viewing brought people together as Americans visited those neighbors who were fortunate enough to have a set, and together enjoyed the antics of Milton Berle, who quickly became Mr. Television. By the time that "Uncle Miltie's" dominance was being challenged by Bishop Sheen, television receivers had proliferated and viewing was no longer a social event. Television now kept people at home, isolated and increasingly alone.

My own observations about the negative social impact of television have been supported by others. Some charged that television viewing reduced sociability, adversely affecting both the quantity and quality of social interaction. There seemed to be less visiting, and when friends visited neighbors who ordinarily watched television at that time, their hosts often insisted that their guests simply sit and watch their program, clearly discouraging attempts at conversation.[1]

Since a large and ever-growing number of American households had two or more sets, members of the same family often watched different programs in different rooms. Thus television often discouraged communication at home and proved detrimental to family life. Worse still, television not only occupied an increasing block of time, but became the chief topic of conversation for many.

The art of conversation, never very well developed in some circles, declined when it focused on such matters as a skit starring Imogene Coca and Sid Caesar on the "Show of Shows," Lucy's latest caper on the "I Love Lucy Show," or the shenanigans of a host of comedians on the "Colgate Comedy Hour." Matters were to get worse, for some of the earlier programs displayed originality and a certain spontaneity. Later, video tape and the voracious appetite of the viewing public combined to produce a series of less noteworthy situation comedies, variety programs, murder mysteries, and westerns.

The level of programming has not improved. Today more than ever television relies increasingly on situation comedy and crime.[2] The insights to be derived from series such as "The Bionic Woman," "Kojak," "The Incredible Hulk," "Columbo," "Delta House," and "Charlie's Angels" are at best minimal, and conversations based upon such programs less than sparkling. Former FCC chairman Newton Minow's condemnation of American television as a vast wasteland is still applicable. It may well be that continual viewing of that wasteland has contributed to the decline in literacy and the vulgarization of taste, as well as the social isolation, that has burdened a generation.

While television addiction has not abated, television's allure has diminished, so that it no longer forms the basis of conversation. This is indeed one of the few encouraging changes that has taken place in man's relationship to the environment of the magic screen. Perhaps this change will contribute to more dynamic social interaction and alleviate the passivity that television has encouraged from California to Connecticut. The seeming unwillingness of people to exercise initiative in social relations and initiate face to face communications without the intervention of the media has no doubt contributed to increased loneliness in America.

It is paradoxical but true that television, heralded as the most complete means of communication, has not encouraged interaction at the most basic levels: family, neighborhood, and the larger local community. "I find it's easier to look at television than to read a book," said one viewer. "I will sit down and watch television when I ought to be doing something."[3]

"Excess viewing also seems to create passivity in children," writes Edna J. LeShan, educator and family counselor, "they are so used to being observers that their natural curiosity is curbed and they don't ask questions in the classroom."[4]

Television has also discouraged family conversation, undermining the dinner hour which used to be a time when parents and children exchanged the news of the day and related their problems and frustrations.[5] Now all too often the meal is hurried to watch a favorite program or worse still, conversation is silenced at the table so that the omnipresent set may be heard and seen. If this is television's contribution to family life, then clearly it is a god that has failed and any diminution of its influence must be applauded.

The fact that prime-time programming no longer serves as a major conversational catalyst is perhaps a first step in curtailing the influence of the tube, even though this is partly due to the decline in originality in program formats, a visible lack of imaginative scripts, and a noticeable absence of articulate television personalities possessed of wit, charm, and intelligence.

Eric Barnouw has observed that "the big show of 1952 was the election. The loser, Stevenson, was verbal. His speeches were eloquent, witty, polished. On television he never used a teleprompter because he always polished his speeches until the final moment, and there was never time to put them on a teleprompter."[6] Although Stevenson did not win, he was listened to, quoted, and earned the respect of millions of his fellow Americans. Only the most partisan and biased would argue that either Jimmy Carter or Gerald Ford proved to be eloquent or witty in their television debates. Presidential candidates, like television programs, have not improved with the passage of time.

Although television has improved vastly in technological terms, it has failed to attract and retain outstanding writers and producers. Paddy Chayefsky is a case in point: one of the brilliant writers of the "golden age of television," he has written the screenplay for the movie *Network,* which is a blistering indictment of the industry. Still, television's loss of talented writers such as Chayefsky and the industry's recourse to mediocre scripts and hack writers may have had some positive results. It may have slowed down the increase in viewing, and it certainly provided precious little for viewers to discuss. Television, which offered so little that was noteworthy or imaginative, thus yielded its monopoly and provided an opportunity for film and literature to once again become topics of conversation.

The steady diet of mediocrity on most of the commercial channels served to turn a number of Americans away from their sets and even led some to rediscover the joy of reading. Of course, some observers have asserted that reading is also fundamentally a passive act. I think not, and some of the best minds support my position. "Reading is a creative art," the late British novelist Joyce Cary wrote, "subject to the same rules, the same limitations, as the imaginative process by which an observer of the arts turns a mere lump of stone, colors scattered on a canvas, noise, things completely meaningless in themselves, into a formal impression."[7] Reading, unlike television viewing, requires an intellectual input as the forces of comprehension are put to some strain for understanding. Participation in sports, whether tennis, handball, skating, bicycling, bowling, skiing or group sports such as baseball, soccer, football or hockey, requires a physical effort which also represents a departure from the passive act of watching others engage in sports on television.

Ben Bagdikian, the distinguished journalist, has noted in looking back on the first twenty years of the medium that it might well have been used more effectively. During these years, he observed, more than 18 million rural people, most of them poorly educated and semiliterate, moved to the urban centers of our nation. There they formed ghetto communities, cells of despair and alienation that have raised doubts whether our cities can survive and our democratic consensus continue to function.[8] Television might have served as an instrument of adjustment, if not of advancement, for these people, but in point of fact did neither. Refusing to recognize its social responsibility it pandered to mediocrity, rather than offering an illiterate population the opportunity to expand its skills or develop new ones. Notoriously indifferent to taste, standards, and quality, and obsessively preoccupied with ratings and profits, it not only failed to educate but effectively increased the number of "elite illiterates."[9] The television newscaster in *Network* who promises to blow his brains out in a week is symptomatic of the medium that will do anything for a rating. "Television is democracy at its ugliest," Chayefsky has said, "give the people what they want."[10] Others, too, have noted that television has served as an opiate of the masses rather than a means of uplifting or inspiring them.

This is not to suggest that an elitist view should dominate prime time. Certainly entertainment should have an important place in the evening hours without a great message or cultural uplift permeating every show. What I find unfortunate and quite unbearable is the near total dominance of mediocrity.

Our current system, virtually mandating the commercial networks and stations to compete with one another seven nights a week, requires that most prime-time programs be geared to a pop culture, which in the line of its logic, is anti-intellectual. The three big networks, more often than not slavishly imitated by individual stations, are locked in a struggle to increase their ratings and their audience. Since pathetically few American stations are innovative enough to originate programs other than the local news, they are largely dependent on network offerings from the three giants ABC, CBS, and NBC, and rely upon old movies, talk shows, or cheap quiz and panel programs to fill their long schedules.[11] Vacuous fluff to fill a vacuum.

Most new programming is seen over the three networks. ABC, CBS, and NBC have for years been locked in a duel for leadership. Each has sought to acquire the largest number of rating points attended by the largest circulation it can muster. Ratings and circulation are equated with income. If a series can attain a rating of 18 or higher (that is 18 percent of all American households with sets and over 30 percent of the viewing audience at a particular time), the television executives will be content, regardless of the quality or aesthetic value of the program.[12]

Thus even though all stations are licensed in the public interest, public service programs are rarely offered by the commercial stations at other than marginal times. For example, a recent offering of CBS-TV's Summer Semester, "The Great Transition: Alternatives for the Twenty-First Century," which I developed, was picked up by about 65 CBS affiliate television stations. None offered it later than 6:30 A.M. to 7:00 A.M. Many aired it at 6:00 A.M.; others, like Minneapolis and Denver, at 5:30 A.M.; Boston at 5:50 A.M.

This project included distinguished scholars from different parts of the country who presented alternative modes of responses to major global problems such as population, war, values, energy, and environment, so that humanity might look forward to the next century with less apprehension. However, when aired at 6:30 A.M. it was impossible for many potentially interested viewers to tune in. Those who might have found it an interesting, cerebral exploration were never given the opportunity to reject it after sampling.

How does this relate to the notion of anti-intellectualism I suggest is so pervasive? Our primary values stress the importance of pop culture and diminish the significance of educational television, sometimes referred to as elitist, and patronizing. This has a very dramatic effect on millions of viewers. Their sensitivity to television makes them aware of the back seat generally given to nonpop culture by the networks; they reflect this attitude in their own value system.

If, for example, Plato's reflection in his *Apology* that "there is great reason to hope that death is good . . . either death is a state of nothingness or as men say, there is a change and migration of the soul from this world to another" was offered in prime time, a sponsor would be hard to get. Without a sponsor, the opportunities for viewers to savor Plato's posit in an intellectual framework would be limited. Even if it were to be offered in prime time it would be the exception rather than the rule and could hardly compete with the impact of the more than forty hours of pop entertainment the average family sees each week.

Just as Homer provided the Greeks with a sense of history and common language through his *Iliad* and *Odyssey*, today's common cultural mechanism is television. Unfortunately, the current popular culture of television does not inspire pride in what most would consider higher values such as loyalty, honor, wisdom, excellence, and unselfishness. If nonpop programs are not even given the occasional dignity of prime-time visibility, the message is clear and loud: intellectualism is second-class. This, I posit, has had unfortunate consequences.

In 1976 college entrance examination scores were reported to be 10 points lower on verbal and 8 points lower on mathematics than the previous year. This precipitous drop in only one year represents a cataclysmic decline in a period of steadily declining SAT scores. One might say there is not enough evidence to suggest that television is responsible, or that to use television as the responsible agent for declining scores is an example of overly simplistic lineal thinking. Yet what else is there to which one may point? A popular prime-time program reaches about 32 million people; the 1978 Super Bowl reached an estimated 75 million people. No other force in our culture is as pervasive as television, or has comparable impact. Unquestionably television is the most significant form of popular art in our age.[13] I would, therefore, unhesitatingly point to television as the force constricting our vocabulary and limiting our perceptions.

On July 5, 1976, President Ford addressed a group of newly naturalized citizens at Monticello, Thomas Jefferson's home, and criticized the "growing danger to this country in conformity of thought and taste and behavior." In a land as vast as the United States a communication network must be operative to bring about conformity. This communication network is our television system, dominated for the most part by the three television networks. So, despite the shift in conversational focus, one must acknowledge that television has increased conformity and encouraged anti-intellectualism.

In a discussion of the influence of TV on social behavior one rarely hears of personnel attitudes in the studios which influence the participants or performers, who in turn exercise their influence over the viewers. It has been my observation that studio personnel generally show a different attitude to entertainers on the one hand, and discussants/lecturers on the other. The gap between control room personnel and studio crew vis-à-vis the participant widens as one moves from the pop-culture performer to the serious discussant or scholarly lecturer.

In television the participant or performer is much more a servant of technology than other media. The technology is so sophisticated, costly, and requires so large a group of personnel that the single speaker becomes virtually subordinate to the technicians and their equipment. For example, in a simple lecture format produced at one of the networks, station and union requirements mandate a control room cluster of about a dozen people whose various responsibilities include video and audio adjustments, directing, announcing, production assistance, and production supervision. Within the studio there are three cameramen, a floor manager, prop, set, and lighting personnel, as well as unseen technicians responsible for recording the offering on tape. In all there are about two dozen staff members.

This crew is rarely if ever responsive to a scholarly lecturer. The easy, friendly interplay that so often takes place between this staff and popular entertainers is all but lacking when the presentation is educational. This often brings about a more rigid, stultified program than originally intended, further turning away some viewers with unnecessarily stilted presentations. The control room and studio crews' frequent displays of open cynicism, parody, and manifest apathy are hardly the instruments needed to develop vibrancy between viewer and program content.

The singular importance attached to television exposure for self has made television visibility a prerequisite for reassurance as to one's importance. Recognition in the world of mass culture is generally acquired by exposure to the mass audience that television controls. The key word here is visibility, for since the end of World War II recognition for any accomplishment has generally been acknowledged by numbers. A motion picture is recognized by its gross receipts, a writer by the number of books he sells, a television program and its luminaries by its ratings. The transition from star to superstar status flows from the public's knowledge of the superstar's salary but even more from its familiarity with his image as outlined by film, videotape, or photo-offset.

In the United States with a population of more than 200 million, preeminence is increasingly achieved and identity is reaffirmed when cameras are trained on you and your image flashed on the screen. The vast majority, unrecognized by local or network camera crews in most situations, feel a sense of worthlessness. Worth is now often correlated with intervening media self-images. In a culture with an ever-increasing emphasis on technology the hunger for recognition becomes ever more painful. Sociologists, psychologists, and psychiatrists have all attested to this.

Thirty years ago Charlie Chaplin, one of the cinema's great comedians, produced *Modern Times*, in which he portrayed man's growing loss of individuality and hunger for recognition. Roland Barthes, the distinguished literary critic and semiologist, wrote, "For Chaplin, the proletarian is still the man who is hungry; the representations of hunger are always epic with him: excessive size of the sandwiches, rivers of milk, fruit which one tosses aside hardly touched. . . . Historically, Man according to Chaplin roughly corresponds to the worker of the French Restoration, rebelling against the machines."[14]

It was this film which gave recognition to man's frustration and quest for recognition. At present appearing on television before a huge unseen audience momentarily assuages this hunger. This is no longer the hunger of the disadvantaged or any minority group. This is characteristic of society on an interactional scale. Aren't they saying "Please recognize me; I'm not an amorphous, impersonal being"?

Michael Arlen vividly depicts today's frustration in writing of our era of communications: "Surely the conditions of depression that occur in so many areas of the modern world—whether clinical or otherwise, and whether they take the form of the 'sullen' East German or the 'apathetic' American voter—derive at least in part from the continued, nearly unrelieved, public situation of *being talked* to by authorities, however sometimes benign, and never being able to *talk back*."[15]

Perhaps the ridiculous costumes and outrageous behavior of the contestants on daytime game shows best demonstrate the extraordinary lengths that people will go to achieve some recognition and appear on television. They are willing to make boobs of themselves to be seen on the boob tube.

Erving Goffman makes the point in *Behavior in Public Places* that there is a "nodding" line that emerges as people move from a densely populated area to a sparsely populated one. "Nodding" does offer some recognition between human beings, though rather impersonal. Now as we see population emerging from a rural to an urban setting, the climate of impersonal existence becomes more severe—the "nodding" line becomes even more elusive. However, the quest for identity, aggravated by its difficulty and compounded by the awareness that if you are anyone (in a superficial value system) that awareness is bolstered and given appropriate recognition through television, continues to be part of our character. On a number of occasions I have witnessed the desire of groups and individuals to appear on television.

Some years ago, during the peak of the student unrest activated by the Vietnam War, camera crews visited Columbia University, where I served as television director, to record several demonstrations against Marine Corps recruiting, Dow Chemical, and the Vietnam War. Continuing adversary relationships had developed throughout the campus, many of which ended in fist fights. In one instance I had suggested to a single remaining camera crew that if they were to depart, the remaining combatants would cease their sparring. The crew was reluctant to leave, believing that they might miss some newsworthy activity. I suggested that if they were to leave, the tension would very likely terminate, and further assured them that if the fighting resumed I would call them immediately. They withdrew, and at the very moment the camera lens was turned away the fighting indeed ended. Apparently the militants were not sufficiently committed to their ideologies merely to resolve their differences with one another; additional visibility was imperative. Here we see one small bit of evidence, which I view as fairly typical, of how the hunger for identity is heightened by the presence of television.

Television sports has created an intensification of the importance of winning. The major live television programming today is sports. Hardly a day goes by in any of the four seasons without an offering of football, baseball, basketball, hockey, or tennis on network and independent station showings. ABC-TV's emergence into its surprising number one positions during the 1975–1976 season was generally attributed to its coverage of the winter Olympics from Austria. The glory and importance of winning, with its applause, medals and press coverage, was evident as the adulating spectators were shown throughout the games. The superstar status accorded to a Joe Namath in professional football, the personal entourage seen at each Muhammad Ali boxing engagement, demonstrate the respect the world has for winners. Media reinforces this worship.

Chrissie Evert, an engaging young lady earning over $300,000 annually as a tennis player, misplaced several $25,000 checks without being too upset, it has been reported. The average tennis buff would be hard-pressed to name the 8th, 9th, and 10th ranking women because they are not at the top; they are not the *real* winners. Reggie Jackson's ability to win has enabled him to sign a five-year contract with the New York Yankees that brings him almost three million over a five-year period. Joe Rudi of California and Gary Matthews of Atlanta will each earn some two million during the same period.[16]

Players who are not top winners, who are not instrumental in persuading fans to watch the game on television, do not receive the same royal treatment and certainly do not get the same spectacular salaries. If you are not number one or its near-equivalent, you don't rate. Television-land emphasizes number one and doesn't like losers. The football Giants were spurned by their local television station in the fall of 1976 after a prolonged losing streak. The station, though licensed to serve greater New York, decided that it was more appropriate for its ratings to telecast an out-of-town football game.

The ever-present accolades and prizes given to those whose performance records are impressive tend to demonstrate that winning is the only thing. The pleasure of participation as an also-ran is given very little recognition in our value system. How can an impressionable person perceive a life in which he is not a super-winner as a satisfying life if his value as a human being is given only token recognition by the most forceful communication medium of all?

The competition for media coverage has sometimes led to tragic consequences. Martin Luther King said "If the media in the early 60s had been able to accommodate the frustrations of the blacks, they would not have had to take to the streets as they did." Media's lack of recognition of the blacks as being sufficiently newsworthy to focus on, or having sufficiently interesting lives to consider them as protagonists of daytime dramas, evening episodic or anthology series led to pressure by blacks to have their frustrations and activities placed in the mainstream of television's soaps, news or documentary programs. Given the importance of television I believe it was tragic for society not to accord its media benefits to one-tenth of its population at least a proportionate amount of time on television. What does this do to behavior? In the case of blacks it tends to reinforce their own sense of frustration at not fully participating as citizens in this country. In the case of whites the absence of negroes on the screen reinforces their ignorance of blacks as part of the mainstream in the United States.

Recently blacks have been much more visible in television commercials, soap operas, and even prime-time programming. However, before we become too optimistic, we must reexamine the situation to see whether tokenism is at work. Are we looking at everyday people or do we perceive representatives of a black elitist culture? If we perceive elitists, our behavioral responses are fairly similar to those prior to the new look. We tend to say "yes, but they're an exception to the rule." Can we always adapt ourselves to exceptions and continue our prejudices virtually undiluted? Also, we must inquire as to whether the writer of programs with black principals is white or black. Can a white writer effectively write about blacks?

"White writers, intentions notwithstanding, cannot write about the black experience, cannot conjure up a true black image, cannot wake the wonderful—sometimes terrible—beauty of our blackness. I have said it before, and I say it again: only club members can sing the blues because we're the ones who have paid the dues—of membership in the Brotherhood of Blackness."[17] These were the eloquent and perceptive words of John Oliver Killens.

Edmund Carpenter, an anthropologist, has stated that "unlike print, television doesn't transmit bits of information. Instead it *transports* the viewer. It takes his spirit on a trip—an instant trip. On live shows, it takes his spirit to real events in progress. But here a contradiction occurs: though television may make the viewer's spirit an actual witness to the spectacle of life, he cannot live with this. Thus, if the viewer sees a criminal making ready to murder a sleeping woman and can't warn her, he suffers and is afflicted because his being is phantasmal. So he participates solely as a dreamer, in no way responsible for events that occur. All television becomes a dream."[18] The impact of television is so transportative and cumulative that the notion of all television becoming a dream is rather precise. In the same interview Dr. Carpenter goes on to state that viewers "don't want to see Lorne Greene in a sports shirt on Maple Street. They expect him to stay in Bonanzaland, looking after those boys, and they hurry home to watch him on television."[19] The *real* world for television viewers, then, is the dream world exacerbated by the viewer's inability to interpose himself in any active way to alter the television screen situation. This elicits the suffering Dr. Carpenter identified.

This interpretation of the correlation of television drama and frustration has made me more aware of this in my own actions. Recently, I experienced what seemed to be a surrealist view of war as I observed either Leftists or Christians shooting at each other in a film clip forwarded from Beirut. Despite the obvious danger to the men pictured on the screen, I could not accept this image as reality. It was almost an illusion for me. And yet I felt the frustration, too, of wanting to tell the protagonists to be rational and settle their differences in a civilized manner through dialogue and an exchange of ideas rather than through bloodshed. This then is another aspect of the problem: the intertwining of illusion with reality and the frustration that results from not being able to alter the illusion. The inability to separate dreams from reality must inevitably weaken such important basic values in our culture as the respect for life and love, if both are presented as cheap and tarnished on prime-time television.

Consumerism and television in our economic system are isomorphic. Our commercial television structure is geared to the selling of products predicated on wants rather than needs. The more products purchased as a consequence of television advertising, the greater are the advertising expenditures designed to reinforce one's purchases based on wants. This is endemic to our economic structure, which insists on growth as an integral part of our existence. To suggest that growth is not always desirable is sometimes considered un-American. Indeed, in the late 1970s those persons positing less growth or perhaps no growth are often accused of being at least unpatriotic, or at the worst, absolute traitors. Our broadcasting system insists that wants become needs.

The ultimate goal for producers in our television system is to secure a prime-time series. In this segment of the broadcasting spectrum the most competitive battles are joined between networks, stations, producers, and programmers, to improve ratings and its inseparable companion, advertising revenue. There is an interlocking of ratings, pop culture, advertising revenue, and program advertising. The sale of products is almost inevitably based on convincing the viewer that he is less than a whole person if he does not obtain the sponsor's product.

Can man ever be at peace with himself in a television culture which is so insistent that the acquisition of goods is indispensable to well-being? Possibly. But the task becomes infinitely more difficult as we are reminded of the pressure to create wants in the television environment. We are locked into an extraordinarily difficult set of interwined factors: our economy depends on growth; growth is a function of selling *wants* as *needs*; television is our most influential and persuasive mass media; we feel frustrated if we do not accumulate goods, many, if not most of which, are not necessary. Frustration is ceaseless as the individual not only feels frustrated if he does not accumulate goods far beyond the standard package (refrigerator, color television, air conditioner, stereo, new car and the like) but too often loses his self-respect if he does not at least acquire the standard package.

Only with an infusion of new values and priorities can we expect our society to alter its emphasis on consumerism, to relieve the frustration of the imagined have-nots created by television advertising. This infusion should spring from television, since for most people the influence of more traditional institutions like family, church, and schools has apparently been weakened since the advent of prime-time culture.

Will television in the United States turn from some of its past errors? Richard Pinkham, vice-president of Ted Bates Advertising, wrote in *Broadcasting* magazine that television's opportunities for innovation have been reduced.[20] Most of the original program formats have been exhausted. If this is so, it augurs even further viewer vegetation as the amount of television viewing continues to rise. Regardless of the quality or originality of programming, hours per day spent in television viewing continue to mount each year. Here, possibly, is further evidence of television's narcotic effect. There is apparently no easy withdrawal from television viewing; as long as the tube projects some—any—sort of image. Whether that image is trite or imaginative, commonplace or innovative—the viewers loyally remain.

The next significant change in television's structure may be a splintering of television programming similar to various radio stations with their all talk, all music, all news formats. It is not likely that television will develop an all music format, but an age of specialization will probably emerge within the next few years and carry into the twenty-first century.

We have already seen some evidence of specialized format operation with all-Spanish television programming (usually in the UHF spectrum). The first stages of network specialization can be noticed with ABC-TV, for example, exhibiting an action type of format. This is evinced not only with its prime-time action, suspense episodic series, but with ABC's telecasts of Monday night football and its commitment to winter and summer Olympic coverage. Although not as specialized as the all-Spanish format, ABC's programming appears to be directed to the younger person with a definite pop culture orientation. It is offset, on occasion, with programming of a less strident nature. ABC suggests to me an effort to be swinging, brassy, vibrant, and "with it." This effort to be "with it" is reflected in the non-network programming of ABC's New York station, WABC-TV, Channel Seven. This operation offers "Eyewitness News," which, again, seems to reflect the youth, brassiness, and vitality of the network. No doubt for every one turned off by this suspense-action format, many more are turned on.

The impact of the ABC format on viewers extends to behavioral patterns as well. This is evident in clothing, speech patterns, and the prevailing modus operandi (speech, games, social relations) in communication between people. A few scholars call this the cultural norms theory. In effect, the theory postulates that prevailing characteristics of speech, attitudes, and dress are reflections of the influence of mass media. I agree, and further suggest that the correlation between mass media (particularly television) and behavior is more deep-rooted than we suspect.

Other mass media theories also offered as being responsible for behavioral traits are the social categories theory and the two-step theory. The social categories theory suggests that we conform to the largest common denominator of behavioral patterns because of our general age, sex, ethnic and socioeconomic group. It infers that we react as a body to mass media stimuli primarily because of the influence of ascribed characteristics such as age and sex, with achieved characteristics playing a secondary role. The two-step theory, in turn, maintains that many of our common behavioral patterns are transmitted by those most exposed to the media. Whether one believes that the media influence us all directly, as the cultural norms theory suggests, or act upon us through the intermediary of media "carriers," who in turn impose it upon others, few would deny the pervasive role of the mass media in shaping modern society.

The impact of television upon society in the last three decades has been influenced by the primacy of the three commercial networks; by the pressure to create needs, sell products, and make a profit; and by the consequent popularization of the medium. In its determination to attract the largest audience television has appealed to the lowest common denominator. As a consequence, television has become so influential in our culture that viewers not only refer to programs in their conversations but actually quote the commercials. Rather than some haunting refrain, Americans are left with the jingles of Alka Seltzer and Coca Cola on their minds. Television has also created stars and superstars and has led to the notion that visibility denotes success. This explains in part the desire of some to appear on camera. To be seen on television has become the new nirvana.

Still I shall conclude on a positive note by pointing to the new vitality in local television and the expanding influence of educational television. Both have shown a certain daring in breaking from the traditions of the big three and their success may eventually have an influence on ABC, CBS, and NBC. Cable television provides another source of competition and may also serve to shake the lethargy of the networks. I am convinced that this fractionalization of outlets will reduce the dominance of the big three and eventually undermine their policy of program scheduling based on the largest, and all too often lowest, common denominator of appeal.

Notes

1. William A. Belson, *The Impact of Television: Methods and Findings in Program Research* (London, 1967), p. 232.
2. Kay Gardella, "The Good, the Bad, and the Doubtful," *New York Daily News,* 10 October 1976.
3. Belson, *Impact of Television,* p. 235.
4. Sandi Cushman, "Parents Should Monitor Children's TV Habits," *New York Daily News,* 1 February 1976.
5. Sandi Cushman, "Family Conversation is a Vanished Art," *New York Daily News,* 18 January 1976.
6. Eric Barnouw, *The Golden Web: A History of Broadcasting in the United States,* Volume II 1933–1953 (New York: Oxford University Press, 1968), p. 298.
7. Herbert Mitgang, "A Case History of a News Story and a Denial," *New York Times,* 31 October 1976.
8. F. H. and L. A. Voelker, *Mass Media Forces in Our Society* 2nd Edition (New York: Harcourt Brace Jovanovich, Inc., 1975), p. 414.
9. See the article by A. Van Nostrand, in the *Brown Alumni Magazine* November 1976.
10. Joan Barthel, "Paddy Chayefsky: TV Will Do Anything for a Rating!", *New York Times,* 14 November 1976.
11. Timothy Green, *The Universal Eye: The World of Television* (New York, 1972), p. 19.
12. Ibid., p. 25.
13. John L. Wright, "Tune-In: The Focus of Television Criticism," *Journal of Popular Culture,* 7 (1974) p. 890.
14. Roland Barthes, *Mythologies,* trans. Annette Lavers, (New York: Hill and Wang, 1972), p. 39.
15. Michael J. Arlen, "The Air, Talking Back," *The New Yorker,* 22 November 1976.
16. *New York Times,* Sports Section, 5 December 1976.
17. F. H. and L. A. Voelker, *Mass Media,* p. 275.
18. "Reality and Television: An Interview with Mr. Edmund Carpenter," *T. V. Quarterly* (Fall 1972), p. 42.
19. Ibid., p. 44.
20. *Broadcasting,* August 2, 1976.

Bibliography

The works which concentrate on or even meaningfully touch upon the subject matter under consideration here are few and far between. Somewhat more has been done in Europe, particularly England, which has produced such works as William A. Belson's *The Impact of Television: Methods and Findings in Program Research* (London, 1967) which has been prepared for students and teachers of mass communications and seeks to provide useful information about the efficiency and impact of television. It will be useful for educators who wish to reach the masses and in turn want to be understood by them. It also delves into the various ways the impact of television can be measured if not controlled.

Unquestionably much of the preliminary work on the nature and impact of communication has been done by people outside the television industry, many of them writing long before the medium materialized.

The progenitors of sociology were the first to provide a picture of mass society as an organism of interconnected parts. The founder of Sociology, August Comte, in his *The Positive Philosophy* (London, 1915) gave us an awareness of the inherent danger of specialization in our structure while recognizing the virtue of interdependency. He was among the first to alert us to mass society with its sense of alienation.

Ferdinand Tonnies, in a number of works and notably in *Community and Society* (East Lansing, 1957) contributed to concepts of Gemeinschaft and Gesellschaft with the latter approximating our present industrialized society's notion that the contract is the basis of most human interaction. We contribute our services to one another primarily as a rational, contractual and impersonal effort and rarely as an act of altruism or community. Emile Durkheim in his tract on *The Division of Labor in Society* (New York, 1964) developed the idea of *anomie* in which individuals in extreme disharmony and intensive disunity are a possible outgrowth of an impersonal organic solidarity in which heterogeneousness is the dominant character.

After following the work of these sociologists, others have concentrated upon the impact of the broadcasting media in the United States. Eric Barnouw's trilogy *A History of Broadcasting in the United States* (New York, 1968) is an important work that takes us from the late nineteenth century to the late 1960s and examines not only the development of broadcasting but provides some rare insights into the important behind-the-scenes activities of broadcasting.

Remote Control: Television and the Manipulation of American Life, by Frank Mankiewicz and Joel Swerdlow (New York: Times Books, 1978) presents an interesting case for the pervasive impact of television and argues that for many the television world has become more real than their everyday experiences. A similar if more negative view is presented by Marshall McLuhan, "A Last Look at the Tube," in the April 3, 1978, issue of *New York* magazine, which also includes the article "Does TV Have a Future? Yes! Will it be as Good as the Past? No!"

Melvin L. DeFleur and Sandra Ball-Rokeach in their *Theories of Mass Communication* (New York, 1975) have attempted to determine: What has been the impact of societies on their mass media? How does mass communication take place?, and What has been the impact of mass media upon society? Finally, Michael J. Arlen's collection of essays, *The View From Highway 1* (New York, 1976) represents a contemporary, critical, and incisive overview of television today.

7. Universality and Uniformity in the Popular Arts: The Impact of Television on Popular Culture

Lawrence L. Murray
Clinton Hollow
New York

As this volume and its numerous predecessors attest, the impact of television has aroused considerable interest. Investigators of all persuasions, from media specialists to psychologists to political strategists, have endeavored to measure and to understand the effect of telecasting on the human condition. The rapid expansion, the pervasive nature and the intense quality of television have fostered great concern, and the literature is seemingly endless. According to one estimate, over 2,300 studies have been conducted during the last quarter century.[1] No other popular entertainment medium has engendered so much examination and analysis, though the motive forces (usually fears of presumed negative influences) and the patterns and trends of research (haphazard and simplistic evolving into organized and complex) first established in reaction to radio and the movies are comparable.

A survey of the welter of materials relative to how television has affected the human condition reveals the uneven quality of what has transpired. Because the subject is both elusive and illusive, as well as controversial, researchers have had difficulty demonstrating their evidence, adequately sustaining their conclusions, and convincing their readers. General studies have a propensity to be overly generalized, as the subtleties and nuances attendant to sound scholarship are minimized. The growing use of the myriad of tools available to the contemporary social scientist, especially those of a behavioralistic/quantified nature, suggests that future efforts are likely to be more satisfying. More frequent participation by detached observers instead of those in the employ of special interest groups, for example advertisers or the television industry itself, should lead to superior analyses with a minimum of subjectivity.

Of relatively greater import in dictating the quality of research, particularly in the area of television's impact on popular culture, is the negative bias inherent in much of what has been done. Whether this situation will improve along with the more general circumstance is more problematic as no new trend has emerged. Many observers approach television from the prejudicial perspective that whatever the influence of "the most popular art," it must be deleterious because of its popularity. The assumption holds that anything with widespread mass appeal, by definition, cannot be good and anything which can so easily influence the masses will probably be manipulated by agents with less than honorable intentions.

Rather than attempting to assess the effects of television while describing and quantifying them, investigators have simply assumed, a priori, that they have been tremendous. Confident in such an assertion, students of the medium have proceeded quickly into the realm of values with most discussions focusing on whether the impact has been good or bad. Almost without fail, the conclusions fall into the negative spectrum. An apt illustration of the value laden tack is Aubrey Singer's pursuit of the question of whether television is and shall be a "window on culture or a reflection in the glass." As he envisions the quandary, the issue is, will television be a positive, creative social force for the improvement of mankind, or will it be a trite reflection of society's lowest common denominator? Not surprisingly, Singer concludes that the latter is the current state of affairs but that the former is possible and should be encouraged.[2]

Singer's conclusion is not surprising, for most of television's examiners, especially those from academia, show a distinct elitist hostility to the medium and its messages. Harking to Newton Minow's observation that television is a "vast wasteland," these critics perceive their function as raising the intellectual, cultural and aesthetic horizons of the electronic image.[3] They have little patience with programming which they believe has a debilitating effect on the mental capacity of the public and which prompts antisocial behavior. To draw a medical analogy, the "talented tenth" is the guardian of the nation's mental and cultural health; doctors who must keep the intellectual infections of commercial television from spreading. That can be accomplished by working zealously to improve privately sponsored programming while attempting to channel interest toward the superior fare offered by educational or public telecasting. As Harry F. Walters succinctly noted: *"Relief,* of course, can be found on public-TV channels."[4] (emphasis added)

Bypassing or ignoring the nature and content of television's impact on popular culture while focusing instead on the quality of that impact is concomitant with a broader debate over the validity and legitimacy of studying popular culture in any of its manifestations. Serious scholarly attention to popular culture as opposed to "high culture" is a comparatively recent phenomenon whose ancestry dates at most from the 1924 publication of *The Seven Lively Arts* by Gilbert Seldes. As with the initial foray of Arthur M. Schlesinger into urban history during the thirties, interest in popular culture remained dormant for a generation until revived and stimulated by David Manning White and Bernard Rosenberg whose edited volume, *Mass Culture: The Popular Arts,* appeared in 1957. Many traditionalists within the academic community and elsewhere remain skeptical, if not actively hostile to coping with popular culture.[5] Whether fearful of the contagion or disciple of the new wave, intensity of feeling runs high. "Protagonists lambast antagonists—who clobber neutralists—in an arena littered with faulty logic, shopworn analogies, dubious data and, over all, the unappetizing remains of a stale argument."[6]

Even among the devotees of popular culture, there is the agonizing dilemma of an absence of definition and thus confusion over just what is being studied. Assuming that all know what the term popular culture means, no one has adequately defined it. Norman F. Cantor and Michael Werthman believe it to be "what people do when they are not working; it is man in pursuit of pleasure, excitement, beauty and fulfillment."[7] Three American historians wrestled with the term before concluding that popular culture is "a process, not a specific kind of product" and that "a lasting theoretical definition is beyond accomplishment."[8] That conclusion is reinforced by two well-known ideological opponents, Herbert Gans— "Popular culture is indefinable because it has no parameters"—and Marshall Fishwick—"The effort to define popular culture, like discovering the abominable snowman, seems like an endless process."[9] Taking a cue from the title of White and Rosenberg's seminal work, the foremost student of popular culture in America, Russell Nye, evades (perhaps begs) the issue by exploring the "popular arts."[10] By implication or inference, popular culture becomes the end result of the popular arts (never defined either) and a logical-semantic circle is closed. To further confuse the lexicographer, the term mass culture is frequently interchanged with that of popular culture, the assumption being that the terms are synonymous if not identical.[11]

Even with an adequate definition of popular culture, the difficult task of assessing and evaluating the impact of television on it remains. Methodological problems abound to confound investigators. For example, data necessary for determining and measuring impact is often fragmentary or unobtainable. Statistics about the number of stations and receivers, average viewing time per person or per household, program classification and so on are informative, but they are insufficient for sustaining cause and effect relationships. The Surgeon General's Office expended nearly $2 million during a three year period for twenty-three laboratory and field studies concerning televised violence and how it affects the behavior of children. In spite of that expenditure, the investigative committee was able to formulate only a "preliminary and tentative" commentary.[12] Successive probes by public and private agencies have not yielded more exacting conclusions, though proponents of one position or another will cite them as the last word on the subject. Perhaps the isolation of one component such as television is an impossibility when so many stimuli are operative and when complex human motivation and behavior patterns are at issue.

The absence of viable, universally accepted research models and designs further exacerbates matters. While acknowledging what has gone before, nearly every researcher launches his project as if he was the first into the territory because his project is slightly, but significantly, different from previous sojourns. New techniques, new paradigms, and new parameters are stacked one on top of the other with small yet consequential variations amongst them. Opportunities for comparative analyses cannot be fully exploited. Lack of a coherent organizational structure leads to needless duplication of efforts while the demands of diverse disciplines frequently work at cross purposes. The American scientific tradition of decentralized research which shows a common focal point or goal flounders without a clearing house for exchanging information. Such an agency is needed by those studying television and its influence.

With these kinds of problems, what can one say about the impact of television on popular culture? What observations will have a modicum of surety about their accuracy and veracity? In America (more will be said of the worldwide situation later), the most important influence of the medium has been the formation of a universal popular culture. For the first time, the populace collectively spends its free time engaged in the same pursuit. Television, by providing immediate and continued shared cultural experiences, has all but completed, in a relatively short period of time, a process that has gradually been evolving for two centuries. As Professor Nye has cogently argued, the popular arts (hence popular culture by inference) are of relatively recent vintage, first appearing in the late eighteenth century. Their existence called for population increases and concentration (urbanization), an educational system which would lead to broader based literacy, and modern technology with its capacity for duplicating and multiplying materials.[13] The electronic revolution quickened the pace, and television is rapidly finalizing a development which had been greatly accelerated by the movies and radio.

From a different perspective, television is responsible for the near realization of the concept of the melting pot when it provides a universal popular culture readily interchangeable with a singular national culture. The long cherished goal of homogenizing the citizenry into one national type appears on the horizon. Ethnic, regional, class, and other distinctions blur as the medium co-opts into the mainstream elements which formerly contributed to diversity. Saying that is not to deny the reality of subcultures or that ethnic awareness, regional consciousness, and a search for "roots" are at the moment experiencing a revival. Nor is this to assert that a perfect and immutable cultural consensus has been achieved. Residual influences can function within an homogenized national culture and are by no means mutually exclusive with the larger whole. But residual influences and the degree of their manifestation have a transient quality about them and America is unlikely to gravitate toward the Canadian concept of the "mixing pot," a national culture which does not mandate the absorption or sacrifice of subgroup identity. That the goal of the melting pot is nearer because of television is ironic, for it happened at a time when social scientists were eagerly endorsing the desirability of cultural pluralism. Fortunately or unfortunately, television sponsors a neoteric universal popular culture which subsumes all in its wake, including high culture, and through a process of natural selection incorporates some elements while discarding others which previously had been endemic in a single group.

Intimately connected to the existence of a uniform popular culture has been the universal participation in an equitable fashion brought on by television. Prior to the twentieth century and, more importantly, the advent of television, mass participation in popular culture was limited and sporadic. Cost factors, accessibility, and minimal leisure time mitigated against universal involvement. Some segments of society, notably the middle class, were able to enjoy the popular arts regularly whereas farmers and urban laborers were only occasional participants. Class distinctions were also substantial. All classes, for example, had theatrical productions available to them at one time or another, but which ones and which types varied enormously. As in the case of reading material, cultural distinctions were maintained in content if not in form. Robert C. Toll's thesis that "common people shaped show business in their image" is intriguing, but the erosion of class diversity did not occur until the electronic era.[14] Furthermore, much of what constituted popular culture was male-dominated and oriented with women and children excluded or relegated to an inferior participatory status.

The appearance of movies and then radio, in addition to other socioeconomic changes attendant to modern industrialization such as increased wealth and leisure time, hastened the destruction of barriers. Television completed the destruction with frightening suddenness. The degree of universality of participation is thought by some to be less than 100 percent, but evidence shows that "there is no discernable variation between the hours spent watching television by the college educated, or by professors and journalists, and the public as a whole."[15] Nor is there a significant difference in what diverse segments of the public watch on television. Countless surveys have found that the typical viewer of both commercial and educational telecasts is substantially the same. Analyses of audiences for specific programs, with rare exceptions, find viewers to be a cross section of the public at large. Certain individuals may decry the vacuousness of television; they may even assert, as was so popular in the fifties, that they have no television or that they only watch educational television. These claims will not bear up under scrutiny. Popular culture, which had been the province of the majority but not all, permeates every type and class in the age of television. In the privacy of our homes, we all show the same experiential phenomena. The average American born today will eventually spend nine years watching television. With approximately 3,000 hours available annually for recreation and with forty-four hours per week consumed by television, no other form of the popular arts exceeds television and only sleeping takes more of man's time.

Nothing intrinsic to television required that it should be a medium with universal participation and impact. Early receivers were expensive, $300 to $500 at a time of $3,000 salaries, and some form of pay television was thought feasible, especially by the film industry. The medium could have been restricted to the affluent, and it could also have been a purveyor of high culture. However, much as had been the case with bicycles and automobiles which began as playthings for the rich, commercial considerations overcame others and receivers were mass produced so as to be affordable by all. Rather than restrict accessibility, every attempt was made to spread the "benefits" of American technology. Previous experience with radio prompted a spirit of optimism for the economic potential of television, and investors were not disappointed. Slightly under 100 percent of American homes today have sets and over one-third own two or more. Worldwide, the spread of television has not been as spectacular, but that too is changing as the mineral wealth of the previously "underdeveloped" world raises living standards.

As television has been a force in the proliferation of an all-pervasive popular culture within America, so too has it been a contributor in forming a vestige of an international popular culture with uniform properties. Transnational homogeneity is far from accomplished, but remarkable strides have been made in a relatively short time span. Domestic producers export 100,000 hours of programming annually, and nearly one-fifth of transmission time in western Europe consists of Yankee material.[16] A more striking illustration is Canada, a nation in which ninety percent of the population resides within fifty miles of its southern border. Domestic telecasting has been stunted because of easy access to United States stations. Buffalo, N.Y., is included in the top ten television advertising markets only because of its penetration of the much larger Toronto metropolitan area.

Before the onset of television, the ingredients of popular culture were fairly well circumscribed by national boundaries. The form of the popular arts had an international flavor, as in the similarity of vaudeville to European musical hall shows. Yet the character of the content varied widely. Particulars indigenous to any country, the composite of that nation's traditions and cultural heritage, shaped the evolution of the popular arts. Now, however, American programming and the propensity to copy imported styles and conventions in native productions combine to alter cultural individuality. In technically backward countries, television has been instrumental in the creation of a popular culture which previously was either nonexistent or in an infant stage. The factors identified by Nye as integral to the development of the popular arts are unnecessary with television. The relative ease of initiating telecasting and distributing receivers, as well as the simple communicative nature of the medium, has caused a veritable explosion of popular culture in the third world, and it is heavily influenced by America.

American conventions did not have to affect the world's popular culture markedly. Theoretically, each country could have established its own telecasting industry with individualized content, and popular culture would have continued to manifest pluralistic dimensions. (Technologically limited nations must be excluded from that generalization.) A meshing of economic factors and an apparent preference in many places to rely on technically superior imports, however, has led to a significant Yankee presence abroad. The circumstance is comparable to that which occurred in film-making when Hollywood's celluloid fantasies engulfed foreign films.[17] The influence of American television on international popular culture is a concentration of a process begun by the movies, and is complemented by American domination of other popular arts such as music.

The fact that state owned and operated telecasting, the norm in most of the world as opposed to the American practice of government regulated but independent commercial operations, often exhibited a decided preference for high culture was a factor in American penetration of foreign markets. Critics may decry the inane nature of American programming, but it has struck a responsive chord in the masses at home and abroad. Legal and illegal stations have sprung up around the world to challenge state monopolies. The British Broadcasting Company waged a twenty year struggle before succumbing to peaceful coexistence with a commercial competitor. Challenged, government facilities have altered their programming to be more reflective of popular desires and less influenced by elitist decisions about what should be telecast. Consequently, "Kojak" draws the highest ratings in West Germany; a generation of Japanese have grown to maturity on a diet of American TV westerns, and Britons have been exposed to paramilitary spy thrillers. Some exchange has taken place; witness the successful adaptation of Britain's "Till Death Do Us Part" into "All In the Family" and public television's importation of BBC productions such as "Upstairs, Downstairs," and "The World at War." Because of the infrequency of exchange and the limitation to Great Britain, Morris Esslin's observation that "the traffic is strictly one way" still obtains.[18] The likelihood of American popular culture being seriously influenced by the importation of television programs is minimal at best.

Attempts by foreign officials to minimize or to halt Yankee influence in their telecasting have yielded limited results. No country has tried harder than Canada to foster cultural independence. Employment of Americans has been discouraged, domestic programming has been encouraged, and commercial stations have been licensed in direct competition with the Canadian Broadcasting Company. Yet when cable television began in Toronto three years ago, retailers were forced to include all of the western New York stations because they had the largest audience appeal. Except for one or two independent operations, the majority of transmission time on commercial television in Canada remains dependent on American imports. There is some evidence which suggests that American programming may have reached a peak in western Europe. However, it is too soon to decide if the circumstance is temporary or permanent. Imitation of formulas and genres continues and, in less prosperous areas, American shows remain the staple.

Most foreign observers and critics, like their domestic counterparts, fear what television's spread of a uniform popular culture may do to their high culture and to a healthy international cultural diversity. A strong sense of nationalism as well as intellectual revulsion breeds apprehension. The popular culture of American television is considered to be as destructive if not more so than other forms of imperialism. That Canadian criticisms of American television began simultaneously with attacks on American corporate holdings in Canada was not coincidental. To the contrary, the criticisms there and elsewhere are only a part of a larger world effort to escape the clutches of the Yankee colossus. A singular exception among the critics is Marshall McLuhan. He remains undaunted by the fears of cultural uniformity, positing the thesis that television and other media with "electronic simultaneity" may well have the opposite effect. "It should not be surprising to discern that underlying any *figure* of cultural uniformity there might be *ground* of greater diversity and discontinuity."[19] McLuhan's thesis, a cultural variation of Newton's law that every action has an equal and opposite reaction, has reassured few critics.

Television's impact on popular culture has been most significant in the areas of uniformity in content and universality in participation, both in America and the world at large. While of lesser magnitude, other effects are observable. One of these is the development of an abundant and variegated popular culture for the masses. Three commercial and one educational network function nationally, and syndication of programming has grown enormously. The Federal Communications Commission has mandated more local programming, albeit with modest results, and independent channels are available in most metropolitan areas. The citizenry does exercise options in allocating its viewing time and there is exposure to a broader number of alternatives. In spite of the penchant for imitation and formula programming, and with the realization that the potential for even greater diversity has barely been plumbed, television has been the richest form of the popular arts. Compared to previous exertions and the immediate competition, television offers far more.

Similarly, television has played a vital if involuntary part in stimulating public awareness of and participation in other forms of the popular arts. Critics debate whether television has made people more active or passive, violent or sedentary, and the debates run on endlessly as definitions and data vary according to the positions taken. However, all do agree that the medium has fostered public recognition of other forms and prompted both active and passive involvements. The most evident instance is that of sports. This country has had a long sporting tradition and sports have had a substantial role in shaping our popular culture. Television has heightened and expanded that role until sports, participator and spectator varieties, have become dominant elements within our popular culture. The booms in tennis, golf, skiing, and even bowling can be attributed in large measure to the pervasiveness of the medium.

A symbiotic, mutually reinforcing association has grown between sports and television. More than anything else, television has been responsible for high salaried athletes, multimillion dollar professional franchises, and "big time" college athletics. Conversely, the insatiable appetite of the public for televised sporting events has altered programming and generated some of the highest ratings in the history of the medium. The progression of the American Broadcasting Company from a distant third to a commanding first in the rating wars can be credited in part to the introduction of sports to prime time, and a general increase in the amount of time devoted to telecasting sporting events.

The widely held assumption that television has been guilty of diminishing public interest in certain forms of the popular arts deserves more study. Those who point to the decline in the film industry and the restructuring of Hollywood into Television City ordinarily offer television as the responsible agent. Television has had an impact in declining theater attendance and the steady attrition in the number of movies produced. How much of an impact is unclear, as several studies have shown that the film industry was declining prior to television and that in the early years of competition theater attendance lagged as badly in areas without television as with it.[20] Further, one could argue that like sports, movies and television have formed a symbiotic relationship as the two media have learned to cooperate. The number of hours devoted to telecasting movies and the steady, frequently spectacular ratings of films are a reflection of that cooperation. Conversely, total revenues for films always include sales to television and more than one movie has moved from the loss to profit column because of such a sale.

Finally, an ironic influence that television has had on popular culture has been the infusion of elements of high culture with the "lower" or inferior form. As the electronic medium has both acquainted many with other forms of popular culture and stimulated participation therein, so too has it introduced high culture to the masses. A survey by the New York City Ballet Company revealed that approximately 40 percent of the audience was first acquainted with the dance form through television. The ratings are not outstanding, but such programs as the "Hallmark Hall of Fame" dramatic productions have persistently appealed to large audiences. The cliche about how many view a Shakespearian play or some other facet of high culture on television versus all those who have witnessed live performances assumes new meaning in this context. The cultural horizons of the masses have been expanded and the cultural tastes of the educated elite have been leavened by the popular fare of television. Cultural standards are in flux and the potentiality exists for a meshing of distinctions between the two expressions. A universality of cultural standards is emerging as the onetime limited appeal of high culture is extended. For good or ill, increasing cultural uniformity, a one-dimensional culture which is neither high nor low but just popular, is on the horizon.

The preceding analysis is offered with a modicum of surety, not as a final answer to a complex question. In many ways, it is far more of a beginning than an end. Much like the printing press, gun powder and other cataclysmic technological advances, the impact of television on popular culture and all facets of the human condition will best be understood only with the passage of time. Perspective is required to appreciate the effect that 18,000 hours of watching television has on the average college student, and another fifty years or more must pass before the entire population will have been born and raised under the influence of the medium. In the interim, researchers must be cognizant of the fact that regardless of their own beliefs and prejudices, the medium deserves the utmost scrutiny under the most objective circumstances. Concerns about the quality of the impact, what previously has been identified as the value laden approach, should be temporarily set aside until we better understand the nature and content of the impact.

Notes

1. "What TV Does to Kids," *Newsweek,* 21 February 1977, p. 63.
2. Aubrey Singer, "Television: Window on Culture or Reflection in the Glass," in *Sight, Sound, and Society: Motion Pictures and Television in America,* eds. David Manning White and Richard Averson (Boston: Beacon Press, 1968), pp. 150–63.
3. For further discussion of hostile criticisms of television's impact on life in general and popular culture in particular, see Horace Newcomb, ed., *Television: The Critical View* (New York: Oxford University Press, 1976) and Douglass Cater and Richard Adler, eds., *Television as a Social Force: New Approaches to TV Criticism* (New York: Praeger Publishers, 1975), especially Richard Adler, "Understanding Television: An Overview of the Literature of the Medium as a Social and Cultural Force," in *Television as a Social Force,* pp. 23–48.
4. H. F. Waters, "All About Kidvid," *Newsweek,* 21 February 1977, p. 66.
5. For a scathing denunciation of the study of popular culture, see "Pop-Eyed Professors," by Thomas Meehan in the *New York Times Magazine,* 1 June 1975, pp. 33–41.
6. Bernard Rosenberg, "Mass Culture Revisited," in B. Rosenberg and D. M. White, eds, *Mass Culture Revisited* (New York: Van Nostrand Reinhold Company, 1971), p. 3. Russell Nye has summarized the debate in *The Unembarrassed Muse* (New York: The Dial Press, 1970), pp. 417-20, while offering his own opinion that "popular culture and the arts included in that culture can no longer be treated with contempt or dismissed as unworthy of study."
7. N. F. Cantor and M. Werthman, eds., *The History of Popular Culture,* 2 vols. (New York: The Macmillan Co., 1968), Vol. 1, p. xxii.
8. D. Burner, R. D. Marcus, and J. Tilson, eds., *America Through a Looking Glass, a Historical Reader in Popular Culture,* 2 vols. (Englewood Cliffs, N.J.: Prentice-Hall Inc., 1974), Vol. 1, pp. 3–4.
9. Quoted in "Popular Culture in the Round," *Cultural Information Service,* February, 1976, pp. 1–2.
10. Nye, *Unembarrassed Muse,* p. 1.
11. The term folk culture also is interchanged by some with popular culture and mass culture. For purposes of this paper, popular culture is defined as a style of socioartistic expression which is not peculiar to a particular society or a class but instead is reflective of the community as a whole.
12. David M. Rein, "The Impact of Television Violence," *The Journal of*

Popular Culture (Spring, 1974), pp. 934–45. See also Douglass Carter, *TV Violence and the Child: The Evolution and Fate of the Surgeon General's Report* (New York: Russell Sage Foundation, 1975).

13. Nye, *Unembarrassed Muse*, p. 2. Marshall Fishwick denies that popular culture is "just the product of the mass media. There was a popular culture in Rome and in Greece." "Popular Culture in the Round," *Cultural Information Service*, p. 2.

14. R. C. Toll, *On With the Show, The First Century of Show Business in America* (New York: Oxford University Press, 1976), p. 2.

15. M. Novak, "Television Shapes the Soul," in *Television as a Social Force*, p. 21.

16. C. W. E. Bigsby, "Europe, America and the Cultural Debate," in C. W. E. Bigsby, ed., *Superculture, American Popular Culture and Europe* (Bowling Green, Ohio: Bowling Green University Popular Press, 1975), p. 26.

17. Thomas H. Guback, "Film as an International Business," *Journal of Communications* (Winter, 1974), p. 94.

18. M. Esslin, "The Television Series as Folk Epic," in *Superculture*, p. 197. For a critique of British television and the larger role played by American imports on both BBC and commercial telecasting, see Paul E. Friedman, "Do We Really Have So Much to Learn from British TV?", *New York Times*, March 27, 1977.

19. M. McLuhan, "The Implication of Cultural Uniformity," in *Superculture*, pp. 53, 56.

20. Belson, *Impact of Television*, p. 277. Another example might be the impact of television on boxing. It is traditionally assumed that twice-weekly telecasts of boxing matches constituted overexposure and resulted in a precipitous drop-off in public interest in the sport. However, each year brings more football games to telecasting and the sport thrives. Very possibly the decline in interest in boxing may have been the result of other factors, such as racism when boxing ceased to be a sport in which ethnic Americans sought economic and social mobility and nonwhites became the majority of fighters. The demise of American's monopoly on the various championships and the corresponding increase of Asians and Latin Americans who claimed the titles cannot be ignored either.

Bibliography

Although the literature on television is of massive proportions, materials specifically related to its impact on popular culture are limited. Most authors have addressed this general association of the medium and mass culture, sprinkling their commentary with references to its impact. Furthermore, some authorities have approached the subject within the context of an analysis of television and others within that of popular culture, and the literature tends to divide accordingly.

From the vantage point of television, the best introductory, survey-like volumes are Leo Bogart, *The Age of Television: A Study of Viewing Habits and the Impact of Television on American Life,* 3rd rev. ed. (New York: Frederick Unger Publishing Co., 1974) and William A. Belson, *The Impact of Television: Methods and Findings in Program Research* (Hamden, Conn.: Archon Books, 1967). Bogart examines the American scene while Belson limits himself to the British situation and makes excellent use of statistical data. A pioneering effort edited by William Y. Elliot has an attractive title, *Television's Impact on American Culture* (East Lansing: Michigan State Press, 1956), but the selections are weak in substance and the emphasis is skewed toward educational television. David Manning White and Richard Averson's edited study, *Sight, Sound, and Society: Motion Pictures and Television in America* (Boston: Beacon Press, 1968) is a superior, better balanced survey.

Narrowly focused but illustrative of what can be done in assessing television's impact, Robert Mac Neil's *The People Machine: The Influence of TV on American Politics* (New York: Harper and Row, 1968) is a useful model. Collections by Allen Kirschner and Linda Kirschner, *Radio and Television: Readings on the Mass Media* (New York: Odyssey Press, 1971) and Horace Newcomb, *TV: The Most Popular Art* (Garden City: Doubleday, 1974) have useful selections, especially the introductions.

Any study of popular culture should begin with Bernard Rosenberg and David Manning White, eds., *Mass Culture: The Popular Arts* (New York: The Free Press, 1957) and their sequel, *Mass Culture Revisited* (New York: Von Nostrand Reinhold Co., 1971). The depth of feeling concerning popular culture is revealed in the symposium "Mass Culture and Mass Media," *Daedalus* (Spring 1960). Russell Nye has attempted to pull together the disparate studies of popular culture in *The Unembarrassed Muse, the Popular Arts in America* (New York: The Dial Press, 1970) while offering his own insights and observations. His is an improvement on Gilbert Seldes, *The Seven Lively Arts* (New York: Macmillan, 1924) and *The Public Arts* (New York: Simon and Schuster, 1956) as well as Stuart Hall and Paddy Whannel, *The Popular Arts*

(Boston: Beacon Press, 1964). *The Journal of Popular Culture* offered a special issue on television (Spring 1974), publishing fourteen articles on subjects ranging from the impact of televised violence to reflections on the videoculture of the future. Very little has been done on the relationship of American mass culture with its international brethren. Of what has been written, much is collected in C. W. E. Bigsby, ed., *Superculture: American Popular Culture and Europe* (Bowling Green, Ohio: Bowling Green University Popular Press, 1975). *The Journal of Popular Film* has recently expanded its purview to become *The Journal of Popular Film and Television,* thus providing an outlet for the disparite research into the interrelationship between television and mass culture.

8. Television as Big Business

Theodore Kovaleff
Assistant Dean and
Director of Admissions
School of Law
Columbia University

Man's awareness that electronic communication could be broadcast through the air without need of a direct wire hookup dates back to Heinrich Hertz's discoveries in 1888. Within the next thirteen years, Guglielmo Marconi had devised a way to send signals long distance, bridging even the Atlantic Ocean. Slightly over fifty years ago, two inventors, Vladimir Zworykin and Philo Farnsworth, utilizing radio technology, developed a method of transmitting images and voices. By the mid-twenties, the medium had evolved from the level of scientific curiosity to that of recognized potential. In 1927, Herbert Hoover, then Secretary of Commerce, became the first high government official to appear on television. The following year the Federal Radio Commission brought the young medium under its control by making provision for experimental "picture broadcasting," but the exigencies of the Depression slowed development, and it was not until 1941 that the Federal Communications Commission (successor to the Federal Radio Commission) drew up transmission specifications.

On July 1, 1941, two commercial television stations went into operation in New York City (CBS and NBC). In contrast to the relationship of radio to World War I, American involvement in World War II delayed the growth of the television industry; but planning, if not construction, continued at a rapid pace. Incredibly, much of the work consisted of preparations for the transmission of color signals, and provisions for compatible broadcasting in both monochrome and color. Channels 1 through 13 were designated in very high frequency (VHF) range, and those above that became classified as ultra high frequency (UHF). As a result of protests from the radio industry, which was disturbed about television's encroachment on the FM band, Channel 1 was taken away from television and reassigned to FM radio broadcasting. The parameters were now established for the successful economic development of television as we know it today.

The early evolution of television was unlike that of radio. Whereas in the first years of the latter there had been little organization and even fewer records kept (even the famous broadcast of the 1920 election over station KDKA is only *remembered*, the "transcription" being produced in the late 1920s),[1] the case of television was opposite. The major radio networks quickly moved into television and took advantage of their expertise and dominance. After a normal period of shakeout, there were four major networks: American Broadcasting Company (ABC), Columbia Broadcasting Company (CBS), National Broadcasting Company (NBC), and the Dumont Network. (In 1955, Dumont terminated its network activities.)

All except Dumont had originally been deeply involved in radio networking. Additionally, each entity was able to draw on other financial bases to support their then unprofitable, but highly promising, new business. ABC, formerly the Blue Network of NBC, owned United Paramount Theaters, the largest operator of motion picture theaters in the United States. CBS was part of Columbia Broadcasting System, a corporation engaged in the production and distribution of records, phonographs, radio receivers and, after 1951, television sets. Radio Corporation of America (RCA), which owned NBC, was a producer of all types of transmitting equipment, tubes, records, phonographs, international radiotelegraph and radiomarine communications systems. By the mid-1950s, each was making a fine return on its investment in the television field.

The networks operated in similar fashion. Each owned a limited (by the FCC) number of outlets, obviously located in the major markets of the country. What makes the network system possible was that each also developed a number of affiliates throughout North America. Stations sought affiliation because it provided regular programming at no cost while yielding a profit. Usually the relationship was set forth in a contract containing clauses concerning the following:

1. Recognition of the station as the network outlet in a specified area, with the station having first call on all network programs.

2. Agreement to carry all programming of the network during certain specified hours (usually "prime time").
3. Rates for time to be sold to network advertisers.
4. Compensation to the station for carrying network programs.
5. Delivery of network programming by transmission facilities (usually provided by the American Telephone and Telegraph Company).

The value of stations and the importance of an affiliation in a multistation market was dramatized by the NBC-Westinghouse case of the 1950s. In 1953 Westinghouse Broadcasting Corporation, a wholly-owned subsidiary of Westinghouse Electric Corporation, purchased WPTZ-TV in Philadelphia from Philco Corporation for $8.5 million. The figure was broken down: $2 million for land, equipment and license, $1.5 million for good will, $5 million for the NBC affiliation. Within two years, NBC attempted to take over the station, offering Westinghouse its Cleveland outlets plus $3 million. Westinghouse demurred, not wanting to trade an entry in the fourth largest market for one in the tenth.[2] At this point, NBC threatened to withdraw its affiliation agreements with the other Westinghouse stations (KDKA in Pittsburgh and WBZ, WBZA Boston-Springfield). Thus intimidated, Westinghouse felt forced to concede defeat and agreed to the switch, with which the FCC concurred.[3] It was not until the Antitrust Division of the Justice Department became involved that NBC experienced any difficulties.[4] Able to convince the Supreme Court that the deal would increase concentration, for NBC would then own outlets in the top four markets, the antitrusters persuaded the network giant to divest itself of the Philadelphia facilities. Westinghouse subsequently reacquired them.

Once interesting programming was available, the public responded by a television receiver buying splurge. This, plus technological development, led to lower prices, better quality sets, and increased screen size. The first national political conventions were televised in 1948,[5] and sporting events were popular programs from the beginning. The first telecast ever of a baseball game had taken place in 1939 from Columbia University's Baker Field; the first major league game telecast was a 1947 tilt between the Brooklyn Dodgers and Cincinnati Redlegs from Crosley Field. Public enthusiasm stimulated advertiser interest, and it was possible to charge high rates for commercials. Individual station profitability increased dramatically in the early 1950s.

In an effort to protect the stations from cutthroat competition and interference, the FCC limited the number of stations in a given area. The guidelines were based on population, geography, and number of television sets. From 1948 to 1952 no new licenses were awarded. Then the Commission began to process and approve applications for cities with no service. In many areas there was only one station in a community. This was a potential gold mine for the owner, for he could have his pick of the available programming from all the networks, and he did not have to worry about advertising rate competition. In time the FCC would allocate other stations to the area, but while it lasted the arrangement was a monopolist's dream. Lyndon Johnson, then senator from Texas, and his wife became millionaires thanks to a lack of competition in the San Antonio market, which lasted for what opponents charged to be an unconscionable length of time.

Partly in an effort to stimulate the UHF sector of the spectrum, the FCC awarded a large number of new stations in that frequency range, which, however, was not as desirable as the lower range. Most of the sets in use were able to receive only VHF, and those equipped for both cost extra and did not sell as well. Finally, the quality of UHF transmission was inferior, and as long as it suffered from the aforementioned handicaps, it was not likely to improve markedly. It was not until 1963 that Congress decreed that all television sets sold in interstate commerce had to be equipped for both UHF and VHF signals.

The American system of commercial television is supported by advertisers who purchase "spots," portions of programs, or entire programs. They make this investment in order to present a commercial message about some product to the show's audience. Normally the company which manufactures the product in question has little to do with the "ad" or the choice of program to sponsor; this is the function of the advertising agency. Network advertising is the chief method, but each station also carries local and regional messages as well. Usually the rates for "local" spots are lower than those for an identical national one. The advertising agency which produces the advertisements generally makes its money on a commission basis—a small percentage of the amount paid to the various stations and networks.[6]

The importance of advertising cannot be overestimated. Not only does it support programming, it also appears to have a major effect on product sales. In 1955, for instance, Revlon was searching for a way to halt the erosion of its market share by other cosmetic makers, especially Hazel Bishop. Serendipitously, a promoter came up with the idea of the big quiz show. "The $64,000 Question" was one of the biggest programs in all television history and Revlon products were quickly bought throughout the nation. In fact, one of its products was almost immediately a nationwide sellout.

One time slot that was not selling was Sunday afternoons. Despite everything that the network executives tried, few people watched television then and so advertising revenues were low. Then one network began to cover professional football and, according to the Nielsen ratings, enormous numbers began to watch the action. Success breeds imitation and sports came to be the programming mainstay for much of the weekend. Today, probably the most popular presentations are sporting events. The size of the potential audience is so huge that the bids for the rights to televise the 1980 Olympics back to the United States came to nearly $100 million.

With such an obvious influence on the public, it was logical that television would be quickly adapted to politics. Now the preelection and, to a lesser extent, the preprimary period is one of the most profitable segments of the year for the television stations and networks, who sell innumerable spot and even whole programs to competing candidates. In the early days of radio it had been recognized that one candidate might be able to buy all the available time, or, worse, that a station might refuse air time to a candidate. Thus, based on the public's ownership of the air waves, according to the FCC's enforcement of the Communications Act of 1934, § 315, if one candidate has been on the station, other declared candidates can compel appropriation of similar broadcasting time for themselves. In 1959, the concept of fairness was merged with the equal time regulation so that now, if proponents of one candidate or idea are given (or buy) time, those of the other side must be accorded equal opportunity. Today the only factor barring total equal usage of electronic media by candidates is their respective financial resources.[7]

The profitability of many stations has led to a large number passing into the hands of large corporations, some being parts of conglomerates, others belonging to newspaper publishers. This circumstance has persuaded the FCC, now more concerned with the problem of monopoly, to consider concentration as a factor in license renewal. All other conditions being equal, a station will have less need to prove that its past broadcast record demonstrates that it has been aware of and has serviced the needs of the community, if it is involved with no other business in the communications field in the same geographical area. An example of this policy is the WHDH case. Owned by the Boston Herald-Traveler Corporation, which also controlled two major Boston newspapers and two strong radio stations in the city, WHDH had been chosen for the license because the Commission felt that the radio broadcast record had been "superior," and that "the applicant is the most qualified to provide programming service on a continuing basis in the interests of the population of the coverage area, notwithstanding that the diversification policy of the Commission would be better served by a grant to [one of the other applicants].[8]

Difficulties began almost immediately, as it transpired that Robert Choate, a WHDH official, had attempted to influence an FCC commissioner. Upon investigation it turned out that Choate had had lunch with the Commission chairman. The entire Commission determined that this indeed was an attempt to influence, so they decided to reexamine the permit. As a result, in 1962, the FCC, after much study, reissued the permit and granted a license, but only for four months. The television station promptly applied for renewal, but, upon invitation of the FCC, two other groups also filed competing applications. In the meantime, Choate died. An FCC examiner then ruled that since WHDH had been administratively penalized and Choate was dead, the station should receive the renewal. Nevertheless, the Commission disagreed, basing its decision on the fact that the station was owned by a newspaper and the Commission policy was to favor separation of the local news media. The Boston Herald-Traveler Corporation naturally appealed the decision, stating that it had been treated differently than any other station in 35 years, but the court upheld the Commission and the Supreme Court refused to hear a further appeal. The new anti-concentration stance of the FCC was extremely shortsighted. Revenues from the television station had been used for several years to bolster the failing *Boston Herald Traveler* newspaper. As soon as the station was taken away, the company sold the newspaper to the Hearst interests, which merged it with their already operating tabloids. Thus the broader communications market became more, rather than less, concentrated.

For years there have been efforts by entrepreneurs aimed at either improving the quality of television reception or of offering additional and better programming. These schemes have almost always involved viewer payment. In order for programs to be viewed only by subscribers, broadcast signals are scrambled. Only those who rent an attachment which reassembles the signal can make use of the service. In 1955, the FCC allowed a test of the pay-TV system in Hartford, Connecticut. Although it was one of the catalysts for the movement of the Brooklyn Dodger and New York Giant baseball teams to the west coast, subscription television did not immediately live up to its early promise.

Cable Television, or community antenna television (CATV), began for the purpose of delivering television programming to people beyond the reach of through-the-air television transmission. Initiated for television in 1949 (it had been used experimentally for FM radio in the 1930s), it grew slowly in the 1950s and early 1960s, then it burgeoned. Since the television set is connected to a shielded cable which runs to the distribution center, there is no interference with the picture. When it became possible to transmit programs long distances, there were legal difficulties, such as copyright laws, which had to be surmounted by the CATV companies. In 1968, the Supreme Court decided that cable systems were not required to pay copyright royalties on programs captured from the air, but in a staff agreement between the National Association of Broadcasters and the National Cable Television Association, the cable group promised to pay some fees.[9] As a result of the decision, the FCC has promulgated regulations designed to avoid possible anarchy on the air waves.

The new FCC rules provide a great deal of protection to the existing network setup. The CATV company had to carry the un-amended signal of all the television stations operating in the area, and no programs could be duplicated on the same day broadcast unless the station itself did the rebroadcast. In the 100 largest metropolitan areas, the CATV systems could not import distant signals to augment programming. In areas where stations overlapped, the CATV companies could only carry the signals of the nearer stations, unless permission to rebroadcast was granted by the other stations. Also, the rules required that any system with more than 3,500 subscribers must originate a "significant" amount of programming. According to the ruling, the CATV companies may sell advertising. Were the quality of the programs good, the income from this source could become substantial. The CATV companies are also subject to other strictures. As it is necessary to obtain franchises from the metropolitan areas in which they operate, the cities have insisted on certain regulations. Thus, for instance, in New York City, members of the public are allowed access to one of the extra channels carried by the company.

The idea of all homes being tied together by cable has led to many fantastic proposals. The "wired city" envisions home learning, data retrieval, data transmission and other services which would make even the science fiction buff of a decade ago envious. So far, however, its only utilization has been to make subscription television possible, for by paying an extra fee, extra channels are now available to all subscribers.

Another invention is Electronic Television Recording. At present there are a number of different systems, all vying for consumer acceptance. There are three major schemes. The first employs magnetic tape similar to that used in an ordinary sound tape recorder; but as it has to record picture as well as voice, the tape is about four times as wide, and it is necessary to use at least twice as much tape as for sound recordings. Probably technological advances will soon cut down the quantity of tape required. Another plan developed by CBS involves regular filming techniques. Several companies, including RCA and MCA, use a video disc. With either a stylus resembling a phonograph needle or a laser, the machine plays the record over a television tube. All the systems have positive and negative qualities. Those using tape are more adaptable to home recording (leading to many copyright infringement suits), while those utilizing the disc are much less bulky. RCA's version, with the stylus, has a record which rotates at 450 rpm, one side playing for thirty minutes. MCA's system, employing optical technology, rotates at 1800 rpm. One advantage here is that one rotation equals one exposure, making it possible to freeze a picture. Thus the MCA system is compatible with other data retrieval plans. To capitalize on this, the company is developing a computerized system which will locate indexed documents immediately. Industry analysts hesitate to predict which mode will prevail in the end; some even suggest that the market is so huge that there will be room for more than one. The only certain statement at this moment is that once production of the devices increases, the price will fall.

In a consumer-oriented society, the role of television is obvious; it has and it will continue to play a role in influencing the wants of the population. As long as the medium sells products, it will be profitable, and the industry will prosper. There are no indications that the formulae which succeeded in the past need be adjusted.

Notes

1. Bill Kaland to author (May 12, 1976). Kaland was a producer of historical radio and TV shows for Westinghouse Broadcasting; he is now self-employed.
2. U.S. House, 84th Cong., 2nd Sess. Antitrust Subcommittee of the Committee in the Judiciary, *Monopoly Problems in the Regulated Industries: Hearings...* (2 pts in 4 vols., Washington, D.C. 1957), Pt 2, I, 3117–20.
3. Kaland to author.
4. Victor Hansen, "Broadcasting and the Antitrust Laws," *Law and Contemporary Problems,* 22 (Autumn 1957): 575–78.
5. As a matter of fact the major parties both chose Philadelphia because it was located on the cable between New York City and Washington, and thus would garner a large audience. Irwin Ross, *The Loneliest Campaign* (New York, 1968), pp. 92–3.
6. See the industry publications *Spot Radio* and *Television.*
7. John Dean III, "Political Broadcasting: The Communications Act of 1934 Reviewed," XX *Fed. Com. B.J.* (1966).
8. 22 FCC 761, 882 (1957).
9. *Fortnightly Corporation v. United Artists Television, Inc.* 392 U.S. 390 (1968).

Bibliography

There are no specific works on the economic aspects of the television industry; rather it is necessary to consult articles on selected areas of the topic. As many of the following citations are from law reviews, the uniform system of citation is utilized.

Besides the Barnouw books mentioned elsewhere, a good overview is provided by Sidney Head, *Broadcasting in America* (Boston, 1972). The growth and mechanics of the network relationship are treated in S. M. Besen and R. Soligo, "The Economics of the Network Affiliate Relationship in the Television Broadcasting Industry," *The American Economic Review*, 63 (June 1973) and Stewart Long, "Television Network Development: The Early Years," a paper delivered to the Business History Conference, February 1977, included in the 1977 *Proceedings*.

The relationship of the regulated industry to the antitrust laws has been the subject of many articles and symposia. Two of the best are a note, "Regulation of business—antitrust laws—effect upon a subsequent antitrust suit of FCC approval of an exchange of television stations," 57 Mich. L. Rev., 885 (April 1959). On May 28–29, 1968, an extremely fine symposium was held on antitrust and monopoly policies in the communications industry. It featured presentations by Frederick Rowe on monopoly policy; Kenneth Cox on competition between broadcasting, CATV, and pay TV; Donald Turner, the head of the Antitrust Division of the Department of Justice; and Charles Mahaffie on mergers and diversification in the newspaper and broadcasting industries. These and other papers have been reproduced in XIII *Antitrust Bulletin*, 861 (Fall 1968).

The WHDH case generated a great deal of controversy, see, for example, Louis Jeffe, "WHDH: The FCC and Broadcasting License Renewals," 82 Harv. L. R., 1693 (June 1969). In the next volume, he is answered in a note, "Spare the Golden Goose—The Aftermath of WHDH in FCC License Renewal Policy," 83 Harv. L. R., 1014 (March 1970).

The equal time question has involved politicians and lawyers since 1934. A very good synthesis and background is John Dean III, "Political Broadcasting: The Communications Act of 1934 Reviewed," XX Fed. Com. B.J. (1966). Also, see L. A. Erbst, "Equal Time for Candidates: Fairness or Frustration," 34 So. Calif. L. Rev., 190 (Winter 1961).

Especially in the case of electronic television recording, to keep up to date, one must read *Barron's, Business Week, Forbes, Fortune, Television, Television Digest* and the *Television Factbook*.

9. Commercial and Noncommercial Television in America and Europe

Elisabeth Joan Doyle
Department of History
St. John's University

If one were to ask the average American television viewer to define the difference between the kind of viewing he does at home and that which he might do in, for example, Great Britain, one would most often get a simplistic answer: "We have commercials and they don't." If pressed to account for this difference, a small percentage of American viewers would probably hazard the guess that a socialist government runs television in Britain.

Though these views are scarcely more misinformed than the ones some Britons hold about American television,[1] such simplism is a long way from accurately representing the situation; and it absolutely fails to take into account the different development of wireless communications not only in Britain and the United States but also in a number of other European countries which have still different systems. In every case, the nature of television broadcasting as it exists today in both the United States and in the countries of Europe is conditioned entirely by the arrangements and structure provided for radio broadcasting in the period between World Wars.

In Britain, wireless radio broadcasting was early judged to be just another form of communication, the supervision of which had always been a prerogative of the Crown. Thus telegraphy had been placed under the supervision of the Post Office in the nineteenth century; and radio, judged to be its wireless cousin, would be assigned to the same department (after first safeguarding the interests of the armed services) following World War I. The British Broadcasting Company (later the British Broadcasting Corporation or BBC) would start out as a joint stock company

operating under Post Office license; but would soon be altered to
become the public corporation, operating under a renewable
charter, which is now the best known (though no longer the exclusive) purveyor of radio and television broadcasting in the
United Kingdom.[2]

In the United States, the nature of the American Constitution
insured that a different approach would be used in the whole matter of the supervision of the air waves. The fact that the Constitution delineates certain clear areas of responsibility for the Federal
government and then specifies that any not so assigned remain the
jurisdiction of the states would make difficult such an assumption
of control by the Post Office. For, though the two departments at
that time had the same name in both Britain and the United States,
the American postal system has never been given control of any
form of communication other than the mails. Indeed, almost from
the beginning of the first experimental radio broadcasts prior to
World War I, such supervision as there was came from the newly
created Department of Commerce, for it was argued that, as airwaves crossed state boundaries, broadcasting was a matter of "interstate commerce."[3]

Even so, radio broadcasting might have come under much tighter
governmental controls in the United States had not its period of
significant development coincided with one during which the government was following a rather extreme "hands off" policy toward
all forms of business regulation. As had been true in Britain during
World War I, radio in the United States had been developed by
private technicians under contract to the Navy Department, which
would have liked to retain control over radio broadcasting in the
postwar period. The idea of government control of any aspect of
business in the immediate postwar years was, however, repugnant
to the new Republican administration of President Warren G.
Harding and his Secretary of Commerce, Herbert Hoover. In fact,
Secretary Hoover felt that the radio industry was best left to itself,
and he assumed that the private companies which quickly filled the
air waves would police themselves.

By the time he became President himself it was clear that this
would not be the case. Nevertheless, the American aversion to big
government insured that, even when a governmental agency to
clear up the chaos in the air was formed, it would not have the
authority of H. M. Post Office in Britain. Indeed, in the years since
its formation as the Federal Communications Committee, the Fede-

ral Communications Commission (or FCC) has performed a function more accurately described as "monitory," rather than "controlling." When it was realized that radio (and later television) would enjoy a very influential place in American society in the broadcasting of news, the industry quickly assumed the protective constitutional mantle of freedom of the press guaranteed by the First Amendment. This has made the entire broadcasting industry unusually sensitive to—and most reluctant to accept—any form of governmental control. Furthermore, the fact that the members of the FCC are executive appointees frequently means that the Commission reflects the political philosophy of the appointing President. They thus may be inclined to exercise greater or lesser restraint in carrying out their monitory functions.

When, after the end of World War II in 1945, the possibility of regular television broadcasting rapidly became a reality not only in America and Britain, but—within a decade—throughout Western Europe, patterns that had been established for radio broadcasting were simply extended to television. This meant that the nature and quality of programming would be dependent on the revenues available to its costs. Thus, in America, the same business groups, the radio networks, quickly expanded their activities to take in television as well, though with some differences.[4] In Britain the BBC, which had been planning for the event since 1938, was ready to move into video programming almost at once—limited only by postwar equipment shortages in the manufacture of enough receivers. And across the European continent the story would be the same. Everywhere television broadcasters were ready to begin transmitting visual programs just as soon as the manufacturers of television receivers could make and sell enough sets to create a viewing audience. And in every case, the structure of television broadcasting would be modeled on whatever already existed for financing and organizing radio broadcasting. Generally speaking, these structures were described as either "public" or "private," though neither adjective was entirely accurate for radio and is not so for television either.

Thus, before going further with a consideration of the background and present status of television broadcasting organizations in the United States and Europe, it would perhaps be wise to provide some definitions. What is meant by the terms "public" and "private" in talking about the interests that control broadcasting here and in Europe?

Perhaps the easiest way to answer is to isolate the source of operating revenues in each case, for it is this—rather than any legislative structure—that actually determines whether a system is publicly or privately controlled. In the United States where, with the exception of the Public Broadcasting Corporation, the networks finance their broadcasting activities through advertising fees from private enterprise corporations, the system is said to be privately controlled or "commercial." (The varying sources of revenue of the Public Broadcasting Corporation represent a unique case and will be discussed in a later segment of this paper.) In Great Britain (and most other European countries), revenues to support television broadcasting are derived for the most part from license fees on individual receivers and from taxes on the manufacturers of television equipment, though in both Britain and most of Western Europe some revenues from advertising also support broadcasting costs. Because of the ubiquitous tax on individual receivers and because government is involved to a greater or lesser degree with broadcast programming, the European arrangement is usually described as "public," though "quasi-public" might be more accurate in most cases. (In Scandinavia alone does one find television broadcasting systems totally supported through government-imposed tax revenues.) [5]

It would be difficult to overemphasize the significance of the source of revenue as a factor that not only controls the structure of the broadcasting system in each case but also imparts to each system its essential character. In the "privately supported" system of the United States one notes almost excessive responsiveness to the attitudes and wishes of the advertisers who sponsor the bulk of all programming. In Britain and most of Western Europe, on the other hand, the fact that taxes paid by viewers and manufacturers cover much of the cost of programming tends to make television in these nations more responsive, if not to the viewers directly, at least to the government that acts as their representative in overseeing broadcast activities. Programming in these countries is therefore more likely to be innovative and informative and less likely to present massive doses of western serials, police dramas, situation comedies, or whatever strikes American advertisers as the universal common denominator of a given viewing season. This being so, it is probably worthwhile to take a closer look at the organization and consequent programming of such leading examples of private and quasi-public television broadcasting systems as can be found in the United States, in Britain, and in several of the nations of Europe.

As has been suggested earlier, the common factors in the organization of American television broadcasting are the networks, which —despite a spate of suggestions made in recent years for reducing their influence—control the largest percentage of broadcast time; the advertisers who, because they are paying the cost of almost all programming, come very close to dictating its content; and, as the factor that provides the binding tension between them, the rating services, which chart the extent to which the networks reach the audience to whom the advertisers direct their message. Though no network may operate and own outright more than five VHF stations (each of the three major networks, NBC, CBS, and ABC, does own and operate the maximum number), "almost all commercial stations are affiliated to a network" and tend to get the bulk of their programming (up to 66 percent) from them.[6]

As of 1972, there were 701 commercial television stations in operation in the United States. Of these, CBS was serving 192 affiliates; NBC, 219; and ABC, 250. In other words, only 40 of the commercially owned and operated television stations were without some form of network affiliation.[7] Though the growth of commercially owned UHF stations was rapid between 1950 and 1962, growth has slowed since 1962 (when 549 UHF stations were on the air), and it is estimated that fewer than ten new stations per year will have been introduced after 1972 "because most communities currently have an adequate choice of stations and programs."[8] The networks, therefore, can be assumed to have reached their maximum growth at this time.

This multiplicity of broadcasting outlets was on the air for an average of 122 hours per week, in the case of commercially owned network affiliates in 1972, and most of these hours were paid for by advertisers who spent a total of $4,110 million in that year.[9] Though this accounted for only 17.8 percent of all advertising expenditures in the United States, it was unquestionably the most important of all the media in which advertising expenditures were made because of the sheer size of the television audience. Reaching into 96.4 percent of all American households, television—and the advertisers who support its operations—is currently recognized as the most powerful medium in this country.[10]

The largest single group of advertisers who tried to reach this market in 1972 were manufacturers of food and food products, who spent $690.5 million, or 16.8 percent of all television advertising expenditures. They were closely followed by manufacturers of toiletries and toilet goods ($567.2 million, or 13.8 percent of all expenditures). A leading television rating organization has estimated that their efforts reached 13.6 percent of all adults during prime time (7:30–10:30 P.M.) viewing hours at an average cost of $1.50 per viewer per minute.[11] The National Association of Broadcasters, an industry-regulating organization to which the networks belong, limits advertising to sixteen out of each sixty minutes of air time except in the prime time viewing period, when the maximum advertising time is ten minutes.[12]

When one computes the size of the expenditures implied by these figures (one television writer sets the total spent on advertising at $4.85 billion per year), it is not difficult to understand the concern of advertisers that their messages accompany the type of programming most likely to reach the highest percentage of the viewing audience—nor the networks' anxiety that they do. Indeed, the advertisers in American television are inextricably concerned with almost *all* programming.[13]

The normal pattern here is for independent production companies to create and mount a program idea, which is then presented for network and advertiser approval. In almost every case the network, acting in the name of the advertisers (or sponsors) maintains a close, though sometimes quixotic, control over every aspect of commercial programming. Needless to say, because the ultimate goal is to reach as many viewers as possible while offending the least number of them in the process, the end result is often a dreary sameness that afflicts most of the programming offered by the three major networks.[14]

To the sometime dismay of American television viewers and creators, decisions about this type of programming are made completely free of outside controls or review. The Federal Communications Commission does exist, of course; but its role, by law, is a limited one.[15] Though its existence is based on the idea that "broadcast frequencies are public properties controlled by the federal government," which can therefore license private individuals and institutions to use them in the public interest, the Commission nevertheless "has no power of censorship," and it is "not permitted to promulgate regulations which interfere with the right of free speech."[16]

Such regulatory power as it has is exercised through its licensing functions. Because licenses are issued for one-year periods, renewable upon application, the Commission can exert some regulatory power over the activities of broadcasters who fail to satisfy their viewing audiences.[17] Other areas in which the Commission has exercised timid intervention in the past decade would include its adoption of the so-called "McGannon Rule," its ban on cigarette advertising, and its establishment of the "family viewing hour" rule.[18]

Aside from these rather mild restrictions, the Federal Communications Commission cannot be said to exercise very stringent controls over the television broadcasting industry. It tends to react more than to initiate, despite the efforts of various interest groups —political, religious, racial—to use it as a means of controlling or changing television programming. Indeed, under the chairmanship of Commissioner Richard E. Wiley (whose term expired on June 30, 1977), the Commission has seemed singularly unresponsive to consumer activists. One commentator has observed, in fact, that "the Wiley commission is noted for measuring social progress in inches rather than in giant steps."[19]

Nor do the manufacturers of television equipment have a particularly loud voice in the operation of television stations in the United States. Here, too, the FCC rule limiting station ownership to five per owner has kept such equipment manufacturers as the Radio Corporation of America (so significant in the development of radio), the Columbia Broadcasting System, or Westinghouse, to a role much smaller than that played by similar firms in other countries. Both RCA (which owns five of the NBC stations) and CBS manufacture television and other electronic equipment; but these operations are not nearly as profitable as broadcasting—to the point where, at times, revenues from broadcasting are used "to offset losses in other company divisions. . . ."[20]

No discussion of American television would be complete, of course, without reference to the Public Broadcasting Service and the Corporation for Public Broadcasting. PBS is often thought of as "America's BBC" because, though it allows the "sponsorship" of its programs through grants from commercial firms, it bans advertising of the type seen on commercial stations. The Corporation for Public Broadcasting, which grew out of a study made by the Carnegie Commission in the 1960s, owes its legislative existence to the Commission report and the resulting Public Broadcasting Act of 1967. The purpose of the Corporation was "to distribute Federally appropriated funds to the [Public Broadcasting] system and also to provide it with spiritual leadership and insulation from possible attempts at government intrusion."[21]

The Public Broadcasting Service was formed in 1970 by the Corporation "to operate the national interconnection of stations, serving in effect as the network." The relationship of the Corporation to PBS changed during the later years of the Nixon presidency when, "in the view of many stations—including New York's Channel 13—the corporation failed its test as a 'heat shield' against government interference." As a result, by 1973 "the 260 affiliated stations in public television made PBS their representative organization; thus it became a trade association and congress of stations." Because the rights of the stations (who are the licensees and directly responsible to the public) take precedence over those of the Corporation, as the representative of the individual stations PBS was able to force the Corporation into a form of "partnership" in 1973. But it has been an uneasy partnership from the start, and by the fall of 1976 the two units were squabbling openly.[22]

The idea of a noncommercial network of television stations was being discussed from the earliest days of American television broadcasting. In 1952, in order to counter the complaint that the choice of television programming was being made without reference to popular wish, the FCC reserved 242 (later 632) television channels for the establishment of noncommercial, educational television stations. Of these, 116 would be VHF channels and 516 UHF. By 1974, 220 of these stations were in operation in 47 of the 50 states.[23]

In assigning these channels the Federal Communications Commission certainly did not evidence undue concern about noncommercial television, however, and—generally speaking—"educational television got what was left—if any. It received no VHF reservation in 69 of the top 100 markets," including New York, Philadelphia, Detroit, Cleveland, and Washington, D.C. In order to get a "VHF voice in the vital New York market," supporters of educational television in 1961 "finally had to buy a commercial station at a price of more than $6 million. . . ."[24]

Because the nature of programming and the desire to provide an alternative for viewers unwilling to settle for the networks' offerings were the major inspiration for the creation of the Public Broadcasting Service, one must ask the question, "Where does it get its broadcast materials?" The answer to that question varies from station to station in the noncommercial network, depending to some extent on the nature of the viewing audience being served and the length of the broadcast day.

In the relatively sophisticated metropolitan New York viewing area, Station WNET originates some of its own program materials as well as carrying most of the thirteen and one-half hours of PBS network programs. These include a number of programs produced outside the United States—more, certainly, than are carried on commercial television. Yet, because language would pose a problem for most American viewers, the bulk of these foreign-produced programs originate in Britain.[25]

Has the Public Broadcasting Service broken the mold of sit-com, drama, and film offered American viewers by the commercial networks? An analysis of the broadcast program of WNET would suggest that it has. In a single week in the fall of 1976, for example, WNET's prime-time schedule showed that 37.3 percent of its 126 hours per week of broadcasting was devoted to children's shows; and the next largest segments of time were allotted to informational programming (10.7 percent); films (10.5 percent); and musical performances (8 percent).[26] Not all PBS stations would try to match the schedule of WNET; but, thanks to grants from the Corporation for Public Broadcasting, most of them can come very close to it. The results, so far as alternative programming is concerned, may not make the PBS the "BBC in America"; but in some respects it may be better.

Certainly, the existence of the Independent Broadcasting Authority in Britain suggests that not all Britons find the commercial-free offerings of the British Broadcasting Corporation irresistible. It would be a mistake, however, for any American to assume that the relationship between BBC and IBA in any way approximates that existing between America's PBS and the commercial networks.

To begin with, despite its name, the IBA is *not* an independent commercial network in the sense that NBC, CBS, or ABC are in the United States. In addition, the advertisers who use its channels to tout their products have absolutely no control over programming. And, finally, as the purveyor of alternative programming for British viewers, commercial television has yet to live up to the promises of its original promoters. But here some background would be useful.

When World War II ended in 1945, British broadcasting interests, like those in the United States, were anxious to go forward with plans for television broadcasting on a national scale; and, as was the case in America, they found it most convenient to use the organizational structure and revenue-producing means that had already served so well for radio broadcasting. This would mean the British Broadcasting Corporation would be financed by license fees on receivers (radio as well as television) and taxes on manufacturers of electronic equipment.

In 1952 the BBC's Charter of Incorporation was up for its regular five-year renewal. The charter *was* renewed—but, 1952 being a year of political change in Britain, with a difference. The new Conservative government of Prime Minister Winston Churchill described the BBC's television broadcasting license as "nonexclusive," suggesting that the government did not envision a television broadcasting monopoly to match the BBC's monopoly of radio broadcasting. Indeed, a few months after the charter renewal, the Assistant Postmaster General announced that twenty-four "enquiries" had been received about the possibility of establishing commercial television stations.[27]

The announcement was not received with much joy by some BBC veterans, who objected that the admission of commercial television to British air waves would subject British viewers to the same low quality programming that American viewers had to watch. The Postmaster General and the Lord Chancellor responded that the comparison was inaccurate inasmuch as British viewers who objected to the commercially sponsored programs would always have the regular commercial-free programs of the BBC as an alternative.

Despite the objections of Lord Reith, a former BBC director-general, that the introduction of commercial television would mean the application of a sort of Gresham's law of television to British programming, the Independent Broadcasting Authority was created in 1954 to provide one commercial television channel in Britain. In addition, in 1964 a second BBC channel began broadcasting, giving British viewers a choice of two noncommercial and one commercial channel. A fourth television channel and cable television also have been considered in the last three years, but no basic change in the general structure of British broadcasting is contemplated.[28]

Programming on the BBC is divided between news and "News Magazines" (10 percent); documentaries and current affairs (7 percent); religious programs (3 percent); adult education (4 percent); school programs (7 percent); children's programs (10 percent); plays, dramas, and serials (20 percent); feature films (13 percent); entertainment and music (13 percent); sports (12 percent); and other outside broadcasts (1 percent).[29]

The Independent Broadcast Authority supervises fifteen independent television companies, organized on a regional basis, "with two for London, one for weekdays and the other for week-ends, which produce programs" and transmit them over Authority transmitters. Programming for the member stations of the IBA is divided among plays, drama, and serials (20 percent); news, documentaries, features, and outside broadcasts (18 percent); education and school programs (10 percent); entertainment and music (14 percent); and religious programs (3 percent).

Advertising on the IBA stations is limited to six minutes per hour of spot advertising, averaged over the day's programs with a maximum of seven minutes in any one hour. Advertisers are restricted to buying segments of five, seven, fifteen, thirty, and sixty seconds in length and are allowed no voice in program production or content.[30]

Commercial television in Great Britain has not been rated an unqualified success by at least one advertising agency, which termed its programming in the summer of 1976 "boring," and charged it attracted only 51 percent of the viewing audience. One significant set of results of this situation, the agency pointed out, was falling audience figures and rising advertising costs—factors which will unquestionably affect the government's decision on the projected assignment of a fourth television channel.[31]

The three present television channels reach into 93 percent of all British households, 90 percent of which are equipped to receive commercial broadcasts. On them viewers can receive 82 hours of programming on BBC 1; 42 hours—mostly in the evening—on BBC 2; and approximately 100 hours per week on IBA stations.[32]

Both the BBC and the IBA are members of Eurovision (or the European Broadcasting Union), which enables them to exchange programs with other countries via satellite links.[33] Thus, in the summer of 1976, BBC experienced a surge of viewership during the satellite broadcasts of the Olympic Games from Montreal.

The Olympic Games were equally popular television fare across the English Channel, where French viewers watched them—often in cafés or department store windows—on one of the three channels of Radio France, the official French broadcasting organization. As was the case with the United States and Britain, the roots of French television broadcasting lie in the radio broadcasting begun there in the 1920s. The first official experimental television broadcasts were begun in 1932; but, as was true of Britian, World War II halted all television transmissions.

With the liberation in 1944, experimental broadcasting resumed; but the pioneers in French television early recognized a problem in these transmissions that might be peculiar to France: the line-definition of the picture being transmitted. Prewar experiments had been broadcast with a 455-line definition, but postwar critics pointed out that this level would be unsuitable for projection sets of a medium-to-large size to be used for community viewing. If television was not to become a divisive factor between the well-off, who could afford the high price of receivers, and the working classes, who could not, community viewing was essential. Aesthetically and technically, too, the French television pioneers wanted a finer picture definition than was available on either American (525-line) or British (625-line) equipment. Hence they opted in 1949 for a definition of 819 lines—a decision which protected French manufacturers of television equipment from foreign competition at the same time that it provided French viewers with a picture of photographic quality.[34]

Since 1950, when the new 819-line transmitter was installed at the top of the Eiffel Tower in Paris, French television broadcasting has grown rapidly. Starting with 20 hours of programming per week on a single channel, reaching 60,000 receivers in 1950, television broadcasting in France has increased to an average of 108 broadcast hours per week on Channels 1 and 2, and 27 hours per week on Channel 3, reaching 63 percent of all French households.[35]

When French television broadcasting was begun, it, like the BBC, was financed out of the general budget of what was then known as the Office of French Radio and Television (ORTF), which was made up from license fees and taxes on the manufacture of radio broadcasting equipment. No advertising was permitted on these early broadcasts.[36]

Starting in 1969, Regie Française de Publicité, a government department, was set up to supervise the introduction of commercial television on Channels 1 and 2. The amount of money which RFP may invest in television advertising is set annually by the French government, and all television and advertising costs "are regulated by the RFP after consultation with advertisers and agencies. The maximum daily commercial time allocated by station is 16 minutes on Channel 1 and 12 minutes on Channel 2." Individual advertisers are severely limited in the amount of advertising time allotted to each annually. As a result, advertising time is much sought after, and orders must be placed a year in advance. At that time, too, would-be advertisers are expected to pay 5 percent of the estimated transmission costs; an additional 15 percent must be paid before the program airs.[37]

In the early fifties, television programming costs ran between $543,000 per annum (1952) and $1 million (1953). By 1972, the total amounts which the government allowed to be invested in advertising had reached $130 million, suggesting rapidly rising programming costs.[38]

From the beginning, both the financing and the programming of French television has been debated in the French Parliament, which approves the annual budget. In 1976, in preparation for the annual debate scheduled to begin in the fall, the Council of Ministers—in discussions that became front-page news and that provoked a spate of letters to newspapers—criticized existing programming and proposed certain changes, among them the augmentation of French-produced programming.[39]

Not too surprisingly, this close government supervision of television broadcasting has meant that Radio France has more than once been involved in controversies in which art, advertising, and politics have become inextricably entangled. In the anti-Gaullist risings of 1968 and again in 1974–1975, Radio France personnel were involved in protests over both programming and administration. The effort made in January, 1975, to improve programming by separating television broadcasting from the radio operations of the system was bitterly criticized by a former director of the ORTF. Another writer, R. Barjavel, declared that "the only workable reform would be to relieve the P[residing]-D(irector) G(eneral]s of *all* their administrative responsibilities in order to give them the leisure to read, seek, detect, and choose new talent and to hire them. What the head of an entertainment enterprise must be is a man of taste, flair, and decision, who has authority and time."[40]

As a result of the action of the Council of Ministers, the subsequent reshuffling of the French Cabinet in August, and this close association between the government and television, it is rather difficult to predict the future course of television broadcasting in France. At the moment, of the three existing channels, Channels

2 and 3, using a 625-line definition, transmit in color, using the French-developed SECAM color system; and advertising is accepted on Channels 1 and 2. Channel 3, known as "France Régions," began broadcasting in 1973 and presents rather limited programming between 7 and 9:45 P.M. Program topics lean heavily toward dramatic presentations and such outside features as Alistair Cooke's "America."[41]

Channels 1 and 2, both of which begin transmitting in the early afternoon (Channel 1 at 12:30; Channel 2 at 2 P.M.), also rely rather heavily on dramatic features. A recent breakdown of programming showed that 28.52 percent of the programs on Channel 1 were devoted to original dramas, serials, theater, shows, and plays and entertainment. On Channel 2, the figure was 18.2 percent, plus an additional 14.51 percent for films.[42]

A different approach to television organization and programming is to be found in the Netherlands, where the household penetration is not even equaled by any other nation in the world. It has been estimated that 98.2 percent of the 13.5 million Dutch watch the programs presented by its uniquely structured television organization. "Television broadcasting in the Netherlands is composite in character: the Post Office owns and operates the transmitter, n.v. Phillips Gloeilampenfabrieken furnishes the technical equipment, and five private organizations, representing different cultural and political groups in the Netherlands, are in charge of programming." The five groups are joined together under the umbrella title of Nederlandse Omroep Stichting (NOTS) "which is in charge of all broadcasting."[43]

When television broadcasting was still in the planning stages in the Netherlands, neither government nor license funds were available to finance it. The five (now seven) groups therefore decided to finance television broadcasting out of their own funds (which, for the most part, represented contributions of their memberships). These groups or associations must have a license-holding membership of at least 100,000 radio and television listener-viewers, and 60 percent of the total broadcasting time is allocated according to the size of the group's membership. (The remaining 40 percent is allocated to the joint NOS program.) Smaller groups, with at least 15,000 license-holders, are allowed a certain amount of time with a view to raising their membership to the required 100,000 level.[44]

Though it was not contemplated originally, the Netherlands' two television channels each accept commercial advertising during the 63 broadcast hours per week; but the positioning and number of commercials is strictly regulated by act of Parliament. These commercial breaks appear during broadcast hours on six (Sunday is excluded) days of the week on both channels at the same time— before and after the news bulletins. Daily transmission hours are from 6:45 to 11:30 P.M., and viewers can expect to see eight commercial breaks in each evening's programming.[45]

As is true of other European nations with limited commercial television, advertising time in the Netherlands is in great demand and must be booked in August of the year preceding the date on which the commercials are to be broadcast. "There are only 48 breaks per week, and competitive commercials are never put in the same break. Therefore, the higher the number of competitors, the lower the frequency will be," reports one American advertising agency. Dutch television imposes restrictions on advertising directed to children, on contests, on mail order advertising, on medicinal commercials, and on alcoholic beverages. Advertising of tobacco products is forbidden altogether.[46]

The breakdown of programming in The Netherlands is one of the most interesting in Europe, for it reflects the lowest number of hours devoted to sports broadcasting (7 percent). Information (news, religion, travel) programs, on the other hand, comprise 40 percent of all programming, with drama—in the form of films and serials—running second (25 percent). Other programming topics include culture (art and classical music), 4 percent; entertainment (light music and comedies), 15 percent; and youth programs for children and teen-agers (4 percent). Educational television programs outside evening viewing hours are provided for primary and secondary schools through the Netherlands School Television Association in collaboration with NOS; and for post-school youth and adult groups by the Television Academy.[47]

As a member of Eurovision, NOS has originated a number of programs, as well as receiving others through the Eurovision network. Both channels broadcast in color, using the 625-line definition.

East of the Netherlands, the German Federal Republic (or West Germany) also operates a television system with an organization roughly representative of various sections and groups in the population. The history of television transmission in West Germany (as well as in East Germany and in Berlin) goes back to experiments begun in 1926—experiments which, within a decade, had achieved sufficient success that it was possible to televise the 1936 Olympic Games live every day. These early transmissions were projected on large screens in television rooms where visitors watched. By 1939, six German cities were linked in a loose network. Picture quality also improved as the definition rose from 180 to 441 lines.[48]

The outbreak of World War II not only prevented the mass production of early television receivers but interfered with the advance of programming—though the service was used to entertain wounded soldiers in German military hospitals until 1945. There was only a brief break in programming between the end of the war and the first meeting of television engineers in 1948. By 1951, television programs using a 625-line definition were again being broadcast for several hours per week from both Hamburg and Berlin. Regular broadcast service in West Germany began on Christmas Day, 1952.

Considerable controversy whirled around the structure of West German television in the early part of the 1950s because of competition between the various radio organizations (such as Nordwestdeutscher Rundfunk, which had initiated the 1948 engineers' meeting) and the Federal Government which, through the Post Office, was also involved in television broadcasting. Ultimately a permanent program committee, made up of representatives of each of the radio organizations (which in *their* turn each represented a geographic and political area in West Germany) agreed to contribute proportionately to the financing of a national German program.

This early attempt at cooperation was further cemented with the 1963 formation of the ARD (consisting at that time of seven regional stations) and Zweites Deutsches Fernsehen (ZDF), the single national station which was established jointly in 1961 by all the *Lander* (the German equivalent of state governments) and financed out of their license fees and advertising revenues. ARD broadcasting consists of a weekday afternoon program, an evening program, and a weekend program, transmitted on equipment of the nine *Land* organizations over the circuits of the Federal Post Office. Early set-owners showed reluctance to pay license fees on their sets (especially if their proximity to a transmitter eliminated need for an outside aerial), so that, in 1955, only 84,278 receivers were registered, while it was estimated that another 80,000 also were receiving programs. More recent figures show that 91 percent of all West German households own the estimated 18,063,882 sets operating in the country.[48]

Television broadcasting in West Germany is financed out of license fees (now more successfully collected) and advertising, which is permitted in the form of four five-minute blocks per evening on both the ARD and the ZDF networks. These four advertising blocks at different times on the two networks appear between the hours of 6:25 and 7:40 P.M. No commercials at all are permitted on Sundays and holidays.[49]

As is true in France and the Netherlands, demand for advertising time far outruns (by two and a half times) the supply; as a result, individual advertisers are normally limited to two spots per week. Time must be reserved by August 31 of the preceding year, and all commercials are previewed. They can be rejected for religious, moral, or medical reasons. No tobacco advertising is permitted.

The typical early evening program on both ARD and ZDF includes (in addition to the four advertising blocks) news (25 minutes) ; a film series (20 minutes) ; a children's program (5 minutes on ARD and 30 minutes on ZDF) ; another film series on ARD (25 minutes) ; and 20 minutes of regional news.[50]

Since 1964 third programs have also been broadcast by the *Land* organizations (separately or jointly) for about three hours in the evening and in morning programs for schools and high schools. Evening programs also include educational programs, such as the successful TV vocational high school "Telekolleg," which began in 1967. In the evening hours on all three channels, at least one foreign program (and often more) is carried. American series such as "Columbo," "Kojak," "Owen Marshall," or "Rio Grande" have been popular in recent years. British-produced series, such as the "Barbapapa" children's cartoon show, and several French dramatic productions were noted during one week in July, 1976.[51]

In only one section of Western Europe can television truly be said to be controlled and financed almost solely by public representatives using public funds—the nations of Scandinavia. Though the state television broadcasting systems of Denmark, Norway, and Sweden differ in such details as the number of broadcast hours per week and in the number of locally produced programs, they are otherwise similar. All derive the revenues to cover broadcasting costs from license fees on radio as well as television receivers, and only one—Norway—carries any advertising at all. As is true of the other continental nations already discussed, broadcasting in Scandinavia was built on existing radio broadcasting organizations.

Sweden, where 94 percent of all households have television receivers, experiences the greatest amount of broadcast saturation of the three countries and, indeed, beams its broadcasts to parts of the rest of Scandinavia as well as to its own viewers. The two Swedish channels provide a total of about 100 hours of programming per week, of which 66 percent is carried by Channel 1, which goes on the air each weekday at 9 A.M for twenty-five minutes of children's programming and then does not resume broadcasting until 6:40 in the evening. Broadcasting continues until 1 A.M. daily.[52]

Sweden produces a larger percentage of the program materials seen there than do the other countries of Scandinavia; but production costs are high there, too, despite the expertise and cooperation of the well-developed Swedish film industry, and about 39 percent of all program materials are imported—chiefly in the form of films from Western Europe or of programs from other Scandinavian countries. A visitor in the summer of 1976 found, however, that the American-produced program "The Virginian" was a popular choice for adult viewing in the period beginning at 9:35 P.M.[53]

In neighboring Denmark, where television broadcasting has been provided since 1954 by Danmarks Radio, the number of broadcast hours is limited to 38 per week. Here, too, the operating cost is paid through the imposition of license fees on individual receivers. Though the fees are said to be the highest in Europe, they are insufficient to support much in the way of locally produced programs. For some Danish viewers the rather short broadcast day is less of a deprivation than it seems, for viewers in Copenhagen and North Zealand can also receive both Swedish channels; viewers living on southern Fyn can get both West German channels 1 and 2; and viewers on such islands as Moen, Lolland, and Falster can receive East German Channels 1 and 2 as well. Of these, however, only West Germany provides a full day's programming, starting at 10 A.M. each weekday.[54]

The thirty-eight hours of programming presented by Danmarks Radio reaches into 83 percent of Danish homes and includes fourteen hours of news, public affairs, sports, and so on; nine hours of cultural and scientific programs; six hours of broadcasts for special audiences; four hours of light entertainment; and about two hours each of programs for ethnic minorities and of an educational nature. A good many programs are imported from other countries, and there is also a program exchange with the other nations of Scandinavia. In Denmark, too, American television programs are very popular, and "Columbo" was rated among the top ten programs shown during the week of 12–18 July 1976—scoring one place above the popular Olympic games. Other United States-produced offerings included "Kojak," "Gibbsville" (which had not yet aired on American television at the time), and "Diana," plus the 1935 Fred MacMurray-Carole Lombard film *Hands Across the Table.*[55]

Finally, in Norway, a single channel operated by Norsk Rikskringkasting reaches 94 percent of the Norwegian population during its forty-five hours of broadcasting per week. Of this, 57 percent is produced in Norway, and the balance is provided by Eurovision, Nordvision, and Intervision in the form of films and other foreign-produced programs. Norway differs from the other nations of Scandinavia in that Norwegian television carries one hour of commercial advertising per week. Main program categories include news and information (12 hours); light entertainment (11 hours); cultural programs and films (7 hours); educational broadcasts (4 hours); and broadcasts for special audiences (3 hours).[56]

To summarize, then, we have seen that the amount and method of producing revenues to cover the costs of television programming has a great deal of influence on the type of programming offered wherever television is seen. Methods are more or less limited either to license fees and taxes on equipment manufacturers (in the case of the American Public Broadcasting Service to public and private grants and viewer donations); to monies realized from commercial advertising; or to a combination of the two. The organizations themselves exhibit far more diversity, of course, running the gamut from the purely public financing of Sweden and Denmark, through the unusual regional or interest-group controls found in West Germany and the Netherlands, and the feet-in-both-camps approaches of Britain and France, to the unabashed (though much decried) commercialism of American television. After admitting that these differences exist, one final question remains: Which is best—at least from the viewers' point of view? Here the answer would have to depend on so many other variables that a clear-cut decision would be impossible. Indeed, one cannot even turn the question around and ask, Which is worst?

American television exports so much—too often of inferior

quality—that an American traveler can usually find something familiar (complete with the original English sound track) wherever he or she may go in Western Europe. Sometimes the local offerings are so poor that even "Kojak" and "Columbo" come off as Art. On the other hand, every one of the state-run services occasionally presents program material of such beauty and sensitivity as to make the peripatetic American viewer cry with envy.

Though the answer might seem to lie in the amount of creative freedom granted to television production people unshadowed by networks or ratings organizations, even creativity can lead to the presentation of some pretty rum stuff from time to time. All the systems strive to present a percentage of entertainment programming for their viewers; but precisely what constitutes entertainment varies widely from country to country. A pair of comics with a broad Lancashire brogue may roll viewers out of their chairs in Britain—and be totally unintelligible in Paoli, Indiana. And a program consisting of a concert of baroque music presented over New York's WNET may get rave notices from viewers and critics there and be rated as one of the "five worst" programs in Denmark.

Americans regularly complain of programming dominated by advertisers and networks which seem to be aiming their efforts at the ratings services' ideal 18- to 49-year-old moron. But in Britain, Parliamentary commissions regularly chide both BBC and IBA (the latter more often) for almost the same thing; and the French are currently going through another of their efforts to improve (and Gallicize) their programming.

No one seems to be very happy with the medium; but neither can anyone say that the answer to the problem lies in the structure or the means of financing it. One can only conclude that there are different approaches to running this most powerful of media—and none of them presently satisfies everyone.

Notes

1. See, for example, Anthony Sampson, *Anatomy of Britain Today* (New York, 1965), p. 666. Sampson speaks of the "frenzied hucksterism of American TV," which, he says, "rose out of an established jungle of commercial radio, salesmen's attitudes, publicity machines, and a vast film business...." See also Timothy Green, *The Universal Eye* (New York, 1972), p. 31.
2. UNESCO, *Television: A World Survey* (Paris, 1963), pp. 23, 162–63.
3. For this material and that on the following page, see Sidney W. Head, *Broadcasting in America* (New York, 1972), p. 139 and Chapters 8 and 9 passim; and Walter B. Emery, *Broadcasting and Government: Responsibilities and Regulations* (East Lansing, 1961).
4. Head, *Broadcasting in America*, p. 153. Head sees a difference in the postwar societies that produced the two electronic media, however, and predicts that the "broadcast commercialism" of the period dominated by radio would "eventually seem ... archaic...."
5. UNESCO, *Television: A World Survey* (Paris, 1953), pp. 11, 16–21.
6. UNESCO, *World Communications: A 200-country survey of press, radio, and television* (London and Paris, 1975), p. 204; Green, *Universal Eye*, p. 29.
7. UNESCO, *World Communications*, p. 204.
8. Ibid.; J. Walter Thompson Company, "Television in the U.S.A. and Europe" ([New York,] 1973), U.S.A. p. 5. (This privately circulated booklet was prepared for the information of employees of the Thompson agency and loaned to the author. It is organized by sections, each dealing with television in a particular country.)
9. UNESCO, *World Communications*, p. 204; Thompson, "Television," USA p. 9.
10. Thompson, "Television," USA p. 1.
11. Nielsen Company (rating service) figures, quoted in Thompson, "Television," USA p. 8. Figures for viewing hours vary; but ratings apply principally to prime-time viewing.
12. Thompson, "Television," USA p. 4.
13. In a few instances the networks themselves own—or have a financial interest in—programs; but the United States Department of Justice has recently sought consent decrees from them that would separate broadcasting and program ownership functions. See *New York Times*, 18 November 1976; also interview with TV writer Danny Arnold on "You Should See What You're Missing," produced by Station WTTW of Chicago and carried by New York Station WNET on 26 November 1976. The theme of this program underlined the fact of extensive

205

network control over program content and types of programming.

14. In 1973 this led to major network emphasis on dramas (32 percent), films (16 percent), and situation comedies (19 percent) in prime-time scheduling. Thompson, "Television," USA p. 3. The picture for 1976 would probably show some changes in emphasis.

15. The applicable law is the Communications Act of 1934, amended to cover television in 1952. See Head, *Broadcasting in America*, pp. 361–65, and WTTW, "You Should See What You're Missing."

16. UNESCO, *World Communications*, pp. 60–61.

17. A fairly recent example of the threatened use of this regulatory power has come with the objections of New Jersey viewers to the saturation of their state's air waves by programs created by the New York-based stations of the three big networks. Led by their Governor Brendan Byrne, New Jerseyites unsuccessfully challenged the license renewals of several New York stations. See *New York Times*, 7 December 1976. Also see UNESCO, *World Communications*, pp. 60–61.

18. This limitation is referred to in the industry as the "McGannon rule," after Donald H. McGannon, president of the independent Group W Network, who persuaded friendly Nixon appointees on the Commission to cut network prime-time programming from three and one-half hours to three. Green, *Universal Eye*, pp. 22–23. Two other areas where the FCC has stepped in has been in banning all cigarette advertising and in a ruling, overturned in the courts in late 1976, which restricted programs featuring violence or "adult themes" to the later portion of the prime-time viewing period, reserving the earlier hours for so-called family viewing. Thompson, "Television," USA p. 5; *New York Times*, 21 and 23 November 1976.

19. *World Almanac* (New York, 1975), pp. 97, 777; *New York Times*, 7 December 1976.

20. *New York Times*, 26 September 1976,

21. Ibid., 2 December 1976.

22. Ibid. See also reports of the settlement of the quarrel. Ibid., 9 December 1976.

23. See Emery, *Broadcasting and Government*, pp. 115, 118–19, 120–21; Head, *Broadcasting in America*, pp. 183, 211, 214–15.

24. Head, *Broadcasting in America*, p. 211. The unique origins of New York's Channel 13—Station WNET—provided it with a welcome protection during the election campaign of 1976, however, when Republican incumbent Senator James Buckley attempted to compel the educational television stations in New York State to carry his political advertising on pain of losing their licenses under application of a little-known FCC rule. Because WNET had originally been a commercial station it had the right to charge a fee for any commercials it might run—and announced it would bill Senator Buckley $1,000 per five-minute spot. Unfavorable publicity given his move caused Senator Buckley to withdraw his threat a day later. *New York Times*, 7, 8, 9, 20, 28 October 1976. He lost the election by a wide margin. See also Jack Gould, "Television," in *New York Times Encyclope-*

dia (New York, 1970), p. 640. Gould, describing noncommercial television as a going concern at the opening of the 1970s, called it "a cultural force that would have seemed like a fool's dream only a decade ago."

25. See television program schedules in *New York Times*, 21–28 November 1976.
26. Ibid.
27. Burton Paulu, *British Broadcasting in Transition* (Minneapolis, 1961), pp. 35, 37; UNESCO, *Television* (1953), p. 162.
28. Paulu, *British Broadcasting, pp. 36–37; Thompson*, "Television," UK p. 1; Sampson, *Anatomy of Britain*, p. 665.
29. See, for example, *London Times*, week of 2 September 1976.
30. Thompson, "Television," UK p. 3.
31. Ibid.; *London Times*, 12 August 1976.
32. *London Times*, week of 2 September 1976.
33. Anthony Sampson, *Anatomy of Europe* (New York and Evanston, 1968), pp. 303–4.
34. UNESCO, *Television* (1953), p. 121.
35. Thompson, "Television," France p. 1.
36. UNESCO, *Television* (1953), p. 122.
37. Thompson, "Television," France pp. 4–5.
38. UNESCO, *Television* (1953), p. 122; Thompson, "Television," France p. 4.
39. See, for example, *Le Monde, Figaro*, et al., 23 July 1976. French sources contacted in New York in November, 1976, could think of no reforms that had been made as of that date.
40. *Journal de Dimanche* (Paris), 25 July 1976.
41. UNESCO, *World Communications*, p. 386. For a fascinating discussion of the politicizing of color television systems, see *The Economist*, 14 August 1976, p. 78, which observed, "The choice of a t.v. system has been decided more often by political and commercial considerations than by technical ones. France's pro-Arab attitude and Israel's choice of [the German system] PAL, helped SECAM in the Middle East, while PAL cashed in on Algeria's differences with France."
42. See for example, *Figaro* and *Le Monde* for the week of 24–31 July 1976; Thompson, "Television," France p. 1.
43. UNESCO, *Television: A World Survey* (Paris, 1954), p. 147; and UNESCO, *World Communications*, p. 425.
44. UNESCO, *World Communications*, p. 425.
45. Thompson, "Television," Netherlands p. 1.
46. Ibid., p. 3.
47. UNESCO, *World Communications*, p. 425; Thompson, "Television," Netherlands p. 2.
48. UNESCO, *Television* (1954), p. 131.
49. UNESCO, *World Communications*, p. 397; Thompson, "Television," West Germany p. 3.
50. Thompson, "Television," West Germany p. 2.
51. Copenhagen *TV Bladet*, 23–29 July 1976.

52. Ibid. (*TV Bladet* carries both Swedish and German program lists but only a small area of Denmark actually receives the broadcasts.) UNESCO, *World Communications*, p. 448.
53. UNESCO, *World Communications*, p. 448; *TV Bladet*, 24 July 1976.
54. Green, *Universal Eye*, pp. 143–44; *TV Bladet*, 23–29 July 1976.
55. UNESCO, *World Communications*, p. 376; *TV Bladet*, 23–29 July 1976, p. 4 and passim.
56. UNESCO, *World Communications*, pp. 427–28.

Bibliography

Because television in Europe, as in the United States, is such a mercurial medium, the only really current information to be found on it is in the television sections of daily newspapers—notwithstanding the fact that books by the hundreds have been written on the subject. Though many of these bound volumes are both thorough and thoughtful, for the most part they demonstrate the superiority of the electronic medium in rapidity of response. Most are out of date before they are published.

For the best historical perspective on the organization and operation of television throughout the world, however, UNESCO's series of studies, published under the title *Television: A World Survey* and *World Communications*, provides the best continuous source of information. The earliest volume, which traces the history of electronic communication facilities throughout the world up to 1952, is more complete and detailed than the later volumes; but all are unique and extremely useful.

Also useful, informative, and broad in scope—though it was published in 1972 and is therefore not as current—is Timothy Green's *The Universal Eye*, a breezy survey of television operations in the United States and most of Western Europe. Some of the information therein appears in another multination survey, cited in this essay as J. Walter Thompson, "Television in the U.S.A. and Europe." This is an in-house publication for the use of the staff of the giant American advertising agency. Because of the nature of its origin, it tends to give greater emphasis to nations whose television broadcasting systems accept advertising. Also, because it is based on data available in 1973, it does not provide current information.

Other bound sources, which were published earlier and which contain extensive, but often out-of-date, information, would include Walter B. Emery, *Broadcasting and Government Responsibilities and Regulations* (East Lansing, Michigan, 1961); Sydney W. Head, *Broadcasting in America* (New York, 1972); two volumes by Burton Paulu, *British Broadcasting in Transition* (Minneapolis, 1961) and *Radio and Television Broadcasting on the European Continent* (Minneapolis, 1967). Wilbur Schramm and Janet Alexander contributed a lengthy and informative essay on "Broadcasting," in Ithiel de Sola Pool and Wilbur Schramm, editors, *Handbook of Communication* (Chicago, 1973), pp. 517–618.

The British journalist Anthony Sampson includes chapters on television in both his *Anatomy of Britain* (New York, 1964) and *Anatomy of Europe* (New York, 1968). In both cases, the chief importance of his contribution is his respectful assessment of the power and influence of television, both in Britain and in Europe. Alfred Havighurst, in *Twen-

tieth Century Britain (New York, 1962), also includes a chapter on television in Great Britain. The major work on one of televisions great pioneers, the British Broadcasting Corporation, is, however, still being written by Asa Briggs. Only three volumes of his—which cover only radio operations—have appeared so far, but, when he finishes, Lord Briggs will have undoubtedly written the definitive work on the BBC. No comparable source is in print for any other nation in the world.

As was stated initially, the most up-to-date source of information of the state of television broadcasting in both the United States and Europe is the pages of such daily newspapers as the New York *Times*, which carries a weekly column of comment on the medium in its Entertainment section on Sundays, as well as extensive daily news coverage of governmental actions related to television; the London *Times*, which carries both daily and weekly stories on the medium; such Paris journals as *Le Monde*, which devotes a page daily to television, and *Figaro*, which publishes comment along with the daily broadcast schedule of French television; and Copenhagen's *TV Bladet*, a weekly insert in one of the daily newspapers that is comparable to the American publication *TV Guide*.

Aside from the printed material listed above, information for this essay was obtained through the viewing of actual television broadcasts (such as the informative WTTW production "You Should See What You're Missing," dealing with American network practices, as well as regular daily programming in Britain, France, Germany, and Denmark), and through conversations with present and former employees of the British Broadcasting Corporation and Danmarks Radio.

Index